THIS HAS ALWAYS BEEN A WAR

THE RADICALIZATION OF A WORKING-CLASS QUEER

LORI FOX

ARSENAL PULP PRESS
VANCOUVER

ARSENAL PULP PRESS
Suite 202 – 211 East Georgia St.
Vancouver, BC V6A 1Z6
Canada
arsenalpulp.com

The publisher gratefully acknowledges the support of the Canada Council for the Arts and the British Columbia Arts Council for its publishing program, and the Government of Canada, and the Government of British Columbia (through the Book Publishing Tax Credit Program), for its publishing activities.

Arsenal Pulp Press acknowledges the xʷməθkʷəy̓əm (Musqueam), Sḵwx̱wú7mesh (Squamish), and səl̓ilwətaʔɬ (Tsleil-Waututh) Nations, custodians of the traditional, ancestral, and unceded territories where our office is located. We pay respect to their histories, traditions, and continuous living cultures and commit to accountability, respectful relations, and friendship.

Cover and text design by Jazmin Welch
Edited by Catharine Chen
Proofread by Alison Strobel

Printed and bound in Canada

Library and Archives Canada Cataloguing in Publication:
Title: This has always been a war : the radicalization of a working-class queer / Lori Fox.
Names: Fox, Lori, author.
Identifiers: Canadiana (print) 20210390212 | Canadiana (ebook) 20210390387 |
    ISBN 9781551528779 (softcover) | ISBN 9781551528786 (HTML)
Subjects: LCSH: Working class. | LCSH: Capitalism. | LCSH: Minorities. |
    LCSH: Patriarchy. | LCSH: Working class—Social conditions. |
    LCSH: Capitalism—Social aspects. | LCSH: Minorities—Social conditions. |
    LCSH: Patriarchy—Social aspects. | LCSH: Minorities—Employment—Social aspects. |
    LCSH: Queer theory.
Classification: LCC HD4904 .F69 2022 | DDC 305.5/62—dc23

For my people, the working classes, who cook the meals and pick the fruit, who serve the tables and stock the shelves, who work the gigs and deliver the orders.

We are the makers and builders and doers of this world, and all that is in it belongs to us.

"A bank isn't like a man. Or an owner with fifty thousand acres, he isn't like a man either. That's the monster."
—JOHN STEINBECK, *The Grapes of Wrath*, 1939

Contents

At Your Service

"SO," HE SAID, "Are you a real Scottish lass?" His cigarette, still lit, burned in the red plastic ashtray.

I paused. The man had paid in cash; I'd been looking down while I made change from my billfold. I'd made him pay up front because he was sketching me out, and I didn't want to be stuck with the bill if he pulled a dine and dash. When I glanced up at him, he was straight-faced, casual-like, as if he were merely remarking on the weather, not asking me if I was wearing panties.

This wasn't the first time I'd heard this question, nor the first time I'd heard it phrased this way. I worked at a pub which billed itself as "authentically" Scottish, so wearing a kilt was part of my uniform. There seemed to be a bevy of men in Ottawa who believed "real" Scottish women did not wear underwear. The question was always posed by a man just like this one—white, middle-aged, professionally dressed—and always in a light, playful voice, as if they were being boyish and charming and not piggy little fucks at all.

It was very late, creeping up on closing time. It had rained hard a few hours before, all the patios had cleared out, and I'd been wiping down the salt and pepper shakers, toying with the idea of closing up when he'd strolled in. He'd ignored the PLEASE WAIT sign at the front gate and seated himself in the back corner, against the wall. The street was empty and very dark. I was working alone. It's a universal truth that any time—in any city in any part of the world—if a server so much as contemplates the idea of closing the bar twenty minutes early, someone will wander in looking for service and be an absolute douche about it, so I suppose it was really my fault he was there, bridging the gap between probable scuzzbag and pervert in under five minutes flat.

He was still looking at me, staring with that familiar, cockeyed expression middle-aged men seem to think makes them look intense and smouldering but really only makes them look like what they are, which is half-cut pathetic horndogs. It's hard to tell a customer—on whose tips and goodwill a server relies for their daily bread—that you'd rather eat a pound of broken glass than fuck them, so I batted my eyes and giggled, trying to make myself appear as small and stupid as possible.

In my very best server voice—a grating falsetto several notes higher than my natural near-contralto—I said, "That's for me and my boyfriend to know." I didn't have a boyfriend, but at twenty-four I had been a queer long enough to know simply saying "I'm gay" is not enough to deter straight men from continuing to hit on me, especially not the kind of man who would ask you what's under your kilt in the first place.

I pocketed my billfold and slipped away before he could reply. He'd already been a total creep, reaching out unbidden to stroke the edges of my bright half-sleeve of tattoos and becoming indignant when I wouldn't tell him what they meant or bend to his request to pull down the collar of my shirt to show him more of the indigo-blue swallow on my breastbone, and I honestly just wanted to bring him the pitcher he'd ordered so I could slink off to marry the ketchups, strategically ignoring him until last call forced him to leave.

I went inside. The bartender, a hulking ex-football player type who could hoist a beer keg over each shoulder like he was carrying a couple bags of garden soil to his car in the Canadian Tire parking lot, was pouring the beer. He asked me why I looked so nervous, and I told him the guy on the patio was a red flag parade. He nodded. Holler if you need a hand, he said.

I took the pitcher and glass and went back out to the table. I made sure to smile, but to keep my eyes fixed on the far middle distance. As with any predator, you need to make sure you don't look a guy like that in the eyes. I could see him looking at the top of my breasts where my shirt was unbuttoned as I bent forward to deliver his drink. The pitcher, sweating beads of moisture, touched the metal surface of the tabletop.

Without changing his expression, without so much as blinking, the man shot his hand out and up under my kilt, reached between my legs, and grabbed my cunt.

He squeezed. I remember that squeeze very distinctly: dispassionate, commercial, as if he were considering the ripeness of a piece of fruit he was thinking about buying a basket of at the farmers' market.

I squealed and, in a motion made smooth by thoughtless fury, upended the pitcher over his head. Sixty ounces of cold, frothy Molson Canadian poured down over him, dousing his expensive shirt, his garish designer sunglasses, his pack of Du Mauriers.

He snatched his hand back, retracted like the proboscis of some startled bottom-dwelling sea creature, sputtering. There was an areola of beer darkening the cement of the patio floor around him.

"*You goddamn piece of shit bitch!*" he roared, standing up so fast he threw the table against the outside wall of the restaurant with a bang, but I was already reeling backward and hollering bloody murder.

In response to my yelling, the bartender came stalking out the front door and onto the patio like a roused bear, seized the grabber by the back of the shirt, and not-so-gently "escorted" him off the premises while the man fumed and cursed and flailed like a bad child having a tantrum.

Once the grabber had been tossed out on his ass around the corner, the bartender came back and poured a pair of Jameson, that old cure-all for a server's ills. We did a round and agreed the man had been an unwashed, ugly prick before we pulled the gate and started closing the place down ten minutes early, because *fuck that*.

When all the glassware was polished and all the chairs were up on the tables and all the silverware polished and rolled and all the trash taken out and all the ashtrays emptied out and run through the dishwasher, I went home. I hadn't seen which way the groper had gone—he might live around there, for all I knew—so I put an empty beer bottle in my purse in case I ran into him—we did that all time, bring home bottles in our purses, because nothing says *get fucked* like screaming and brandishing a broken bottle of Coors Light. I got in around three, had a couple drinks, and was in bed and asleep by 5:30.

I had a *clopen* the next day—when you close the bar at night and open in the morning—and I arrived at the restaurant at ten, bleary but dressed and ready for work. As I was putting on my apron, the day manager came up to me and told me our boss, the pub's owner— we'll call him Hank—wanted to speak with me. I was just cinching the knot on my apron strings when he told me this, and I stopped to warily ask him why. Hank's office was downstairs, and when he wanted a meal or a pack of cigarettes or a beer he called up to the kitchen and someone brought it down to him. He rarely wanted to see anyone, and when he did, it was never for anything good.

The manager shrugged and sighed.

The man from the night before—the man who had reached under my kilt and grabbed my cunt, the man who had been picked up like a purse and hucked out into the street because he couldn't keep his fucking hands to himself—had called in to complain about the quality of the service he'd received.

—

For seventeen years, I worked as a server in various bars and restaurants across this country, slinging beers, flipping tables, and tossing drunks to earn my living. If my career as waiter were a kid, it would have a learner's permit and be bugging me to buy it a used Corolla by now.

From 2003 to 2020, I was employed, more or less continuously, in family diners, nightclubs, fine dining establishments, greasy spoons, blue-collar dives—once, even, in a whiskey bar where the top-shelf liquor cost the same as a year of university tuition. Even when I worked full time as a reporter in a newsroom, I bartended as a side hustle, partly because, as you may or may not know, community news pays shit, and partly because it's hard to leave serving once you've done it for a while. You get used to it, the cash-in-pocket, the stress, and the camaraderie.

By his own report, Hank—hands down the best boss I've ever had, a snaggle-toothed, sinewy old man with merry eyes and skin jerkied by forty years of late nights, liquor, and cigarettes, who removed the filters from his smokes and puffed on the denuded ends—had listened to the groper rant about what a rude, disrespectful bitch I was and how he was never coming back there again and how Hank had lost himself a customer for about ten minutes before telling him to go fuck himself and hanging up. The bartender had left him a note about the incident in the log, so Hank had known the man was lying, and lying was one of the many things Hank had absolutely zero patience for. I didn't get in trouble, for which I was grateful, because there are plenty of places that would have reprimanded me, if not fired me outright. Hank actually thought the whole thing terrifically funny; the bar was said to hire only the meanest and toughest servers in town, a reputation Hank enjoyed cultivating. At that bar, it was *de rigueur* to pair a new would-be server with one of the oldest cats, who, unbeknownst to the newbie, had been charged with being as unkind, demanding, and shitty as possible. If you made it the day without punching her in the face or dissolving into tears, you were in, but if you broke and lost face, you were told to hit the pavement.

But—the groper. *Why?*

Why would he grab me by the cunt and then make a call like that?

He might have sobered up, been embarrassed by his behaviour, and sought to rationalize it by punishing me, or perhaps he'd thought he might get in legal trouble and was trying to discredit me. Both plausible explanations—except he had paid in cash. I had no way of knowing who he was. *Not* calling would have been in his best interest.

What he wanted to do, why he'd really called, was to have me punished for what he considered a genuine affront. My response was contrary to what he—consumers in general, but especially men and especially men of means—was taught to expect when he was served in a restaurant. *Served* being the keyword.

As a consumer, he felt entitled not only to my service, but to look at, even touch the body committed to that service, because my body (or, at the very least, my feminine attention) was viewed as part of what he'd paid for when he bought that pitcher of Canadian lager. This perception was not entirely imaginary; in my little kilt and knee-high socks, my sexual availability, real or feigned, was part of the business model of the bar I worked for.

My resistance to the implied contract was an insult to him, my outright refusal by dumping beer on him instead of merely swiping his hand away and laughing it off, an act of violence. By dousing him with beer, I not only responded to his aggression with aggression—something men do not expect or accept from anyone but cis men—but broke a rule of customer service: I behaved as a person and not as an object. It's as if he had turned on a Roomba and it had told him to eat a dick instead of going about the room, sucking up dirt.

From his perspective, that of the consumer, I was in the wrong, and grievously so.

Which is why he called.

Capitalism is not simply an economic system; capitalism is culture. Specifically, capitalism is *our* culture. And under capitalism—within our culture—working-class bodies are property.

If you want to understand this relationship, you'll find no better case study, no place where these values are more deeply lauded or enmeshed, than the service industry.

—

In the summer of 2003, at the age of sixteen—an awkward, acne-pocked, pigtail-wearing sixteen—I took my first job as a server, waiting tables in a family-run diner nestled in a strip mall next to the hockey arena in my hometown of Belleville, Ontario. It was the kind of place that has the same cook wearing the same grease-smeared apron for twenty years, where customers sit in booth seats upholstered with crackling vinyl under bad oil paintings of boats and order "the usual" without opening the menu.

There's an order to service—some large chain franchises will try to teach you their own corporate (usually stupid and inefficient) version of these steps, but at the privately owned establishments many young servers start out in, you're expected to just pick it up yourself. Serving is one of those things that has to be learned on your feet through practice, like car repair or fishing or any other skill that blends the physical and the technical.

You begin like this: At each individual table, you greet, bring menus, and take a drink order. You get the drink order, bring it to the table, take the food order, and punch it in the computer, where it gets sent to the kitchen so it can be made. When the food is ready, the table is "up" and you "run" the meals out to the appropriate place, giving each customer the correct plate, which could be one among dozens waiting to go out at the same time. It's your job to remember which is which, and to ensure that you don't take the wrong plate to the wrong person, as this kind of error seriously fucks things up not only for you and your tables, but your fellow co-workers, who either end up missing plates or else waiting while the kitchen fixes your error and the orders for their own tables are delayed. When your table has taken a few bites—only a nibble is too early, halfway through the meal is too late—you pop by to make sure everything is tasting good, refilling drinks and topping up condiments as required.

These steps may need to be repeated, depending on whether or not they order appetizers or dessert, as each course necessitates a restart of the process after the greeting. When they have finished eating, you clear the table, bring the bill, take a payment, and then "flip" the table (bus the remaining dishes, wipe down, and reset it) for the next round of customers to be sat.

Each table in your section—typically between six and ten in a casual setting, although fine dining, which requires more intensive and detail-oriented service, usually has fewer—is apt to be in various stages of this staggered process. You are always keeping a list in your head of which table is at what stage, as well as who needs another beer and which beer, and which table has the peanut allergy, and why hasn't the blackened salmon for the two-top in the corner come out yet and has the family with the four kids gotten their chicken fingers, all the while answering sudden requests and clearing tables and cleaning up spills and answering the phone and handling the unpredictable tempers of fellow co-workers, managers, and customers alike.

A confident and experienced server, which is to say, a server who is good at their job, glides through these steps, wheeling between tables like a ballroom dancer. An inexperienced, unskilled server gets bogged down by ever-accumulating small errors—forgetting to bring a knife for a steak, not cleaning tables as you go, neglecting to properly reset tables—which compound into larger and larger errors—a burger ordered without the requested cheese, an appetizer that comes out too late, three fish and chips ordered when they needed four—until, eventually, you find them hiding in the walk-in, crying behind a box of romaine lettuce, their section in irritated shambles.

At the diner where I first worked, I learned to do all these things, and quickly, because aside from a week or two's grace for training, a server who cannot hold their section is quickly fired. I had another additional incentive in that the owners of the restaurant, a cantankerous couple of curiously similar height and build, like they'd come off the same factory line, one right after the other, would absolutely fucking terrorize you if you weren't performing up to standard.

The wife, who handled the kitchen, made more than one server cry over a misordered sandwich or a broken coffee cup—both of which you had to pay for out of pocket, although this was and is illegal—and even the most inconsequential slip-up was sure to be met with acid (and very public) criticism. The husband, who handled the front of house, was quieter, but he had a ticking-time-bomb temper. In addition to having a very thick accent, a few years before I started working there, he had suffered a stroke that left him with a wicked lisp, and he was very sensitive about it. As a result, he was extremely difficult to understand, but when he gave you an order—clean this table, bring this drink, sweep that corner—you had to gamble on whether or not you had understood him correctly; if you asked him to repeat himself, he would be furious, and if you guessed and did the wrong thing, he would also be furious, screaming at you in front of customers or seizing you hard by the wrist and dragging you off to complete whatever task it was you had either bungled or not even realized you'd been asked to do.

For this labour, both physical and emotional, the restaurant paid me $6.85 an hour before taxes; an eight-hour shift cost the owners $54.80.

How much a server makes an hour varies, sometimes dramatically, from province to province and state to state. Although it's often the minimum wage of wherever you live, some places allow for tipped employees to be paid a special lower wage. In Canada, three provinces— British Columbia, Ontario, and Quebec—pay servers less than the minimum wage, and in the United States, although the federally mandated minimum wage is already an abysmal US$7.25, employers are permitted to pay their serving staff a wage as low as US$2.13 an hour.[1] This works out to about seventeen dollars for an eight-hour shift.

In part, the low wage servers make is linked to that keystone of capitalism, patriarchy. Service is ultimately the art of anticipating and responding to the needs of other people, an act of emotional labour which is culturally coded as inherently *feminine* work, and therefore not worth paying very much for. Women are expected to do this kind of emotional care work for free every day, after all, which is probably why, although about 70 percent of servers are women,[2] male servers still make more than women,[3] especially at management levels.[4] Anecdotally, women make more tips than men, but we aren't talking about tips right now (we will); we're talking about what servers make on paper, which is the amount restaurants feel their labour is worth.

More broadly, however, restaurants pay servers (and cooks, bussers, and dishwashers) as little as they do (which is to say, as little as possible) because we culturally devalue the kind of work they and most other working-class people undertake by labelling the physically, emotionally, and cognitively draining work I just described as "unskilled labour."

Unskilled labour is a funny (by which I mean stupid) idea. Economically speaking, it's defined as work which requires a low level of education and a generalized skill set, which produces labour of "minimal economic value"⁵— a strange way to think about the people and work which provide the fundamental goods and services upon which our entire society turns. It's like saying flour is the least important ingredient in a muffin because it's the simplest and most plentiful, even though without it, there's nothing holding your breakfast pastry together. You can't eat (or wouldn't want to) a muffin tin full of scorched blueberries, sugar, and melted butter.

Moreover, if every investment banker and POS systems analyst and digital advertising executive—occupations considered "skilled"— were suddenly struck dead, you probably wouldn't notice much difference in your day-to-day life. If, however, you were to remove every single supposedly unskilled labourer from the picture—every cab driver, every server, every meat packer, every fruit picker, every delivery person, warehouse worker, grocery store clerk and barista— you'd notice it pretty fast. In fact, we *did* notice it pretty fast. During the COVID-19 pandemic, these unskilled workers were relabelled "essential workers," because the work they do is fucking *essential*—

a label many businesses and governments were equally quick to do away with when it led to calls for increased pay, paid sick days, and access to vaccines.

The people with money have their money, in part, because they don't pay their workers what their labour is actually worth. Part of how they get away with doing that is by telling working-class people that not only is their work not worth very much, neither are they.

In other words, there's no such thing as unskilled labour. It's capitalist bullshit.

—

My experience with the pussy-grabber was neither isolated nor out of place, but just one of many fucked-up things done to me or that I had to do while working as a server.

Once, when I was nineteen, I caught a man old enough to be my grandfather with his dick out, sitting at the bar jerking off to the shape of my ass as I stocked the beer fridges; on another occasion, I quit a job I needed very badly because the head chef, drunk, threatened to cut my face with a sushi knife because I refused to touch his cock. A customer once handed me a pint glass full of her child's vomit—regurgitated chicken fingers floating in a brine of strawberry milkshake—without so much as a warning and then complained to my manager when I, in turn, vomited in surprised disgust. I've cleaned the word "cunt" written in menstrual blood off a patio window and scrubbed human shit out of carpet because someone had squirting diarrhea in the middle of the dining room during Friday night dinner service.

I've had bottles thrown at my head for refusing service to drunk customers, walked into bathrooms where full-grown men have passed out and pissed themselves, witnessed a (rightly) irate sex worker trash a table because her john, hiding in the bathroom, refused to pay her what was owed. Once, on Saint Patrick's Day, I cut a guy off because he came in too drunk to serve, only for him to walk out into the street and beat one of my favourite regulars, a fiftysomething partially retired nurse, in the face with the door of the cab she'd been about to get into because she refused to give it to him. We dragged her back inside to hold a bag of ice to her smashed face while waiting for the police to arrive; at the end of the night I mopped her blood out of the cracks in the floor behind the bar.

Honest to god, being a server is just plain fucked a lot of the time, but at the end of the day it's not those big, scary, disgusting, or violent things that make it truly degrading. It's the small daily humiliations, the dehumanizing way owners are constantly trying to milk every single drop of productivity out of you for as little as humanly possible, and, worst of all, it's the way you come to feel that this is normal and what you deserve.

One of the biggest problems is in the industry is the inordinate amount of power managers and owners have over staff; management tells staff when to come in and when to leave, what to wear and how to wear it, when (and if) they can take a break, have a smoke, eat, take a piss. Hours and pay are never guaranteed, and the best shifts usually go to the people management likes best. Your manager has a bad day, throws a tantrum, and yells at you—you'd better not shoot off your mouth back at them, or else you're apt to find yourself working the worst, slowest, and least profitable shifts, and there's absolutely nothing you can do about it. You can fire a server for pretty much any reason at all without much fuss or fanfare. Even if you know full well it's a wrongful dismissal, the resources—not to mention the time and education—needed to argue your case are beyond the reach of most staff, whose main concern at that point would be finding a new job before they get evicted or run out of groceries. Once, I was told I'd be fired if I didn't "adjust my attitude" and "mind my own business" because I'd had the gall to get visibly upset with the chef-owner when my customers found shards of glass in their fettuccini alfredo—twice, at two separate tables, on the same night. He'd broken a wineglass over the pasta station and been too cheap to throw the cream sauce out.

Perhaps the most malevolent force of all within the industry is how the culture of serving—which is an incarnation of the larger culture of capitalism—makes these day-to-day indignities seem *okay*; exploitation of your time and emotional labour are built directly into the job. Senior serving staff, for example, are often expected to train new staff members through a practice called "shadowing." In a shadow shift, a new server is given to an established server to train, something that takes time and emotional energy: you're stopping to explain things, you're showing them where things are, you're teaching them new routines, you're navigating the social niceties of meeting and working with a new person. The new server may or may not be paid for their time. I've seen some places require up to three full unpaid training shifts before you are officially "on the clock."

If the newbie is being paid, however, their wage will almost certainly be the same as their trainer's, which means the server doing the teaching is doing the labour of training a new employee for the good of the restaurant with absolutely no additional compensation. There's no good financial reason for them to do this training, let alone to do a good job of it. Management, however, often frames being asked to train a new server as a kind of reward—you're really great at your job, so we only want *you* to do this, so the new server can be as good as you—or as a duty to your fellow servers, because if the new person doesn't start working as quickly and efficiently as possible, your co-workers on shift with them will just have to work harder. It's a white elephant; you know you're being had, but refusing the "honour" has social consequences.

These expectations have other, more immediate (and for the industry, quite lucrative) applications, as accepting time theft is an unwritten expectation of continued employment for servers. It's a common mandatory requirement that staff be "on the floor" (fully dressed and ready to work) *fifteen minutes* prior to their scheduled shift. This is time for which servers are rarely paid; the meter starts ticking when you're scheduled. For staff, this practice is practical; you are coming on the floor to replace someone, or else preparing for a shift with colleagues, and to facilitate this smooth transition and not inconvenience others you need to be a bit early. But managers don't build this into the schedule; you're just expected to come in and start working.

Fifteen minutes of unpaid labour does not seem like a lot, but if you work five shifts a week, you lose 1.25 hours a week, which works out to sixty hours—1.5 standard workweeks—in lost wages a year.

Servers also rarely receive their (legally mandated) breaks—I certainly never did—and yet you'll always find them deducted from your paycheque. Even if you're shorted just fifteen minutes each shift you work, that's another sixty hours a year, which, including the time lost at the start of your shift, brings the annual total of unpaid labour to a full three workweeks. When you factor some of the other scuzzy shit many restaurants do—making servers pay for uniforms or foot the bill for misordered meals or customers who have dined and dashed—that's a lot of coin employers are siphoning back out of the pockets of the people they're supposed to be paying.

Basically, both customers and restaurants tend to treat servers as pieces of rented equipment which they are obliged to pay for, but not to maintain. Sick or tired? Shoes worn out and too broke to get new ones? Had it with the guy at table 10 eye-fucking you? Too bad—that's all part of the job, and if you don't start looking the part of the numbly smiling, put-together servant, they'll can you and find someone whose flats still have tread left. Like most consumer goods, a server is cheaper and easier to replace than to keep in good working order, or to repair.

———

Unpopular server opinion: tipping is fucked.

I say that as someone who, for most of my adult life, survived on tips. Tips paid my rent and bought my groceries and kept beer in my fridge. You can't live on minimum wage in most cities anymore, because the disparity between it and the actual cost of being a bare-bones alive person—a person entitled not only to food, shelter, health care, and safety, but also *pleasure*— is huge. In Toronto, for example, Canada's most populous city, minimum server wage is $12.55 an hour versus a living wage of $22.08—a disparity of $9.53 an hour, or around 55 percent.[6] Tips are quite literally a server's bread and butter.

Tips are also a massive fucking scam.

From a server perspective, tips appear—if you don't think about it too hard—to be a great deal. You walk into work and walk out with cash in your wallet, cash that supplements the meagre, some might say insulting, wage the restaurant itself pays you. Tips do what capitalist businesses and governments won't, namely, create a living wage.

Tipping also create fractures between employees within the industry. Because of tips, servers have higher earning potential than back of house employees, who earn a fixed (albeit higher than front of house) hourly wage. This creates long-standing and well-established divisions between back and front of house workers; cooks, bussers, and prep cooks (rightly) maintain that they do the bulk of the manual work, for which they are grossly underpaid, while servers and bartenders (also rightly) maintain that the emotional heavy lifting and routine sexual and verbal abuse they receive as the face of the industry entitles them to the tips they work for.

By fostering income inequality, tips create an artificial class division; both front and back of house are underpaid working-class groups, but neither feels much solidarity with the other because the tip system allows servers to feel superior to back of house, while at the same time giving the back of house a genuine class grievance that is, rather conveniently, not directed at the business itself. Allowing front of house to be paid largely in cash tips not only saves the business money, it also discourages a unified labour force, one which might, say, strike, unanimously demand better hours and wages, or even work together to steal back the fruits of their labour by passing a round of cold beers back to the kitchen and writing it off as spillage, or sending a plate of "misordered" nachos out to the front of house staff.

To surface-offset this manufactured inequality, most restaurants institute a "tip out"; servers tithe a portion of their nightly sale to the back of house. When a server cashes out, they give a percentage (usually 3 to 5 percent, although I've seen as high as 8 to 10 percent, and in one particularly crooked joint, it was 40 percent) of their sales to the kitchen. To do the math, on a 4 percent tip out of $1,000 in sales, the server gives the kitchen forty dollars. This percentage is applied regardless of whether or not the server actually got tipped on every bill; even if a server gets stiffed on a $100 bill, for example, they still tip the kitchen four dollars, which means they've actually *lost* money to serve that customer, at no cost to the house.

The money goes into a tip pool that is usually divvied up to the back of house based on how many hours each person works (provided management, who is entirely in charge of this largely unaccounted-for cash money, doesn't dip their fingers in, which they often do). Although no server would ever claim the kitchen doesn't deserve a share of the cut—they absolutely do—it's a solution that satisfies no one; all it does is dip into the income of one group of poorly paid people to top up the income of another group of poorly paid people without the house, who is making all the profit here, having to actually pay for any of it.

Moreover, the modern tipping system in the United States— keeping in mind that Canada uses a very similar, if not nearly identical, model—is rooted in racism. The practice, which first took off following the American Civil War,[7] allowed employers to pay their Black employees—many of whom were newly freed slaves—a subpar (or, in some cases, nonexistent) wage. Although tipping is now a socially accepted practice across the board, it's still steeped in and encourages racial inequality, with servers of colour earning less per hour in tips than their white counterparts[8] for doing the exact same work, and servers engaging in racial profiling of their customers based on beliefs around racial practices in tipping. It also, as I mentioned earlier, perpetuates worker exploitation by both customers and management, along with gender inequality and pervasive opportunities for sexual harassment.

In short, it's a dick situation all around.

—

So, why not just pay everyone a fair living wage and do away with tipping? Restaurants say they can't afford to do so without upping the cost of their meals, and honestly, with the average profit margin in a restaurant a slim 3 to 5 percent,[9] maybe they can't. Customers generally balk at raised prices, and in North America we rarely pay the real value of the food we eat, on everything from a Pink Lady apple grown in the Okanagan to an apple tart at an upscale restaurant. We're used to having working-class (and, in the case of produce and meat production, largely BIPOC) bodies subsidize the cost of what we eat by working for less than their labour is worth.

An alternative to raising prices directly is to include the gratuity in the bill, a common practice outside of North America which basically has servers working on commission. What happens when North American restaurants try this, however, is fascinating and reveals the true nature and function of tipping itself.

A standard North American tip, depending on where you live and where you're dining, runs anywhere from 10 to 20 percent. Logically, then, if you included an automatic 15 percent gratuity on a bill—even

18 or 20 percent—staff should make exactly what they made before, and customers should be paying pretty much what they were paying before, only with without the messy power imbalance. Basically, if consumers were to pay what service at a restaurant is actually worth, it would be about the same—slightly less, even—than what they're paying now, when they tip.

Better for everyone, right?

Apparently not. Because it's not about money for the customer and it's very much about money for staff.

Starting around 2015[10] (although there were a handful of earlier adopters) there was a push within the restaurant industry to address the inequality created by tipping, led by big names in dining such as Comal of Berkeley, California; Trou Normand of San Francisco; and New York City–based Union Square Hospitality Group, which as of 2021 includes eighteen well-known New York eateries, including the much-lauded Gramercy Tavern. Many of the participating restaurants abolished tipping and replaced it with an included-gratuity model.

By 2018, most of the restaurants that attempted this had dropped the no-tipping idea and gone back to the original, admittedly unfair and imbalanced, gratuity system, most notably the Union Square Hospitality Group. Even though diners were paying the same, maybe even less than what they would have paid under the traditional gratuity system after tip, they were ordering less, dropping profits for both the restaurant and the staff.[11] Not only did customers reject the higher (on paper) prices, they also tended to give restaurants with a no-tipping policy lower ratings[12] on social media review sites like Yelp; they were less satisfied with their experience even when nothing other than the tipping policy had changed.

That's because tipping isn't about service, nor even necessarily price for many consumers—it's about class and power.

As someone who served for most of their formative adult years, and who inhabits a perceived-female body, I can tell you that a tremendous amount of the pleasure many people get from eating out is in having power over another person. Consciously or unconsciously, part of the experience of eating in a restaurant, whether it's pancakes at Denny's or crème caramel at 21, is knowing you can tell someone to do something—bring you a fork, cook you a steak, refill your coffee—and they will not only do it, but do it with a smile because *they have to*. And if you don't get *exactly* what you want when you want it, you have the power to economically punish them without ever having to say anything at all.

Although many diners are kind and reasonable humans, there are also many people who relish the opportunity to display their social status over another person. That, ultimately, is why the man on the patio grabbed my cunt.

Tipping is a cultural-capitalist display of power. It's a physical signal of class and status, without which the dining experience loses value for customers.

To that end, many servers didn't like the new system either—some restaurants reported reduced earnings and huge staff turnover—because it often meant (against all logic) less money in their pockets. Because the majority of restaurants were still using the traditional system, and because staff makes such low wages to begin with, it was often not in the staff's best interests to stay. Having a wad of cash in hand at the end of the day also creates the illusion of prosperity, the feeling that you're somehow getting away with something, when in fact you're just making what your labour is actually worth.

As a server, you have to buy into the system to survive, or go make minimum wage somewhere else.

That doesn't mean—and I cannot stress this enough—that you shouldn't tip your server. You absolutely should. Until the low-wage system is addressed, all you're doing by not tipping is stiffing someone who is already underpaid. The problem isn't servers going home with money in their pockets. The problem is that to do this, businesses exploit a corrupt class-based system which pits working-class people against each other to fight for whatever bones the upper classes will throw them, without regard for their human dignity, safety, or security, so that the businesses don't have to pay what their labour is worth.

The North American cultural practice of tipping is a physical manifestation of the way capitalism tricks—and needs—everyone to buy into the system it creates, even when it benefits no one but the people at the top.

This buy-in-or-starve mentality is at the core of cultural capitalism itself: the illusion of choice and freedom where there is none.

———

I loved being a server. I know that sounds strange, given everything I've just said about the industry, but I did.

I liked it best when I worked in places where the food was beautiful, where the kitchen really loved and cared for each plate they sent out, where the front of house staff watched each table with parental affection, stepping in only when needed, hanging back most of the time. There are few things more lovely than a full dining room, empty and perfectly set before the four p.m. service, everything still and white and clean, the cutlery just so, the curtains drawn, and the light coming in over the hung glasses over the bar, over the brass of the rail. I love a busy kitchen, tattooed arms sweating under their rolled-up sleeves, pots clattering, people shouting to one another, "More greens! Five fettuccini all day! Eighty-six the veal parm!"

By the time this book comes out, I will have stopped being a server for two whole years—the longest I have ever not worked in a service profession since I was old enough to legally work at fourteen and started out at Pizza Pizza as a cashier. I didn't actually quit my last serving job; when shit hit the fan hard and we all went into lockdown following the global outbreak of COVID-19 in March 2020, I was furloughed like everyone else. I managed to hustle myself a different job, working as the editor of a small entertainment magazine in the Yukon. When the world opened back up again—slowly, step by step—I chose not to go back, because shifts and tips were scarce. I already had work, and even though I loved the people I worked with and had grown so accustomed to serving that it seemed impossible I would never *not* do it, going back to the bar would have meant taking money directly from the pockets of my fellow workers. Never mind that fact that on top of everything, it didn't feel very safe to be serving in the middle of a global pandemic.

Feeding people, giving people good food and good drink and a place to sit and talk and laugh, or a place to be alone and have someone take care of them so they can just enjoy and think, is a genuinely beautiful thing. That's true whether you're serving truffle risotto and locally farmed hanger steak or grilled cheese sandwiches and BLTs. It's just a *good* thing to be doing, and a good, honourable way to make your living. More honourable and more useful, in my opinion, than working in public relations or trading stocks or designing marketing campaigns.

Likewise, not all managers and restaurateurs are capitalist shit-eating pieces of scum; a lot of them really care about the work they do and have a love of good food and good drink and good service. Some of them are even good people who want to do right by their staff and see them as whole human beings with lives and worth and meaning. And then, there are those who don't, but people have been perfectly capable of being prolapsed anuses long before the advent of capitalism and probably will be long after it's nothing more than a sour memory in the history of human civilization. Provided we can survive as a species before it destroys us, anyway.

There are good and beautiful things in the world: There are rabbit stews and Brussels sprouts roasted in bacon fat, there are hamburgers with golden french fries, and cold pints of beer and bottles of champagne. There are perfectly polished forks and kind people who will notice it's your birthday when you give them your ID at the door and have dessert sent over, and staff who will bring over a round of tequila because they have been laughing, just right howling, while you and your friends run a half-cut arm-wrestling tournament at table 9.

There are also people who work really, really hard and still don't have enough to pay the rent and buy groceries. There are people who don't get to go to the doctor when they're sick because they can't afford to take a day off, and people who don't go to the dentist because even though they work and work and work, they can't afford it. There are people who could never eat the food they make and serve if they didn't eat if off the discarded plates of the people they serve—that's the way I first tasted real truffles, as earthy and fragrant and intoxicating as sex.

There are men who will reach under the kilt of a young person and grab their cunt, because the young person is alone and because they are a servant and because the man thinks that means he can.

Capitalism teaches us that working-class people are not as important as the businesses their labour creates goods and services for.

Likewise, capitalism tells us that if you are working class, you *deserve* to be working class—and so, by extension, you deserve however it is you are treated, because the people treating you that way are not only your economic superiors, they're also your *moral* superiors.

And that's a motherfucking lie.

So many people, good, hardworking people, working-class people, deserve better than this. But we just accept this as not only normal, but right—even though it's glaringly obvious that even if it's the former, it's not the latter.

We are all stuck doing things we would rather not be doing, treating people in ways we know we shouldn't be treating them, in a culture that encourages us to both exploit others and to be exploited ourselves.

It's a system of learned helplessness.

And it doesn't have to be this way.

Creatures of Impossible and Tremendous Beauty

CARLA SASHAYS DOWN THE ALLEY, turns around at the Dumpster, and sashays back.

"Like *that*." She wiggles her ass from side to side in exaggerated demonstration, sucks the smoke from the last of her cigarette, and tosses the butt into the plastic bucket—it once contained sliced pickles—which serves as an ashtray for the cooks and floor staff. The bottom of it is covered in a grimy brown slurry of nicotine and rain. "It's got to come, like, from the hips."

I try a series of uncertain steps down this impromptu catwalk. I'm wearing a pair of Payless flats. There's a hole in the sole where I've worn through it, running back and forth from the kitchen to the patio a thousand times a day.

It's the end of my shift, nearly midnight. Mid-July in Ottawa, and one of those impossibly hot city nights, sticky and close with humidity and fumes. I work on Sparks Street at a greasy dive where a tourist once left a Tripadvisor review claiming our burgers "slid through [him] like a rat through a drainpipe." I believe that, as the entire floor staff got food poisoning from sharing a plate of chicken nachos at the beginning of the summer.

"Fuck, girl, kick out those hips … you're not going to the fuckin' barn. Tits up, ass out!"

On the street beyond us, a stream of Friday night taxis come and go. What Carla is trying to do with all her commands and her smoking, all her trotting me back and forth, all her instructions, is teach me how to walk.

Or, more specifically, teach me to walk "like a girl."

———

I really hated being a little girl.

My mother, an accomplished seamstress, sewed me little dresses in flower-patterned fabric and lace trim, wove ribbons into my hair. I used to pull the ribbons out at every opportunity, using them instead as magic rope for my toys to tame wild horses or subdue dragons with. When I was caught, my mother would braid them right back in, often tighter the second time.

I didn't like the little dresses. I couldn't run or jump or leap or crawl in a dress. I couldn't pretend to be a wolf or a hawk or a deer in a dress. I couldn't make snow forts or steal the old archery set that hung on the wall of my father's den and pretend I was hunting in a dress. Worse, dresses seemed to invite people, even total strangers, to touch me, to fawn over me, to tell me (or, more often, my mother) what a *very pretty,* what a *very beautiful little girl* I was—attention, I quickly learned, was an unforgivable rudeness to refuse. It is as if little girls are somehow the common property of everyone but themselves.

By contrast, my younger brother, with his shirts covered in dinosaurs and a ball cap tucking back his short-cropped brown hair, seemed to have every freedom I desired; he was an adorable little boy, buck-toothed and kittenish, but I don't ever recall him being manhandled the way strangers felt inclined to do to me. I was often jealous of his clothes, which, as I was older and already more than five feet tall by grade four, were at first too small for me to steal, and then, later, suddenly too large. I was especially jealous of his Sunday clothes, which included a little blue-and-black-striped clip-on tie with a perfect glued-on Windsor knot.

Ironically, my brother, who would grow up to be a gay cis man, was not happy with his lot, either. As the pair of us grew older, it became painfully clear neither he nor I was particularly well suited to the roles we were expected to play, not as a *boy* or as a *girl*. Where I was too rough, my brother was too soft; where I was always being told to lower my voice, he was admonished for not speaking up; where I was punished for getting detention for fighting, he was reprimanded for "being a sissy."

As children, we often joked that we had been born out of order, that our souls had gotten mixed up standing in line to be incarnated (or, more likely, that I had cut in the queue), and we'd accidentally come to inhabit the wrong bodies. This was never quite the correct analogy, however; my brother never wanted to be a girl, he just wanted to do things more suited to his tastes, which happened to be "girl things." Likewise, I never wanted to be a boy—I just didn't particularly want to be a girl, either.

One of my earliest and happiest memories as a child is of a game my brother and I used to play called Princess and Tiger. My brother, the eponymous princess, would befriend a wild tiger cub, played by me—sometimes feeding them, as they were on the brink of starvation, sometimes rescuing them from a trap, sometimes saving them from poachers. Thus allied, the young tiger would in turn have to rescue the princess, who would be stolen by a great eagle, or a monster, or a band of brigands. We would play this game for hours, my brother hiding behind the couch, awaiting saving, while I pranced around on all fours, my fingers tucked under my palms to better simulate paws. We never traded places, nor fought about who would play what. I had no more interest in being a prince than I did in being a princess. I had already selected the role I wanted for myself, a form that was neither obviously male nor female—a body, in other words, that had no readily assumed gender.

Long before I had the words for it—and let us be honest, in the queer community, we hold our words over heads as talismans of fate or fortune which we believe might somehow save or absolve us—I was a non-binary person. When I eschewed girl things, it was not because I found them inherently more objectionable than so-called boy things, but because I was repulsed by the idea of being viewed as something I was not. I was not a little girl, and I was also not a little boy. I was a little *person*.

Which is exactly why at that same age, my favourite movie—the one I watched over and over and over, so often that the vhs began to wear out and a blue line formed at the top of the screen when it was played—was *The Last Unicorn.*

—

It was a Friday. I had worked a double shift, as I often did, two five-to-eight-hour sets back to back, separated only by an hour or so during which I usually ate something down the street at a different restaurant, had a beer, napped for fifteen minutes on a pile of clothes in the break room, then hauled my exhausted carcass back out onto the floor. The kitchen was down a flight of stairs, so you had to run up and down, up and down, up and down whenever the little bell rang to tell you an order was ready. There was a huge dining room that led into the bar, and the bar led out to the patio, which in the summer was almost always full, and we had those huge cruise ship–style trays on which we would often carry seven or eight full plates at a time because it took so long to get back and forth between the two points. It was hard, tiring, physically demanding work. We were always short staffed.

Earlier that day, during my noontime shift, while the house was buzzing with the hum of full seats, of diners ordering, eating, talking, the owner of the restaurant—an elderly, bottom-heavy man with a white Yosemite Sam moustache and a well-documented proclivity for eye-fucking the servers while they worked, the younger the better— had been in for lunch. The restaurant had at one time been much grander than the shabby, outdated thing it was now, and it had a second-floor mezzanine. The owner had offices on the upper floors of the building, and he would come down, seat himself in this other- wise closed section above everyone else, and wait to be served by one specific server, who was the only one permitted to take care of him. It was always tense when he was there, because from this vantage point (he always made me think of a vulture in a cartoon, perched with his scaly feet about a branch, smugly waiting for something to die) he'd observe the staff, making a mental list of things (which is to say, servers) he did not like. He would later turn these complaints over to the head manager, a middle-aged man with a red face, a constantly nervous expression, and a tremendous gut slung over the belt of his pants, for "correction."

Hours later, long after the owner and the head manager had gone home—as the top dogs, they worked regular daytime hours, like real people—Carla caught me in the kitchen as I was bringing a chin-high stack of dirty dishes down to the pit. The owner had seen me today and complained about me, she said. The head manager, who would later claim he knew absolutely nothing about Carla's mission, had asked her to speak to me. Carla was the only woman manager on staff.

I frowned. I was a strong server. I worked very hard. I came in on time and I always took extra shifts whenever I was asked without complaining. Customers and staff generally liked me. What could I have done?

The problem, Carla explained, was not the quality of my work, it was my appearance. I was "unfeminine." Why was I not wearing more makeup, a better cut of clothes, some earrings?

Really, though, Carla said, the real problem—well, the biggest problem, anyway—was the way I walked.

"Like, I know you're gay," Carla had said as I stood before her, dirty dishes still stacked on a tray now held against my chest, a blush of shame burning up my throat to my ears. "But you clomp, girl. You walk like a dude."

This was not the first time I had been told that I didn't walk the way I should. When I was a child, my mother had often complained of my stride, which she said was too "wide" and too "heavy" to be "ladylike." More flattering descriptions had been given to me by lovers, namely that I "strutted" or "loped" in a quick, purposeful, long-legged stride. Either way, it was how I walked and had always remembered walking.

The owner had demanded my mannish gait be corrected, Carla said. I was to come see her when my shift was over.

I went back out onto the floor with a kind of detached numbness, as if I were watching from a distance while a rather clumsy actor played a rather clumsy version of me. When the time came, Carla summoned me into the back alley to work out this unsavoury personal defect off the clock, without pay. The owner was quite willing to retrain my unsavoury step, but he most certainly wasn't going to pay me minimum wage to do it.

So here I am. Trotting back and forth amid the pungent odour of garbage and fryer-grease like a show dog.

———

Released in 1982, the animated fantasy masterpiece *The Last Unicorn* is based on the novel of the same name by Peter S. Beagle, who also wrote the screenplay adaptation. On the surface, it's a classic romantic fairy tale replete with monsters, heroes, and a grand and noble quest: the Unicorn (voiced by Mia Farrow, no less), who lives alone in an enchanted forest, learns through an overheard conversation between two hunters that all the other unicorns have disappeared—no one has seen one in years. Fearing they may indeed be the last of their kind, the Unicorn sets out to find out what happened to their kin and, ultimately, to rescue them, making friends and battling enemies along the way in classic fantasy-adventure style.

And yet, just below the surface of this simple-seeming narrative broods something darker. More existential.

The movie has a lot going on—a love-besotted sentient tree, highwaymen waiting to prey on unsuspecting travellers, vengeful monsters, a poetry-collecting butterfly, a talking cat who is as helpful as his nature will allow him to be (which isn't very), a wine-loving dead man, a handsome prince in love with an impossible-to-obtain maiden—but it is the Unicorn around which all this revolves, who acts as the moral and emotional linchpin of the story. Once out in the real world away from their forest, the Unicorn discovers that, with a few notable exceptions, most people literally *cannot* see them for what they are; instead, they are seen as people would prefer to see them, which is to say, what people *expect* to see: an ordinary, if particularly beautiful, white mare. For anyone to see them as even a pale approximation of themselves, a sorceress has to put a spell on them to give them a *fake* horn; they are either invisible, or a cheap parody of how other people imagine they should be.

"If men no longer know what they are looking at," the Unicorn says, baffled by being taken, over and over, for something they are not and yet grateful for the safety it provides them, "perhaps there are still unicorns in the world yet, unknown—and glad of it."

While it's unlikely Beagle was thinking particularly hard about us when he penned the novel in 1968, for queer people who, for time out of mind, have been hiding in plain sight among the cis-straights, often for the sake of our own safety, the metaphor is obvious. This is doubly true for trans and non-binary people like me, whose identity—and the validity of that identity—is often challenged to the point of questioning whether or not we exist.

For reasons I couldn't articulate at the time, as a child I was absolutely in love, enraptured with the Unicorn. Sometimes I would sit on the living room floor, rewinding the tape to a specific scene of them racing along the sea, watching it over and over again. I loved the way they moved—they had power and grace, were delicate but fearless—and I loved the way they interacted with the world. They didn't ask anyone permission to do anything. They went where they liked, when they liked. They got angry without consequence or reprimand. The Unicorn is both an animal and a person, and yet neither of those two things entirely, inhabiting an in-between body which allows them both power over men and solidarity with women; they are simultaneously desired and in control, the antithesis of the way women (and little girls) are taught to think about their bodies. They control who does and does not touch them—Schmendrick the Magician (Alan Arkin), despite all his power, apologizes when he slips and accidentally lays a hand on the Unicorn's flank, while humble Molly Grue (Tammy Grimes) is permitted to walk side by side with them, one hand on their neck.

Throughout both the film and the novel, Beagle refers to the Unicorn—who does not have a name, never having needed one—as *she*. I've referred to the Unicorn here as *they*, for two important reasons. Firstly, because the Unicorn is, for all intents and purposes, a *she* only in terms of their biological sex, and even that doesn't really seem to matter; there seems to be no discernable physical difference between the Unicorn and any other unicorn. Their gender, realistically, is a moot linguistic point. Regardless of their sex, unicorns are not men or women any more than a stallion or mare would be.

Secondly, and more important, it is only when the Unicorn is forced against their will into the shape of the Lady Amalthea, a woman, that the real horror of the story makes itself known.

The Unicorn is a creature of impossible and tremendous beauty beholden to no one, unconcerned by (perhaps even unaware of) the desires or expectations of other people.

Until, suddenly, they're not.

—

I turn on my heel and come back, standing before Carla. She's in her late thirties or early forties, tall with black hair and bleached highlights, in a short skirt and low-cut top. I am twenty-three, short, with a rough pixie cut that grew out from an unspeakable buzz job I got from a student barber. My pants are too large and too long for my frame, and my shirt, an ugly orange thing with the name of the restaurant emblazoned across the breast pocket like a brand someone would actually recognize, is also too large. I'm always buying my clothes too large, as if I expect that someday I will wake up and actually be as tall and broad as I think I am. It has never bothered me before, but standing in front of Carla's appraising, mascaraed eyes, I feel like a child wearing my parents' clothes, awkward and ugly and small.

"We'll keep working on it." She fishes a lighter from her pocket, starts another cigarette. "You've got nice curves, you know?"

She blows smoke and crosses her arms.

"You'd be so pretty if you just did a little more with your hair, if you wore a little makeup."

She shakes her head slowly, looking me up and down with a pitying expression, as if I have just told her something very sad, but for which I am doubtlessly to blame.

"Really," she adds, as if trying to reassure me, "you could be a very pretty girl, if you put some effort in."

———

A drooling, mindless behemoth, the Red Bull gave me nightmares as a child—although his master, the selfish and bitter King Haggard (Christopher Lee) is the real monster in the film, not the Bull himself. The Bull lives in a cave beneath the castle (whose rounded, slanted towers possess an oddly phallic shape), a furious, unrelenting force of dominance and will. As his name suggests, the Bull is specifically and unrelentingly *male*, and Haggard uses him for a particularly masculine purpose, even for a patriarchal society such as our own: the subjugation of other non-male bodies for his pleasure.

Having been stirred to joy by the sight of a unicorn as a young man, in his old age Haggard (that proto-Chaser) bade the Bull round up each and every unicorn in the world and force them into the sea. They remain there, coming in and out on the idle foam of the tide, captives under the guard of the Bull, so that Haggard can stand at his window, presumably in his boxers while swirling a martini, and look at them whenever he likes. It's basically the Playboy Mansion, but with a horse fetish. When the Unicorn and their companions first encounter the Bull, he's furious to discover he's missed one and attacks them—not to kill the Unicorn, but to round them up and push them into the sea with the rest of their kind.

The Bull's intention is not to destroy the Unicorn, but to subdue, control, and, ultimately, assimilate them.

In the name of saving them, Schmendrick accidentally casts a spell which transforms the Unicorn into a preternaturally beautiful but very much human woman, in which the Bull has no interest. Schmendrick, a man, is overjoyed by the result of his magic; that he can do such a thing is a mark of his tremendous power, he claims. Only Molly Grue, a woman herself, sees the true nature of the terrible thing he has done, good intentions or not; in this shape, which is the antithesis of all they are, she says, the Unicorn will surely go mad.

"What have you done? *What have you done?*" Molly demands. "I didn't know you meant to turn her into a human girl! You are an idiot! Do you hear me? You lost her!"

Seeing what has been done to them—now a *her*—the newly made Lady Amalthea is outraged and terrified; she falls to her knees and demands to be returned to her proper form, but Schmendrick doesn't know how to return her to her old shape, nor does he seem very interested in doing so; this is the only shape in which she might have a chance to rescue her kin, he says. What he's done to her—to *them*—is for their own protection, he says, and the way it has to be right now. A forced conversion: in order for the Unicorn to walk about safely in the world, they must cease to *be* themselves, the Unicorn, and become *herself*, the Lady Amalthea.

But Amalthea will not be comforted; they wish he had let the Bull take them. They would rather have been captured, or even killed, than forced into this shape, a shape in which people still cannot see them for what they are, and, worse yet, is not of their choosing.

They are in the wrong body, and they are horrified.

As a child, no moment was more terrible to me than this. Sometimes I had to fast-forward through it.

———

Dismissed, I go back inside, gather my things in the staff change room, which, as always, smells of fried food and damp feet. Tears prickle at the corners of my eyes, but I force them back; I am alone now, but I don't know when someone else might come in. I don't want to be caught crying, with snotty nose and red eyes.

I change out of my uniform. It needs washing, but there won't be time; I need to be back in before ten tomorrow morning to open the restaurant again. I ball the uniform, greasy with food stains, damp with sweat, in the back of my locker. It will need to be ironed in the morning before I can wear it, but I don't care.

Still in my socks, I go over to the cracked, cloudy mirror over the sink, splash a little water on my face, and run my hands through my red-blond hair, slicking it back. I've never possessed anything even remotely approximating classical feminine beauty, but I like my face: I have a good strong jawline, a nice mouth, eyes that are a very bright, very sharp blue.

I've been a server for nearly seven years at this point, and this isn't the first time a manager has commented on my appearance. Usually it's more subtle: snide remarks about my hair or clothes, the suggestion that I try a little makeup, things you'd never say to a man. This, though, this walking me back and forth, this enforced *correction* of something as fundamental as my walk is new, and deeply, deeply degrading. I have never been very comfortable working as a server, here or anywhere else. I have always felt judged because I don't look or act quite like the other girls, who seem to know, with an intuition I have always lacked, how to *be* girls.

Sometimes I try to emulate them, these "natural" girls, by wearing a little makeup, more jewellery, more dresses, new shoes, but it never works. Makeup, no matter how carefully selected and applied, always seem to be the wrong colour for me, I totter in heels like a drunk, and any dress I wear looks silly, ridiculous even, like putting pants on a horse. Still, I've tried; over the past few years I've wobbled back and forth between femme and butch many times, not finding either quite the correct fit. In my head, I am six feet tall, broad-shouldered, and breastless. Female, but not a woman—not the way people think of *women*—but not a man, either. In reality, I'm five foot four and lightly built. I have a very strange relationship to my breasts, which I am sometimes uncomfortable about, but more often wilfully oblivious of. Sometimes I get in trouble at work for unbuttoning my shirt to just below my sternum; this is "inappropriate" as it's possible for some customers (if they're really looking) to see the space between my breasts. The restaurant is often hot, the kitchen not air-conditioned; I get sweaty and simply forget that my breasts are there, because in my head, they're not.

The boys walk around with their shirts unbuttoned in precisely the same way, but boys get to do whatever they want. Likewise, the most beautiful female servers could probably come in topless, and the manager wouldn't do anything but rush to stand behind the counter to hide his erection. It isn't lost on me that the most beautiful (which is to say, the most feminine) servers get the best shifts, nor that they often make more money in tips than me, nor that my male co-workers are forgiven their slights more often, get more flexible schedules, and move up to management positions faster and more often than the women.

I stand awkwardly somewhere in between, *persona non grata*, in a body that must be policed—or punished—into conformity. And so, we get Carla's little skit, meant to humiliate me into obedience, into becoming something more tasteful to the owners and managers, into something not only malleable, but also palatable, which for my body means *feminine*. The implication is that not only is something wrong with me, personally, for which I should be ashamed, but also that I might be punished again, even fired, if I continue to look and behave as I do.

Anxiety twists in my gut.

I need this job. I can't afford to lose it. They know that.

What will happen if I can't be the way they want me to be? What they expect—demand—me to be?

What will happen to me if I can't fix whatever it is that's wrong with me?

———

After her transformation, which is really a kind of imprisonment, the Unicorn largely drops out of the plot, leaving the action to Schmendrick and Molly as they seek to discover a way down to the lair of the Bull to rescue the unicorns.

Stripped of her proper body, Amalthea is subdued. As time passes, even she starts to forget she was—is—something other than she appears, and she begins to acquiesce to what is expected of her new form, namely that she be winsome and comely and quiet. Prince Lír (Jeff Bridges), who spends much of the movie writing bad poetry, killing innocent animals, and failing at basic tasks such as peeling potatoes, fancies himself in love with Amalthea, despite never having held a single conversation with her. He pursues her relentlessly despite her initial obvious disinterest. When she finally begins to return his affections, it seems to be more because she is *expected* to than because of any great external or internal change within her; that's just how the story is supposed to go. For Lír's part, he's not really in love with *her*, he is in love with the body and the role she has been made to wear. He has never even seen her real form, nor does he really understand who or what she is—the *they*-ness of who he perceives as Amalthea is obscured to him by the inherent *her*-ness the Unicorn is forced to wear.

Eventually, the erasure is so complete that when Schmendrick begins to talk of changing her back into her correct form, she begs him not to—she wants to marry Prince Lír, and that's all she wants, unicorns be damned. She is so used to being seen and treated as a woman that *she* can no longer see herself as anything else.

Not only does the Unicorn-cum-Lady cease to be an active participant in their own story, they cease to be themselves.

They have been effectively obliterated.

———

At home, I turn on the television, get a beer from the fridge, roll a joint, and sit down on the couch, feet up on the coffee table. I crack the beer, light the smoke.

I wiggle my toes and look at them. I have strange feet; they are wide and rough and the second toes are longer than my big toes. I have always thought them a little ugly. I have never liked them.

You clomp, girl.

Friends is on, because it's the aughts, and so *Friends* is always on somewhere. Rachel and Monica are sitting in their impossibly large New York City apartment which they would never actually be able to afford, being sexy-pretty in that somehow approachable, somehow unattainable, but always seemingly effortless way beautiful women on television are.

You'd be so pretty if you just wore a little makeup.

I sit sucking on the joint like it's going to make me feel better, even though I know it's not. I'm embarrassed, and I'm angry with myself because I let them humiliate me, because I didn't know what to say in the face of such sexism and queerphobia, because at that age I never knew what to say, because even if I had I wouldn't have said it, because what if they fired me?

I fall asleep with the television on and my bare, traitorous, ugly feet still propped up on the coffee table.

———

It's not made explicitly clear precisely what allows Schmendrick to change Amalthea from a woman back into their true form and bring them back into their power. The magician was never fully in control of the spell that turned the Unicorn in the first place, but, in an unexplained reversal, he *does* appear to be in control of it when he undoes it. Whatever the reason for this *deus ex machina*, the Unicorn is abruptly returned to themselves.

In the final, pivotal scene, Lír is wounded, and the Unicorn is left to fight the Red Bull alone. We are led to believe it is the Unicorn's love of Lír that gives them the courage to fight, but they've also simply been freed to do so; with Lír dashed to the stones by the Bull, the dynamic that Lír brings to the story, that of maiden and hero, is broken. The Unicorn, now the only combatant capable of taking the field, stands their ground and refuses to give way to the Bull, a steadfast position that allows them to turn and drive the mindless, snorting animal into the sea, extinguished—precisely the fate the Bull had intended for them.

And then it's over. The Bull is gone. Along with his magic, Haggard's castle collapses into the ocean, taking the evil king with it.

The other unicorns are freed. Prince Lír, near death, is healed by the Unicorn and takes his father's throne with the aim of restoring the scarred kingdom. Schmendrick and Molly, in love, ride off together for other adventures. The Unicorn, once again themselves, goes home to their forest.

Although restored, the Unicorn, by their own admission, is unable to be exactly the way they were before this dysphoric and traumatic experience. They've gotten to experience love, yes, something they would not take back, but with it comes regret, because they cannot be with Prince Lír now that they've been restored to their true form.

Lír loves a woman, which is not what they are.

———

In the morning, I wake, stiff, on the couch. The light is coming in through the little window in the living room of my rundown apartment. The television is still on. A woman is chattering away about the benefits of a juice cleanse. I turn it off.

Overnight, a curious thing has happened: all my fear and shame is gone, evaporated. Mist on the dank Rideau Canal, burned away by daylight.

In its place, distilled fury, hot and sharp as liquor.

This is fucking bullshit.

——

The head manager is in his office when I come in. Directly below the dining rooms, the office is windowless and dark, an airless lair in which the heavyset man sits, filing the paperwork for paycheques. I knock once and let myself in without waiting for a reply.

"Lori—you're early," he says, looking up in surprise. He is wearing a tie that's slightly too short, dangling from his thick neck like the leash of a loose dog. He smiles, but the smile does not reach his eyes; he is talking to me, but not thinking about me.

I cross the floor. There's a hard-backed chair on my side of the desk. I pause a moment, considering it. I turn it around, the legs scraping the tile, straddling the back.

"I understand," I say, "that you have a problem with the way I walk."

He blanches. I can see the bob of his Adam's apple as he swallows. He rolls on his chair a little, away from me, his back against the wall. The smile falls from his face.

The Happy Family Game

MY GRANDMOTHER DIED YESTERDAY. She was ninety-six.

When I knew her, years ago, she was already one of those impossibly frail, paper-skinned elderly people who have begun to collapse in on themselves, as foreign and pale as evening stars. She had a hump and walked with a shuffle, but I remember her being quite spry and mobile when I was little. She had beautiful, slender-fingered hands that looked as if they should belong to a pianist. There was a piano in the old farmhouse, out in the red shield country of Napanee, Ontario, a forlorn, uncared-for thing sitting by itself under a patina of dust in a little room no one went into much. I don't know if she played—if she did, I never heard her. We were not a family who cared much for music, although at one time we must have been.

I learned of my grandmother's death second-hand, via a terse text from my brother: FYI—*grandma died this morning*. I don't blame him for his shortness. He's exhausted, being the only child left in my family to whom my parents can turn, and probably equally exhausted by my own stubborn insistence that this be the case.

55

I've had virtually no contact with any of the relatives on my mother's side for nearly fifteen years. Most of the relatives on my father's side are long dead. In the last ten years, I've only seen my mother a handful of times, perhaps three or four hours all together. In 2016, I stopped speaking to her entirely.

I realize my refusal to break this silence—even now, when my mother, herself in her early seventies, is most certainly grieving and alone—could appear cold at best, even wantonly cruel. I would understand if someone thought that of me. Sometimes I think it of myself.

The last time I saw my grandmother was in the summer 2010, when my grandfather died. I went to the funeral. I won't be going to this funeral. Even if I could get there—as I write this, Ontario is in the middle of its third and arguably worst wave of the pandemic, and I live some 5,600 kilometres away on the other side of the country—I doubt I'd be welcome there, not only because my family (devoutly Christian, right wing, gruesomely racist, sexist, and homophobic) are inherently opposed to my queer, non-binary, anti-capitalist, tattoo-covered existence, but for a more personal, arguably even more fundamental reason. It's the same reason I can no longer speak to my mother, why I never call my cousins. It's the same reason it's increasingly hard to talk to my father and sometimes, even, to my brother. It's the same reason I, for all intents and purposes, am without family, kin, or history.

It's because I won't nod, smile, and keep my fucking mouth shut.

I won't play the Happy Family Game.

—

Growing up, my mother always told me the one thing she wanted more than anything else as a young woman was *a happy family.* She would often say this with an air of disappointment, which both unsettled and confused me. She had a family. I was her family. My brother and father were her family.

Were we not a happy family?

I didn't understand that not all families had fathers who threw vicious temper tantrums over nothing—a dropped dish of popcorn, a lawn mower blade hitting a stone, the cancellation of a television program—spitting and screaming and putting holes in the walls. I didn't understand that not all families had mothers who wept but said nothing when these things happened, who came to you afterward and asked *why do you always have to antagonize him, why can't you just behave, can't you just be good?*

I didn't understand that not all families had secret, bad things they knew about but would not talk about, secret, bad things they did to each other and the people around them, confident the rest of the family would turn a blind eye, even absolve them of the bad things they did.

We were *not* a happy family, although that was not quite what my mother had meant.

The "happy family" of which my mother spoke with such unful- filled longing was actually something much larger, both more solid and more ideological—not a happy family, but a Happy Family.

A Happy Family is not simply a contented family unit, but a social institution and, more importantly, an object of capitalist desire. Like the latest iPhone, a Gucci purse, or a Mercedes-Benz, the idea of the Happy Family has more value (and signals more about the owner) than the actual function of the object itself. It's a consumer good and, like all modern consumer goods, from headphones to sexual partners, from IKEA furniture to housing, from Nike sneakers to mental health care, it can be bought.

If you are willing to pay the right price. To make the right sacrifices. To stand in the right lines and sign the right papers. To turn your head and look away at the right times.

If you are willing, as it were, to play the game.

———

The dog wasn't allowed in the kitchen, so she lay in the doorway with her nose pressed hard against the line where the living room carpet turned to tile. A black spaniel mutt, floppy and soft as a child's toy.

She watched us eat jealously, the dozen of us: my father and mother, my brother, my mother's sister, my three cousins seated next to each other in descending age, getting smaller and smaller, like babushka dolls. My grandfather, hulking and pale, hunched over at the head of the table, the grand patriarch, clutching his spoon with fingers already thick and clumsy with calluses, getting thicker and clumsier by the day with the onset of arthritis.

It was Christmas. The tree was in the other room, a blue spruce whose top just barely avoided scraping the ceiling of the farmhouse, bedazzled with janky old decorations, dangerously buzzing coloured lights, and dusty tinsel hauled up from the basement where they lived the rest of the year amid the kaleidoscope of old rugs, broken tools, and other nameless junk. At home we always had a plastic tree, a cheap affair with a faintly chemical odour, and I liked to stand next to the real tree and breathe the spicy, citrus scent of its needles. It had been cut from the back forty lot somewhere on my grandfather's fifty acres of red, bare rock and scrub grass. At one time he had been a farmer, and although he still raised cattle—shaggy, red-maned Highland cattle with horns like scimitars and gentle, sweet-timothy breath—in all my childhood I never saw one goddamn good green thing grow there but hay, thistles, and oily-leafed poison ivy so thick it was like a wave lapping at the shore of the fields from the sea of the woodlands.

The dining room table where my grandparents ate, tonight and every other night of the year—they rarely, if ever, ate out—was a farmhouse table, a long, thick, solid piece of wood meant for farm-sized families, with an extra leaf in it tonight to accommodate the additional bodies. Scratched, the varnish peeling, a white tablecloth thrown over it and arranged on top, the good china, items reserved for only the most special of occasions—Christmas, along with Easter and a midsummer annual family reunion and church service, were the trinity of yearly events around which my mother's side of the family revolved.

We were having what we'd always had for Christmas dinner for as long I could remember Christmas dinners: plain mashed potatoes (no butter, no garlic, no sour cream, just a splash of milk and a tablespoon of Becel whisked into them) in a huge porcelain bowl, white and stiff as plaster; boiled carrots and peas; cranberry sauce in a beautiful glass serving dish, the ridges of the can still visible in its malleable wiggliness; Jell-O (served with dinner, as if it were a condiment and not sweetened boiled joints and hooves) in an ornate crystal bowl, canned fruit and grapes suspended within it, topped by a perfect white chemical froth of Cool Whip; gravy in a gravy boat, getting a skin on top;

two-dollar grocery store rolls, the sticky-soft kind that come attached to one another, still in the shape of the square industrial pan they were baked in; and turkey, its golden-brown exterior belying its pallid, spongy interior, overcooked and underseasoned, sitting in the very centre of the spread on a faux-silver serving dish. I didn't know this until I was much older, but absolutely no one in either of my parents' families could cook.

At the opposite end of the table, my mother sat next to her mother, a thin grey woman who rarely spoke. She had married my grandfather when she was sixteen, only three years older than I was; one of my earliest memories was attending their fiftieth wedding anniversary, at which my grandfather had taught me to dance the waltz by allowing me to stand atop his feet and shuffling me about like a tiny marionette, one-two-three, one-two-three, one-two-three, across the dance hall floor.

"Here, mum, let me help you with that," my mother said, and she stood up at the same time as her sister. They are identical twins, and they wore their hair—brown, thinning hair they artificially curled into a Hepburn-style boy-cut—the same. They went into the kitchen to fetch something, and when they came back my mother sat back down and leaned into her mother and said something which made the old woman smile.

On the opposite side of my grandmother, my grandfather continued to chew loudly. He absently forked mashed potatoes into his mouth as I watched with nervous disgust, sitting stiffly in my jeans and soft, dark-blue sweater that was already pilling, both of them new and unwashed and smelling faintly of formaldehyde. I picked at my food, turning a slice of white meat over with the tines of my fork, nibbling a carrot.

The dog still lay in the doorway. I wanted the dog in my lap. This was not allowed. I wanted to leave. This was also not allowed.

My mother glanced at me from her end of the table. She frowned. The look meant *eat*. I didn't want to eat, but I put a bit of mashed potatoes on my fork, lifted it into my mouth. My mother looked away.

Those were the rules. Smile. Eat. Don't talk too much. Do what you're told. Don't ask questions. Don't draw attention to yourself. Get along.

You can only win the Happy Family Game when everyone plays by the rules.

—

The Happy Family Game—played by millions, arguably enjoyed by none—is, like any other game, simple in its concept, complex in its application.

Do you know how to play? You might. Like me, lots of people grew up with the Happy Family Game and are intimately acquainted with the rules. If you're not, don't worry. I can teach you.

The objective of the Happy Family Game is to create a nuclear family unit which, either in reality or in appearance, looks to outside eyes to be financially, socially, romantically, and physically successful, capable of doing their moral duty to purchase and enjoy the products and services that capitalism creates. This is "happiness" in a capitalist society.

This standardized consumer model is what "respectability" and "success"—i.e., "winning"—look like in the Happy Family Game. Ideally, these families are composed of a cis-heterosexual, able-bodied, middle- to upper-middle-class monogamous.couple producing children with the same characteristics. Players who don't meet these criteria (i.e., people of colour, those who are poor, queer, disabled, etc.) can also try to play the game, but they start play with significant penalties.

There is only one way to win the Happy Family Game: get married, have babies, buy lots of stuff, and keep smiling until you die. However, there are myriad ways to lose at it. There's also a moral implication: good, productive, socially respectable consumers belong to good, productive, socially respectable families.

All Happy Families are families, but not all Families are Happy. All Happy Families are the same, and if you're *not* in a Happy Family, we are told, then there's something wrong with you.

—

Just as very few people are born with the correct combination of physical prowess, skill, social supports, discipline, and luck necessary to be a professional athlete, few families actually meet all the requirements necessary to be a Happy Family. That's all in the spirit of the game, though, because as long as you can make it *look* like you're a Happy Family, you can receive all the social benefits of actually *being* one. When you're in a Happy Family, you're a part of the North American dream. For women, this means that you have a biological, social, and economic role as a wife and mother, as well as a *moral obligation*, and it's from this defensive position that the Happy Family Game is played.

To be as successful at the game as possible, the player needs to develop two specific skills: the ability to alter their perception of reality to make it fit the reality they would prefer, and a willingness to deceive, control, and manipulate others, including themselves.

The two most important rules of the Happy Family Game are the suspension of belief and don't think, don't tell.

My mother was—is—an expert and highly skilled player of the Happy Family Game.

—

We were in the bathroom when I told my mother her father had raped me.

Our bathroom fixtures were a soft, pastel purple, and my mother was kneeling on a shag bath mat in front of the toilet, cleaning the lavender-coloured bowl with a scrubber. We had been fighting; my mother wanted me to go stay on the farm with my grandparents again. I didn't want to go. She demanded to know why I didn't want to go and I didn't want to tell her, but she kept pushing me until, finally, I did.

I cried. I shouted. I shook. I said *Pa hurt me Pa touched me Pa did things to me*. And I shouted and cried and shook some more.

My mother, on her hands and knees, bent over the toilet bowl, brush still in hand, stopped what she was doing, and looked at me. She did not rise to embrace me. Her face was blank and her lips were pale. Then she asked me if he had penetrated me.

This is not the right question to ask your twelve-year-old when they tell you your father has goddamn raped them, but she asked it a couple times.

I declined to answer it then, and I decline to answer it here, because "penetration" is not the point.

After a few minutes my mother asked me what I wanted to do.

I said I didn't know. I genuinely did not know. I was twelve. That's what adults are supposed to be for.

My mother began to explain, slowly and carefully, as if her words were a bramble she was picking her way through, that if we went to the police, bad things would happen. I might get in trouble and my grandfather would definitely get in trouble. He would probably go to jail and the family would be torn apart. Did I want that? she asked.

I didn't know what to say. I didn't understand what she wanted from me. She was still kneeling in front of the toilet on one of those awful shag bath mats, damp looking and ragged.

This tactic—to silence the victim with fear and blame—has often made me wonder as an adult how much she knew when she sent me to stay with my grandparents. Was she merely protecting her father because that was what she had always been trained to do, as a daughter? Was she covering for a larger pattern of abusive behaviour, one she should have known endangered me? Had she known full well what would happen when I was left alone with him and had this line of defence at the ready for if and when I ever spoke up?

In other words, was I a casualty, or a sacrifice?

I said very quietly, in a small voice, no, I didn't want that.

Okay, my mother said. She stood up, went to the sink, and washed her hands under the tap. *Don't ever tell anyone about this. Other people could get us in trouble. The family needs to stay together,* she said.

Then she walked out the bathroom.

———

In the Happy Family Game, men are the only players who matter. They need the Happy Family Game to maintain their power, which comes not only from their physical and economic strength—even today, men earn more money on the dollar than women do for the same work—but from the moral concept of the game. Women are trained from birth to believe that motherhood is their highest biological calling, the pinnacle of their femininity. To "fail" at achieving a conventional family unit is to "fail" at all they are taught is good and beautiful and expected of them. To accuse the father is to accuse the very concept of the Happy Family, and by the time children have come along, many women have sunk so much of themselves—their careers, their love lives, their reproductive capacities, their bodies— that it becomes socio-economically difficult (if not impossible) to question their partners, without whom they would be the sole providers. Furthermore, females with children but without partners are considered less sexually, romantically, and socially desirable to new male mates—"damaged goods." There isn't a sitcom around that doesn't play with the hot-woman-but-she-has-a-kid trope at one point or another.

Likewise, capitalism cashes in on patriarchy, setting it—along with racism, classism, and queerphobia—as a cornerstone of its empire. The Happy Family creates a neat, dependable, ordered consumer unit—two parents, 2.5 kids, and a dog—one which can be both sold as an idea and easily marketed to. Controlling women, queers, and people of colour through the rigid white cis-heterosexual, male-dominated patriarchy of the Happy Family Unit also further pushes down working-class and other "non-conforming" bodies to feed the reliable, cheap labour force which a capitalist culture needs to thrive.

Capitalism needs the patriarchy just as much as the patriarchy needs the Happy Family Game. They're all tied up together, coiled about each other, a Gordian knot of longing and power and greed.

And, like the Gordian knot, the only way to unravel it is to cut it apart.

—

In many ways the effect of my mother's unwillingness (her inability?) to act on or acknowledge the impact of her father's actions—which is to say, raping me, a child, his blood relative—was equal to or possibly even worse than the assault itself. In the years that followed, not only did we not speak of the event, I was also made to continue behaving as if nothing had happened. Although I was no longer left alone with him, I was still expected to go to family events with him, including Christmas dinners and church services. I was expected to sit and be nice, to smile and say nothing at these events, and to embrace, even kiss the man who raped me. Thinking about it now, it still makes my skin crawl—the disgusting male scent of him, straw and sweat, the scratchy feel of his stubble against my cheek, the rancid odour of his breath, and the feel of his hands on waist, always seeming to linger a little too long, to wander a little too low, although no one ever said anything about it.

No one ever said anything about anything, in fact.

As I grew older, I kept looking to my mother (or my grandmother, or my aunt, or someone) to help me, to support and protect me against him, until one day I just stopped and accepted that *no one* was going to protect me. It was only later I would learn that more people than I'd thought possible knew, that a choice had been made to say nothing in order to protect him—to protect the family—at my expense.

My mother was not only *not* a mother to me, she was an active participant in my abuse by virtue of her willingness to allow it. Moreover, she was, depending on whom you ask, potentially criminally at fault. Although Canadian law varies from province to province and territory to territory, there's still a "duty to report"—to go to the authorities if someone has reason to believe a child may be in danger—which is "uniform across the country," University of Calgary law professor Jennifer Koshan told me.[13]

"The wording of these different requirements will change from one place to the next, but all Canadian child protection statutes have this duty to report when a child is in need of protection, in need of intervention, whatever the case may be," said Koshan.

"In turn, I think it's also fair to say that statutes across the country define a child to be in need of protection when they are experiencing sexual abuse," she said, although who has the duty to report varies. In Alberta, for instance, it's literally anyone who thinks a child might be in danger.

Although duty to report definitely "could apply to a parent, and if they fail to report they could be liable for an offence and have to pay a fine or even face imprisonment," it's not as simple as simply charging a parent with failing to report. Although the abuse itself is often a criminal matter—it's obviously a crime (and an abomination) to fuck a child—a failure of duty to report is a civil matter. A spouse also can't be made to testify against their partner in most cases, although there are exceptions to this which would likely apply when it comes to the possible endangerment of a child, Koshan explained.

My mother's father, of course, was not her spouse, despite his penchant for incest.

A parent could also be liable for failing to report a sexual assault under the civil doctrine of fiduciary duty, which arises in relationships involving trust and dependency, and this includes the duty to not abuse them as well as to protect them from abuse, Koshan added. This was established in a Supreme Court of Canada case called *M.(K.) v. M.(H.)* in 1992 and "has been used to hold bystander parents liable where they knew or ought to have known about the abuse."

"Breach of fiduciary duty is something a child could sue a parent for, either the sexual abuse itself or failure to protect, and could result in compensation from the parent to the child," Koshan said.

The duty to report can be legally—as well as morally—nebulous, however, and as Koshan is quick to point out, there are a whole bunch of reasons why a parent, especially a mother, might be reluctant to report, including fear for their own safety, fear of having their children taken away (a particular issue of concern for Indigenous mothers, as the Crown's inherently racist policies have and do disproportionately remove Indigenous children from their rightful homes[14]), and financial dependence on their partners.

"It may be that that the woman is also experiencing abuse from her partner; there could be all sorts of other factors that that go into whether it's safe for her to report … What I'm saying, I guess, is that there needs to be some attention on the broader context as well. Because if we started to penalize parents for not reporting, in some circumstances, they're in fact victims themselves," Koshan said.

In short, a parent's obligation to report is a complex, emotionally and financially fraught enterprise which does not lend itself to easy answers, simple legal convictions, or cut-and-dried moral conclusions. You could argue that perhaps my mother was afraid of my grandfather at one time—he was almost certainly a domestic abuser, in addition to being a pedophile—but by the time this was happening to me, I can't really see how a man in his early seventies who lived over an hour away could be a physical threat to a full-grown adult woman with her own family. Based on what I know about him and the way my mother reacted to various conversations about him when we were still speaking, however, I do believe my grandfather most likely sexually assaulted her as well. I highly doubt the idea to fuck a child was one that just popped into his head as an old man; looking back, I could see he had been grooming me for some time. He knew perfectly well what he was doing. This wasn't his first rodeo.

If true, does that make my mother any less culpable? Any less reprehensible? Does that make her actions more justifiable?

I don't know. Sometimes I think yes, and sometimes I think no. I know that I, personally, having grown up in the kind of house I did, with my unstable father, would rather eat brass tacks and shit a bulletin board than leave any child of mine alone at my parents' house.

Moreover, I don't think my mother's choices had so much to do with her own fear of her father than it did with her fear of what her life would be like without him—or of the social stigma that comes from having a child-fucker in the family. If her father were sent to jail—and, worse, held publicly accountable—it would have been impossible for her to have the Happy Family she envisioned for herself.

Whatever her motives, it was more palatable to her to allow him to continue to do whatever he wanted to do to her children than to confront him and hold him accountable for his actions.

My mother.

What does that even mean?

—

The thing that made me stop talking to my mother, that made me cut her out of my life like the bad spot in an apple, was a single phone call.

I was having a very hard time in the winter of 2016; six months prior, I had been sexually assaulted, for the second time in my life, by the man who was at the time my boyfriend. I had fled to Montreal, where I was living on a friend's couch, out of work, exhausted, and experiencing symptoms of severe, crippling, all-consuming depression. I was trying to press charges with the police—a nightmare of ineffective bureaucracy, objectification, queerphobia, and sexism—and I was terribly afraid that my now-ex, who had friends in Montreal, would send someone to hurt me.

In the midst of this crisis, I called my mother—for what, I can't recall, maybe to talk, maybe I needed a loan. I was a fucked-up mess, all-broke and half-drunk on shitty depanneur wine most of the time. We were fighting. I think she wanted me to come down to see her, maybe go to the farm to visit her and her mother, my grandfather having been dead for some time. I said I didn't want to do that; it upset me to be there, on the farm, and I didn't want to go ever again.

My mother, a mousy little woman, chubby and inoffensive as a marmot, who rarely raised her voice, suddenly snapped at me with surprising ferocity.

"Why can't you just get over this! He did it to your cousin, too, and she's forgotten all about it! Just let it go!"

He did it to my cousin, too.

I was very silent for a long moment. On the other end of the line, my mother was quiet too, although I could feel a kind of rising panic, an understanding on her end of what she had just said, of the mistake she had just made.

"Lorianne," she said, because that was my name then, although it is not my name now. "You have to let this go. He's dead, so what does it matter?"

There was another pause. I still couldn't find anything to say.

"You have to trust in the Lord," she said firmly. "Jesus will sort everything out in the end."

And then I knew: There would never be any reasoning with her. It would always be this way. Her making excuses, dodging responsibility, calling down some folksy morality or looking to a fucking magical dead-ass zombie carpenter to fix the things she, herself, refused to fix.

"Fuck you," I said, and hung up the phone.

———

I called my cousin. Although we are only six months apart and our mothers are identical twins (we look quite a bit alike—genetically speaking, we could be similar to half-siblings) we aren't close. She was surprised to hear from me, but not surprised by my question.

It was true.

Putting together our timelines, it turned out I had been first. When I'd stopped coming around, my grandfather had not stopped his predatory behaviour. He had simply switched targets.

My mother had known, and she hadn't told. It seemed, too, that *everyone* had known—both my mother and my aunt, anyway—and not only had no one said anything, they had not *done* anything. All those years, everyone had been politely smiling, covering it up, pretending it hadn't happened and wasn't still happening.

I thought about the last time I had seen my cousin, at my grandfather's funeral. The two of us in our nicest dresses among the mourners, side by side. Our grandfather had had a stroke years before he died, one that left him senile and mostly paralyzed in a wheelchair, during which time he had been the apple of the family's eye, doted on and beloved even as he drooled and shit himself and swore at people with the immunity of an infirm once patriarch. Now, in the coffin, he was bloated and pale. His flesh looked waxy.

We sat there and the reverend came in his black suit and white collar and said nice things about him, about how loved he was in the community, about what a good Christian man he was, about what a good example he set for others. And everyone just sat there, thin lipped and weeping, saying fucking nothing, while the two grandchildren he had goddamn *diddled*, the godless pervert, sat in the front row.

And our mothers knew.

To protect their father's good name, they had sacrificed the safety of children, and those children's right to peace and justice.

After that phone call in Montreal, I blocked my mother's phone number and email address, cut her out of my social media, and instructed her that further contact with me would result in my seeking a no-contact order. My mother didn't even tell her own husband what her father had done. In a rare show of solidarity and empathy, when I told my father why I would not be speaking to my mother ever again, he fully supported the decision and was horrified by the deception.

And that's been it. I did not draw a line in the sand between us. I blew up the bridge, burned it to the ground, pissed on the ashes, salted the earth where it had stood, and walked away. I haven't said one word to her since then, and I can't see a way to ever say one again. I stopped, in that moment, playing the Happy Family Game, then and forever. I won't play the game, and she can't seem to stop.

Let Jesus sort that out if he can. I certainly can't.

———

These things—these family matters, these stories that we tell, the rules of the Happy Family Game—are complicated, and painful, and near impossible to navigate toward anything that might resemble a truth everyone could agree on.

My grandfather was a much-beloved family man, a farmer, and an active member of his church, well respected by his community, a man of and for the land.

He was also a fucking pedophile who groomed and assaulted at least two girls in his care on more than on occasion, not to mention a racist, sexist, misogynist pig.

My mother was a schoolteacher who dedicated most of her career to helping children with learning disabilities learn to read, who baked gingerbread cookies—spicy, sweet, chewy, fragrant—year-round, who loved *Dr. Quinn, Medicine Woman* and *Dirty Dancing* and desperately wanted to be a mother.

She is also a cowardly, weak, irrational woman who has lied to herself her entire life and believes God will somehow sort out the unsortable atrocity of her late father's behaviour, along with her own culpability.

I am a non-binary tattooed queer who strongly believes in social justice, the demise of capitalism, gender equality, and the objective virtues of science and reason, and in journalism as a means to disseminate those virtues.

I am also a child who, in writing this essay, in rejecting the Happy Family Game, has betrayed the family that birthed and raised them (however inadequately)—a snake, striking from amid a basket of plucked fruit, venomous and terrible.

—

Cancer is what killed my grandmother; she was diagnosed with stage 4 lung cancer sometime around Christmas and died in the spring, shortly after Easter. As a devoutly Christian woman, she probably would have liked that, the symbolism of it. She lived through both World Wars, through the Spanish flu into another pandemic, and now that she is gone, I deeply regret that as a youth I never thought to get to know her better, that in the selfish, ugly way of children, I never asked her a single question about herself.

And then, too, I wonder—I try to stop myself from wondering, cannot stop myself from wondering—*did she know*?

Did she know what her husband was doing to his grandchildren?

Did it matter? Would she have stopped him if she did?

I think, too, about her cancer, about what cancer is: Cells inside you that, damaged by inside or outside forces, mutate, shift, and turn against you. A creeping, ugly sore starting small, unnoticed, then blackening and hardening even as it devours the body that contains it, feeding on it to their mutual, inevitable demise.

Her cancer—and I want to be clear here—is not a moral judgment. People get cancer. It's just that cancer and the Happy Family Game, the lies it makes you tell, the self-deception you must partake in if you are to play, the rot of it, have a lot in common.

It starts small. A cough, a little tiredness. A white lie, a blind eye turned at the right moment. Minor indiscretions of the flesh and the mind. You don't want to look at them, to acknowledge they are growing, worsening, becoming more serious. By the time you can't ignore them anymore, it's too late.

Something has to be destroyed—either the cancer or the host, the lie or the family.

Something has to be irrevocably, heartlessly, ruthlessly cut out—if you are to survive.

Every Little
Act of Cruelty

ONE AFTERNOON, around the time I was seven or eight, I came home from school to find the living room full of camping equipment: tents and sleeping bags, water jugs and purification tablets, propane stoves, knives, an axe, sleeping pads, rifle ammunition, fuel canisters, tarps, survival manuals. Hundreds of dollars' worth of outdoor gear.

For one hot minute, I was wildly excited. Other kids in my class went camping with their parents all the time, started every school year with stories of roasting marshmallows over campfires and fishing for bass, and going canoeing out on the big, flat lakes of Southern Ontario. I *desperately* wanted to go, too, but when I had asked my father, the answer was always no. When he could get all 500 satellite channels in his tent, he'd take us camping, he said. That had been the end of it. I knew better than to ask my father for anything twice.

Looking at all this gear piled up next to the couch, though, the bright red-and-white Canadian Tire price tags still hanging off the various items, I was overcome with a burst of childish optimism that he had changed his mind and was going to take us, maybe even *right now*.

And then I remembered it was March—far too early for camping, none of the parks would even be open yet—and my excitement evaporated in a wave of anxiety and suspicion. Something was not right here. Nothing ever changed in that house when I was a kid … until it did, and when that happened it was never good.

From the kitchen, my mother called me. My brother was already in there. He was still very little then, still had a *Leave It to Beaver* cowlick in his baby-soft brown hair. He was sitting at the kitchen table, he looked up at me nervously, searching for some kind direction or confidence I couldn't provide.

In an odd, calm voice—I did not like this voice, I knew this voice and it made me nervous—my mother said we both needed to pay attention, because my father had something very important tell us. Then she took my hand and my brother's hand, the same way she sometimes did when we were in a big crowd, and ushered us out into the living room, where we were made to sit cross-legged on the floor next to the couch—it was too covered in gear to use—and told to wait.

My mother went into the dining room and got a chair. We had an antique dining room set, and the chair that sat at the head of the table had an ornately carved wooden back and armrests, unlike the other chairs, which were plain. It was this special chair that my mother brought into the living room and placed against the wall.

From another room, my father suddenly appeared, a tall, thin, dark-haired man whose face always seemed to be unnaturally sharp and drawn. He approached the chair and, without saying a word, sat down, placing his hands on the armrests and curling his long, big-knuckled fingers about them, as if he were taking a seat on a throne. My mother came to stand behind him, on his right ride, and laid a hand on his shoulder.

Speaking in a low, even voice, my father explained with ministerial certainty that he had received a vision from God: the world would end soon, and we needed to be prepared to survive the coming apocalypse. Only God's chosen would be spared, and he was God's chosen, and we, by virtue of being his children, were also God's chosen. Things would be difficult, but we'd all make it as long as we listened to him and obeyed the word of the Lord.

My mother stood behind him, nodding in agreement, but not speaking.

My brother and I looked at each other. We said nothing. My father, not seeming to sense that anything was amiss, leapt right back into the empty space of our silence. He was talking about the end times, the Four Horsemen of the Apocalypse, about rains of fire and plagues and the word of God, who had appeared to him as a ball of light in a dream. His eyes were distant, faraway, but feverishly bright.

My mother was standing behind my father still smiling beatifically, eyes half closed, nodding gently, as if the absolute zany nonsense tale my father was spinning—that when the end days came, we would all retreat into the forest, and hunt for our food, and live on rabbits and wild plants until the Lord told us it was safe again—was the most wonderful thing she had ever heard. Now that I am older, I can see that it was much more palatable for my mother, as a devoutly Christian woman, to believe her husband was indeed special as all shit, rather than simply off his rocker.

A little pang of fear ran through me, and suddenly, with adult clarity, I thought, *this is crazy*.

A queasy certainty moved through me, and I thought, *these people are crazy*.

I reached out, took my brother's small hand in my own, and squeezed it tight.

—

The world did not end, as I'm sure you know.

I'd like it to be known, before I tell any more of this story, that I really loved my father. He was—*is* (he's still alive, although I've had to make the difficult decision not to have him in my life anymore)—"crazy," a word I use here not in the derogatory mental health sense of the word, but rather to indicate that his relationship with reality—whatever your definition of that is—was at best casual. Throughout the course of my childhood, he believed that he had heard the voice of God or spirits, that he was in some way destined to do some intensely special and significant thing—something which would occur through no physical, emotional, or intellectual change on his part.

I do not mean to in any way to suggest that strange and wondrous things—things which cannot be entirely, rationally explained—cannot and do not happen in this world. I've been alone on too many back roads and spent too many weeks in the bush to be so arrogant as to believe the world is limited to only what is immediately perceivable. I do, however, mean to suggest there is a difference between experiencing something and *wishing* to experience it; there is a difference between *fact* and *belief*, and to this I can only say that I know my father *believes* in certain things which seem to happen only and specifically to him, both in terms of how he relates to the world and how the world relates to him, in aspects both spectacular and mundane. Sometimes that meant believing the world was ending, and sometimes it meant believing that when my brother and I whispered, as children will whisper together, we were whispering unkind things about our father. Neither of these things was ever true at the time he believed them, but he *did* believe them and often acted on those beliefs.

I can only relate these beliefs through the behaviours he exhibited when inhabited by them and their impact on me as a child—namely, they were deeply unsettling and disturbing and made it hard to feel safe. Whether daddy becomes obsessed with a set of keys he found in the alleyway which he claims may open a door to hell, or he sends you to a psychic because he believes you may be attracting evil spirits coming through a portal at the end of the hall, or he screams at you and punches the door of the freezer because he thinks you're saying he's stupid behind his back, it all has the same effect of making it impossible for you to feel secure as a child. That's all I'm saying.

The most severe bouts of my father's unreality—when he believed God had grandiose and highly improbable plans for him, for example—were for the most part relatively infrequent. Looking back, I can see they were likely the result of extensive periods of mental distress, part of a wider and more insidious pattern of mental health issues, which impacted our family—and me—much more generally and regularly. My father's mental health was a subject of constant concern in our household. Although it was rarely, if ever, discussed directly, it was something I knew implicitly I had to work around.

A lot of the time when he was home—and he worked a lot, was gone often, even though my mother was the breadwinner of the family—he was preternaturally quiet, saying nothing, working with his hands in the yard or the shop, or watching television. This outward calm belied the wellspring of anxiety that flowed just below the surface. If you were looking carefully, if you knew what you were looking for, you could see it in the too quick, too tight motion of his hands, in the way he jerked his head and clenched his jaw and snapped to attention, looking gaunt and hunted, when someone else came into the room.

Constantly restless. Agitated. Deeply, deeply depressed.

And so very, *very* angry.

There was never any telling what would set him off—a glass of grape juice spilled on the rug, a giggle when I wasn't supposed to find something funny, losing a video game, a cancelled television program. My father hated noise; he often worked nights, sleeping through the day or watching TV on the couch in the cool, subterranean dark of the basement rec room. When he was home, the air in the house thinned, and my mother, brother, and I ran between the rooms on mouse feet, skittering along the corners by the walls, creeping about the rooms for fear of waking him.

And then, sometimes, my brother and I would forget, and play, and laugh, and run around the house with our shoes on, and jump on the bed, and watch *Mighty Morphin Power Rangers* with the volume on high.

And then bad, scary things would happen.

He swore. He punched things. He stomped his feet and pounded on walls. He screamed the way baboons scream, jaws open, lips pulled back, canines bared. The veins would strain against the skin of his neck, purple beneath his sweaty skin, and spittle would fly out of his mouth, spraying you with a white, wet foam. He shoved and pushed you, got in your face and *raged* at you, so close you could taste the hot, metallic odour of his breath—coppery, like a warm penny, tinged with cigarette smoke. He took you and shook you so hard your eyes rattled, and his furious voice became a dizzy sensation in which your brain was wrapped.

Living with him was like living with a toddler—a 180-pound toddler in charge of the chequebook, with access to firearms. He turned his wrath on anything and everything within range, including, if no one else was available, himself. Once, while having a total meltdown over a dropped bowl of popcorn, he jumped up and down so furiously that he fractured the heel of his own foot, something that usually only happens in car accidents or falls because it requires such tremendous force.

You were extra quiet, extra good, extra respectful when daddy was home, because if you weren't, daddy would *fucking well make you wish you had been.*

When he got like this, when something (usually me) set him off, he could not be talked to. He could not be reasoned with, was immune to both empathy and logic. He was inconsolable with rage.

He was, in other words, completely insane.

What was really well and truly mad, though, was that when it was all over, when the house had descended into tense silence, like the dull ringing that follows a gunshot, it was as if it had never happened.

We never talked about it. We skulked off to dark corners of the house to lie in the hazy grey aftermath of his fury, a cassette in the stereo playing on low. Our mother in the kitchen, nervously banging around pots and pans amid a tension like the kind just outside an operating room. The de facto peace broker of all my father's outbursts, my mother had two tactics for dealing with these incidents:

wilful blindness or blind acceptance. Either way, when the outburst was over, it was my mother's unspoken job to make everyone in the household behave as if my father had not put a hole in the wall, screamed and thrown plates, or professed to be the direct recipient of the divine wisdom of Christ his own damn self. Whether this task was one my mother had willingly adopted or my father had assigned was unclear. There were times, though, as with my father's living room apocalypse scenario, when she seemed to not only tolerate his delusions, but believe them herself. As a child, I found this deeply unsettling, but as an adult I can see her behaviour for what it was: a survival strategy, one helped along by her own strong Christian faith. It was easier, in some way, to believe her husband might really be hearing the voice of god than to believe he was deeply imbalanced, especially when the former might excuse him of his other unstable behaviours.

Either way, when the hour came, our mother ushered me and my brother, sullen and sometimes bruised, into the dining room, where we sat and ate rubbery chicken breasts and mashed potatoes thickened with margarine and frozen peas as if our father hadn't just put a hole in the wall, as if I didn't have bruises on my upper arms, as if my brother and I hadn't just come out of our rooms where we had been crying and crying silently to ourselves, as if we weren't ourselves seething with impotent, unacknowledged, helpless rage.

Everyone sat where they always sat, my mother and father on opposite ends of the couch, kids on the floor with the dogs. Everyone eating off of plastic fast-food trays pinched from one of my father's night jobs.

My father never apologized for his actions; it was as if they had been perpetrated by someone else, some Slenderman who had slipped under his skin, imaginary but real enough to take the blame, and he took no responsibility for what had occurred in his absence. To speak of it would have been to acknowledge his culpability. Unthinkable. Forbidden.

Smile.

Eat your peas.

There's pie for dessert.

—

In my memory—our memories, of course, being a kind of mirage, real only from a distance—my father stands huge, impossibly tall and dark, long as an evening shadow, strong and handsome and capable.

In reality, he was under six feet, spindly as a buckthorn, a thicket of elbows and knees whose wife did virtually every daily task for him: laundry, cooking, cleaning, arranging his appointments.

He had large, broad-palmed hands, thick with calluses and speckled with sores, because he had a chronic case of palmar warts, which he would cut out himself with an X-Acto knife. The wounds healed slowly, would sometimes blacken and ooze, although the warts always came back.

People were always saying hello to him when we were out as a family—the clerk at the cigarette shop, an acquaintance from the school board where he worked as a janitor, an old high school classmate— but he never went out for "a beer with the boys" or played a round of golf or went bowling or fishing or even to the movies with anyone, not even once, not ever. He had no friends, no hobbies, nothing he was passionate about. There was always a guitar in the house, and although my mother said he'd not only used to play, but had been an incredible singer and picker and had even written songs, I never once heard him so much as pluck a chord.

Why exactly my father had children is a bit of a mystery to me. He wasn't particularly fatherly, took no interest in our education, didn't come to plays we were in or attend our band recitals or track meets. Sometimes, he would drive us into town and take us out for ice cream at Reid's Dairy, which had particular appeal because it also had a petting zoo, or he'd take us with him while he browsed at Sam the Record Man at the Quinte Mall and get us McDonald's to eat on the truck ride home, greasy fingered and salty lipped. There were no games of tag in the backyard, however, no books read in squeaky falsetto character voices, no afternoons fishing or paddling, no paternal heart-to-hearts. When he interacted with us, it was always from a distance, always from a place of remove, where he could watch but not have to participate, the way that shy teens at dances often hang back along the wall while their bolder, better adjusted classmates dance and sneak first kisses.

Honestly, I don't think he really liked children, and I don't think he really knew what to do with us—and yet while we were growing up, my mother, who was nearly forty when she gave birth to me, often told my brother and I just how hard she and my father had worked to get pregnant, how badly wanted we'd been. He was a man, though, who never quite seemed to know exactly what it was he wanted, often developing interests that became furious obsessions to which he devoted all his time and mental energies—starting a family band, owning a food truck, goat farming—only to drop them at the first difficulty, the first moment it became clear it would not be *precisely* the way he had envisioned it.

Perhaps this was how he felt about us, his children: something he'd thought he wanted but was disappointed by the reality of having.

——

Love—perhaps familial love, more than any other—is complicated. We are capable of loving people even when it is decidedly not in our best interests to do so, even when they hurt us over and over, even when the loved one is a threat to our physical, emotional, and mental safety. This is true not only of children, but also—as anyone who has ever loved an abusive partner knows—under the right circumstances, of anyone, with any kind of love.

As a child, I loved my father, but I was also terribly afraid of him. Now, as an adult and a transmasculine person, someone who occupies the vast and wild country in between *man* and *woman*, I am also terribly afraid of *becoming* him. Of becoming a man like him.

There is no denying, even for me, that there are substantial similarities between us; I have his high cheekbones, his strong jawline, the cool blue of his eyes. I've inherited his sensitivity to pollen and other allergens, his boldness, his determination and drive. I've inherited his athleticism, his love for working with his hands, and the same habit of running those hands through his hair while he talks. I even walk the way he walks: a long-legged, winding lope, a sure and crafty coyote-like strut.

I have also inherited other, less tangible traits.

A tendency toward depression. Chronic, near-crippling anxiety. Panic attacks. Dissociation. Suicidal ideation. Hypervigilance.

Certainly, many of these health issues are the result of accumulated trauma, the symptoms of learned coping mechanisms gone wrong. I have severe PTSD, after all. For much of my adult life I have struggled to live with and treat the condition. While the events of my life have certainly played a major role, there's almost certainly a genetic component, just as there is with cancer or high blood pressure or diabetes. The cracks in my foundation were there from the very beginning.

Most times, I have myself together. But sometimes I don't. I've got my shit together, mostly—until I don't. I often wonder if this is how my father felt, like he was just walking around trying to keep the lid on the flaming garbage fire of himself and that at any moment, that lid could come flying off to reveal the disgusting, hot mess inside.

The major difference is that my father was not just a danger to himself, but to other people as well. His illness was allowed to mushroom, to take charge of the family, to overtake all our lives. His illness was allowed to hurt me and damage me in ways that I will probably never be able to fully repair.

And I'm terrified that deep down, somewhere inside myself, that same thing is in me.

How much of my father's abusive, angry behaviour was the result of his illness? How much of it was the result of misogyny and being a white, middle-aged man who didn't feel he got what he was owed? How culpable are we for the ways we behave when we are unwell? How responsible are we for the ways our trauma hurts us? For the ways that hurt can make us hurt other people?

I don't know.

I just know that my father was a real and present danger for most of my young life. I just know that it terrified me then and it continues to terrify me now. I just know that someone should have helped him, stopped him, taken responsibility for him when he was unable—or unwilling—to take responsibility for himself. But no one did.

———

You are not going to like this story. I'm telling you right now: this will be difficult to hear.

When I was in grade eight, our old dog, Duke—a neurotic, cataract-riddled Shetland Sheepdog so inbred from the craze for apartment-sized Lassies that he barely learned his own name—died.

My parents decided a new puppy was in order, and my father, who believed very firmly in the value of having something everyone else said was worth having, selected a golden Labrador Retriever puppy from a breeder. Her parents were Canadian show dogs, but we got her for a little less than the usual rate for such a pedigree, because she had a show flaw: a brown nose, the colour of a just-starting-to-melt Hershey's Kiss, instead of the Canadian Kennel Club's standard black nose.

It was 1999, and my father christened our new puppy Sabrina after the titular character of the nineties incarnation of *Sabrina the Teenage Witch*, played by Melissa Joan Hart. We drove home with Sabrina in the back of my father's purple Honda Civic hatchback, the puppy wedged between my me and my brother, and we took turns holding the squirming, pudgy, honey-yellow animal. I remember her being so, so soft and surprisingly heavy, pliant and sleepy-limp the way all babies are, regardless of species, for the first few months of their lives.

Sabrina quickly proved to be everything a lab is supposed to be: good natured, irrepressibly joyful, rambunctious, and highly trainable.

She was also, unfortunately, completely, totally, *utterly* insatiable when it came to food, an obsession which was not limited to actual food, but included anything that had been even briefly in contact with food. She got in the garbage, she filched scraps off the dining room table, she swallowed whole huge lengths of used Saran wrap, creating inconvenient messes—going in and coming out of her—that exhausted my mother, but that my father, rarely home and not at all invested in domestic chores when he was, largely ignored.

Until, one day, Sabrina went downstairs to my father's den, pulled the TV guide off the coffee table, and tore it to pieces. Maybe my father, who often ate while he watched television, had left some tasty trace of food on the page, or perhaps she was after the glue binding the pages, which some dogs adore the taste and odour of, but either way, she reduced it to hamster bedding.

My father watched television obsessively; it was his sole occupation and interest outside of his job as a janitor and pizza delivery driver. He watched it during the day on weekends and late into the night on weekdays, long after we had all gone to sleep. Sports, sometimes, and movies, but also *Seinfeld*, *Friends*, *Cheers*, and—until she came out as a lesbian and he disavowed her—*Ellen*, consuming hours of television every day. To this end, we didn't have cable, but rather an expensive satellite dish with hundreds of channels, a subscription service which mailed the guide—about the size of our local white pages—to the user's home each month.

It was my father who found Sabrina lying in the remains of the guide, bits of paper strewn about her like confetti, the booklet shredded and wet and chewed up, waggling her tail amid the carnage. It was me who heard him scream with uncontrolled, seething rage, and when I ran downstairs to see what was going on, he was cursing and kicking at Sabrina's cage, taking it his hands and rattling it so hard the veins on his neck and arms stood out blue and ugly against his skin.

Sabrina was huddled and shaking in the corner of her crate, uncomprehending. She had shit and pissed herself in terror.

Seeing me standing there, my father stopped shaking the crate, stuck out his finger and laid into me, face red and spitting with fury. Why wasn't I watching the dog, why wasn't my brother watching the dog, why wasn't his wife watching the dog? Were we *stupid*, was I fucking *stupid*, what the fuck was wrong with this whole family?

There was no reasoning with nor consoling my father when he was like this, and I knew it; he was unpredictable and dangerous. There was never any telling if he would just scream and scream and scream or stomp and throw plates or put his hands around your throat and choke you until you couldn't see. He wasn't merely enraged, he was insane, and the only thing you could do was stand there, keeping as still and calm as possible, never turning your back to him, but never looking him in the eye, either—like with a bear.

Was the problem that we didn't love the dog? he screamed. Did we not *want* the dog anymore?

He pushed past me and stomped into the next room—he had this way of walking when he was like that, stepping quick and high-kneed, that would have been comical if it hadn't always meant something really bad was about to happen. By now his raging had summoned the rest of the family; my mother and brother stood away from me, blinking and silent with fear in the doorway that led from the upstairs kitchen.

When my father came back, he was holding a shotgun. My mother made a sound of protest, but he was pushing past her, panting, lips wet with saliva. He reached the crate again, bent down, reached inside, and seized the dog by the scuff of her neck. He dragged her out, squirming and whimpering, tail between her legs, one of which was covered in shit. He carried her to the door and went outside.

The family rushed after him, my mother pleading with him to stop, but he did not stop—you knew that things were truly desperate when the unabashed insanity of his behaviour could cut through the wilful numbness my mother wrapped herself in and move her to action, although it never seemed to have much effect on him. He went into the backyard—we lived in the country, on four acres. Still holding the dog in one hand and the gun in the other, began to *rant*: incomprehensible, unintelligible, rage-filled animal gibberish, like when people say they are speaking in tongues, but *angry*. Hideously, unstoppably, uncontrollably angry.

My brother and I sobbed and sobbed, begging him to let the little dog go, pleading that we loved the puppy, we would watch her, would keep her quiet.

Please don't kill her.

Fear. The kind that tastes like a cold copper spoon in your mouth.

After a time, his rage began to flag, fade, then dissipate, curling off him like steam. His screaming became more coherent, his sentences less fragmented, until eventually he lowered his voice and lowered his gun.

"If she ever touches my stuff again, I'll shoot her," he said, handing my brother the puppy.

He walked away and went back inside as if nothing had happened. We all stayed behind for a moment, on the unspoken understanding it was better—safer—to give him space. We were all very quiet. I had been crying, was now wiping my running nose on the sleeve of my shirt. My brother was holding Sabrina, who had curled into his chest like a pill bug.

My mother took my brother's arm, then my arm. She was standing very straight. She was very pale.

"Don't tell anyone about this." Her voice was soft. Her grip was hard.

We went back into the house.

Our father was already settled down in his armchair in the den, muttering to himself, flipping through channels, feet up on the recliner. He didn't turn to look at us as we crept past him, one by one.

———

So much of my family's life was built around keeping my father's behaviour a secret. As far as I know, my mother never told anyone about my father's mental instability, his bouts of aggression, his manias. And yet there were neighbours, other family members, teachers around at times—it would have been impossible for someone not to have seen (or, in the very least, heard) a full-grown adult waving around a shotgun and howling and cursing like he'd just caught his balls in a meat grinder. But if someone saw, they said nothing, called no one. It wasn't the only time something like that had happened, either—on another occasion, my father had stood in the backyard with the very same shotgun, ranting and raving in the summer dusk and threatening to shoot this or that or himself, although I don't remember why.

From a very young age, I was an unusually quiet, exceptionally unhappy child at school, the kind of obviously disturbed kid who asks for too many hugs from teachers and never has any friends, the kind of kid who cries about everything—a kicked-over snowman, a bad grade on a paper, being called a mean name—until one day they just stop and never cry again about anything, even when they should be crying.

My mother was a teacher at the public school I attended. Probably none of the teachers who taught me ever stopped to think that my mother's strange, maladjusted kid might be so strange and malad-justed because they were fucking *terrified* at home. My mother—a quiet, demure woman, a shy teetotaller who never drank more than a single glass of Baby Duck wine and who rarely went out with the other teachers—did not seem the type to be hiding something. It would have been hard, I think, for her colleagues to imagine the great lengths she went to, in order to hide the extent of her husband's illness—and his abuse.

As much as humanly possible, our parents kept us away from other children, other families. We were rarely granted permission to go over to other kids' houses—I had my first sleepover in grade eight—and were discouraged from going out for after-school activities. The first time I ate dinner with a friend's family, I was at a loss for what to do with myself; they ate at the table, talking and laughing easily with each other, not sitting on the floor or the couch in stone silence before the television, forbidden to speak unless a commercial was on. We never made friends over the summer either; my father had a landscaping business, and from the age of seven until I was twelve or thirteen, my brother and I worked from sun-up to sundown, June to September, cutting lawns, planting, watering and weeding flower beds, picking up garbage, and trimming hedges. Often, we worked so many jobs for such long hours that for days on end, we would eat nothing but McDonald's, or else have supper at eleven p.m. or midnight. Sometimes we'd be so tired we couldn't even eat, and we'd fall asleep on the car ride home.

Even during the school year, we were largely forbidden from having friends over; even my cousins were rarely invited over. I didn't have a friend over to the house—not one single playmate—until I was in grade six, a young boy named Allan, an event I remember ending immediately when my father came home early. My father claimed this moratorium was because he didn't want people snooping around the house and stealing from us. When he wasn't around, my mother explained that his nerves simply could not stand the sight or sound of other people. Likely, that was true, but there was a second, unacknowledged reason for this taboo: having friends over meant my father would have to watch how he behaved. If he slipped up and lost his temper in front of someone outside the family, someone who had not been forcibly conditioned to excuse him, no matter what he did, they'd probably tell their parents, and that could start people asking questions.

Questions which might lead someone to discover the severity of my father's illness—and his abusive behaviour.

All this secrecy and misery, all this abuse and suffering and loneliness, was allowed to continue with one thought in mind: to protect my father, not from himself, which actually would have been useful, but from losing face in the eyes of the world.

Why?

Because my father was a straight white man in a straight white neighbourhood where you did not question the things straight white men did in their own homes. A king in his castle.

Capitalism needs patriarchy—specifically, it needs a family unit headed by a patriarch. This kind of father-knows-best mentality of obeying the person at the top of the socio-economic structure purely because he must, by virtue of having been placed there, deserve to be there, is the backbone of the class struggle. Children obey their mothers, and their mothers obey their husbands. Wage workers obey their bosses and accept whatever pay they're offered because their bosses have to make a profit, or else the people who run the banks will take their businesses. That's how things are *supposed* to work.

You obey, or there are consequences. When you fail to play by the rules set for you by the people at the top, both in and outside of the home, you are punished. If you question the father—no matter how unfit he is to be a father—you are questioning patriarchy, heterosexuality, and the capitalist balance of power. Capitalism is culture, and the culture requires a standardized, easily controlled, and regulated product: the patriarchy and the family unit.

There are certain systems that benefit when you suffer. There are certain systems that function *better* when you—when working-class people—are suffering. Patriarchy is one of those systems. Happy people and productive consumers are not the same thing and, in fact, each may need very different conditions in order to thrive.

Our culture doesn't make a lot of space for this kind of self-reflective, self-responsible thinking—and when you think about it, why would a capitalist society value those qualities? Emotional intelligence and the capacity to think about how our actions impact others—and to take active, physical responsibility for those actions, even when we ourselves have been harmed in the past—often impede capitalist ends. Thinking about what it means that your cup of coffee costs two dollars because the person who serves it to you makes a wage too low to actually live on, and because the coffee farmer who grew it was paid far less than their labour is worth, and because the land the beans were grown on was exploited and mistreated does not sell cups of coffee.

There is an idea in our culture that the way we are as individuals, as a society, as a species is a fixed and static thing. Even when we know bad things are happening—climate change, poverty, pollution, the systemic destruction of Indigenous peoples and cultures, mass extinctions, rampant overdoses—we are told that we can't change things, because what *is* happening is what *should* be happening, or at the very least, it's the only way things *can* happen. Things and people simply are the way we are; therefore, change is impossible, and we are somehow absolved of responsibility for our actions. It's okay to buy sneakers made in sweatshops and to drive gas-guzzling, carbon monoxide–spewing SUVs and to live guiltlessly on stolen land, because *that's just how it is.*

——

On the dresser in my parents' bedroom was an old photograph of my father: a young man in a leather jacket, clean cut, smiling warmly, leaning up against the side of a black-and-chrome Harley-Davidson motorcycle. I would creep in and take the five-by-seven dollar-store plastic frame in my still-growing hands and think *this is how I want to be when I grow up.*

I think about that photo a lot, about how there's no one story, no one straight narrative that can be told about a person, no matter how much we would like there to be. Everyone you know, including yourself, is a shape-shifter, some of us more so than others. No person is ever just one thing.

There are several truths about my father. He was a musician who never played, a man who loved working with his hands and mowing the lawn and watching *Wheel of Fortune* while eating a huge bowl of buttery popcorn.

He was also a deeply unwell man who refused to accept responsibility for nor take any action to correct the serious mental health issues which coloured every interaction we ever had.

He was a motherfucking asshole and not a good parent at all, an unhinged, unstable, misogynistic, violent prick who was a threat to himself and to others, especially to the well-being of his children.

He was a family man who tried his best to provide for his family, despite the hurdles his mental health presented him.

He was a middle-aged man disappointed that his life didn't turn out the way he'd thought it would, a man constantly struggling to get back to who he'd been when he was that young man with the motorcycle, a man who, unable to do so, became a warped, blurred version of himself, one he did not recognize and did not like.

There are a couple of truths about me, too, and one of them is that I am a hell of a lot like my father. That often terrifies me, but in rejecting my father and the values he represents, I've been able to take responsibility for my own actions and choose new values for myself.

I love my father and am afraid of him. I have compassion for him and am determined to be a better man than he ever was.

———

When I was a kid, they said men like my father—men who screamed and yelled and broke things, who cornered you and threatened you and called you *whore* and *cunt* and *stupid ugly bitch* over a carton of milk left out on the counter or an accidental scratch on a car door, men who terrorized their families with the unpredictable winds of their moods—"had a temper."

My mother would say this all the time, *your father has a temper*, the way other people might say *Bill has severe arthritis* or *Harriet is allergic to peanuts*, like it was not his fault, but something to pity and be mindful of. Something you, as a decent human being, were expected to accommodate. Something my father was never expected to be accountable for.

The effect this had on me was profound.

Every little act of cruelty, whether intentional or not, makes us a little less than we were, than we would have been. It takes something from us. That's what patriarchy is. That's what capitalism is. Taking from the many to empower the few.

The way I grew up, under my father's unstable, sometimes violent temper, under my mother's wilful ignorance, was not the way things had to be. It wasn't the way things should have been.

The way the world is today, right now, is not the way it has to be. It's not the way things should be, either.

So many things, really, are the way they are because we are taught—because we assume—that the way things are is the way things have to be.

I think it's really important to remember that.

Where the Fuck Are We in Your Dystopia?

THERE IS NOTHING MORE PLEASING TO ME, more vindicating, more enrapturing, more sublime, than a woman who is absolutely fucking *furious*.

I love it when femmes lose their shit in bars, spitting insults and slapping unwanted hands away and throwing drinks in people's faces. I love it when butches throw that hard-jawed, stony stare at some guy who calls them *dyke*, that look that means *fuck you, breeder*. I love the trans women calling out TERFs like J.K. Rowling, fanning the flames of the pyres on which the Harry Potter books burn,[15] the literal smoking ruins of cis-heteronormative mediocrity. If I could, I'd feed the wood stove in my cabin exclusively with second-hand copies of *The Deathly Hallows*, Dave Chappelle headshots, and yard sale Margaret Atwood novels—the only way to draw any warmth from the latter's lifeless prose would be to burn it.

All our lives, we—and I say here "we," because although my gender is androgynous, for most of my life thus far I have been treated as a woman and probably always will be by certain people—are discouraged from anger. Women are supposed to be "nurturers" and "caregivers," which is man-speak for "physically and emotionally available doormat who never says no and always puts other people first, men especially." An angry woman is a "bitch," a "cunt," a "hysteric"—but even if that's true, *so what?* What's wrong with being a bitch when being a bitch is called for? There's so much suppression, so much malice, so much disdain and dismissiveness for female rage that our every justifiably angry word and wrathful act is an act of defiance and rebellion.

In some ways, the social censure of women's anger seems to be loosening; the #MeToo movement has brought toxic masculinity and male privilege to the fore, with public accusations of sexual assault, misogyny, and misconduct against big-name men like Hollywood producer Harvey Weinstein, actor Bill Cosby, and literary biographer Blake Bailey. And yet, even as women push forward, men push back, and push back *hard*. Abortion rights rolled back, vicious attacks on trans women, court cases against abusers lost or overturned, not to mention the COVID-19 pandemic, which has impacted women's employment, earnings, and careers disproportionately to their male counterparts. The misogynist culture of incels—increasingly and inextricably tied to racist, fascist, queerphobic movements and political ideology, as portrayed in Talia Lavin's 2020 work, *Culture Warlords*—is becoming alarmingly mainstream and violent.

As Louise Erdrich[16] says in her 2017 novel, *Future Home of the Living God*, men have become "militantly insecure."

Basically, shit's all fucked up and getting worse all the time.

With the way things are, it's not surprising there has been a huge surge in dystopian literature, largely written by women, for women, about women's issues in the last decade. As publishing reporter Alexandra Alter wrote in the *New York Times*,[17] "This new canon of feminist dystopian literature ... reflects a growing preoccupation among writers with the tenuous status of women's rights, and the ambient fear that progress toward equality between the sexes has stalled or may be reversed."

I *love* dystopian novels. A good dystopian novel is a translation; something large and frightening and abstract is made personal. Dystopian fiction is both exposure therapy and catharsis, and in early 2018, healing from a recent sexual assault, frustrated and exhausted by the apathy and impotence of both the law and the men who make and enforce it, and just generally weary of the day-to-day misogyny having a pair of tits gets a person, I began to devour feminist dystopian novels, one after the other. I've always turned to books when I feel alone, and I was feeling very, very, very alone at that time in my life. It was vindicating to hear voices as angry, as frightened, as disturbed by the world as my own.

I started off with Margaret Atwood's *The Handmaid's Tale*—a natural choice, as in recent years Atwood has come to be recognized as the founder of the modern genre. In it, the once-United States becomes the totalitarian regime Gilead following a coup by right-wing Christian extremists dedicated to controlling women's bodies in the wake of a fertility crisis. Later, I read *The Testaments*, Atwood's follow-up novel in which a full generation has passed and grown up in Gilead, which is beginning to show cracks in its control, and *The Power* by Atwood's protege, Naomi Alderman, in which all the women in the world suddenly evolve the power to blast electricity from their hands, like electric eels, upending the traditional power balance between the genders.

I chewed through Leni Zumas's *Red Clocks*,[18] in which new draconian laws on abortion, IVF, and adoption alter the lives of three women; and Helen Sedgwick's *The Growing Season*, set in a parallel world where technology has "freed" women from physical pregnancy in the name of equality, but the company that controls it is keeping a dark secret from its users. Later, I read Louise Erdrich's aforementioned work, *Future Home of the Living God*, written as a series of letters from a pregnant woman to her unborn child in a near future in which creatures—humans included—are evolving backward, birthing long-extinct versions of their species ancestors, causing the government to begin capturing and imprisoning pregnant women.

More and more and more novels. I read and read and read. As I did, a pattern started to emerge, one which, as a queer person, as a working-class person, as a non-binary person, as a feminist, began to disturb me.

I felt I was on the trail of something, so I read some more.

In Sophie Mackintosh's *The Water Cure*,[19] a family sequesters themselves from a world torn apart by a mysterious disease carried by men that may or may not be imaginary, but which sickens women nonetheless, causing the women of the family to subject themselves to cruel and bizarre "purification" rituals levied and governed over by their all-powerful father, King. Later, I read Mackintosh's second novel, *Blue Ticket*,[20] in which women are either allowed or prohibited by the state to have children—with dire consequences for anyone who attempts to change their lot.

I read Christina Dalcher's *Vox*, in which a far-right Christian American government has forbidden women from working, reading, or writing and fitted them with shock-collar devices to enforce a limit of a hundred spoken words a day.

On a road trip to Keno, Yukon, I chewed through Jennie Melamed's debut novel, *Gather the Daughters*, in which an isolated island community, having fled a disaster on the mainland generations ago, forces girls to marry the year they begin menstruation, and men are granted complete authority over their households—even though the world beyond the island may not be all that they have been told.

I read ten books in all, most of them written in the last five years. I primarily consume novels as audiobooks, so I know exactly how much time it took: 100 hours of words.

One hundred hours of words in which queer people are almost entirely absent.

One hundred hours of nightmarish scenarios of incredible danger for women and female bodies in which no one bothers to explain—to think about, even—what happens to *us*.

One hundred hours of imagined futures in which we, apparently, do not exist—or perhaps, simply do not matter.

If this is feminist dystopian fiction, for whom is the "feminism" it depicts?

How can you have feminism without queer women and non-binary people?

Where the fuck are we in your dystopia?

—

To be clear, it's not that I would expect *all* of these works to include a queer character, or even to mention queerness as a thing that exists in the world. Not every book has to be everything to every person. I'm the whale shark of readers, just swimming around out there in a blue-green sea of books, opening my mouth and letting them drift on in, and I love lots of books that are written by straight people about straight lives without even the whisper of queerness about them. These novels, however, are special in that they are designed—and marketed—as inherently *feminist*, i.e., about the rights and issues of women generally.

Only four of these ten novels, however, mention queer people of any gender, even in passing.

Only three feature lesbian characters, and of those, only one shows those women actually engaging in same-sex romance and sexuality.

None feature non-binary or openly trans women at all, in any context, at any time.

Once is an accident, twice is coincidence, three times is science, and this is a motherfucking *phenomenon*, baby.

What the fuck is going on here?

—

So, what are these books, these supposedly feminist *1984*s and *Brave New World*s, about?

Universally, every single one of these books is about the way men, individually or as a gender, seek to control, confine, and subjugate women and their bodies at a personal, social, or government level—sometimes all three. Women in these (mostly) imagined worlds are held captive, sometimes against their will, as in *Vox*, *The Handmaid's*

Tale, and *Future Home of the Living God*, sometimes without their even knowing that they are prisoners, as in *Gather the Daughters*, *The Water Cure*, and *Blue Ticket*. Across the board, there is an inherent, innate fear of both religion and the state, as one or the other (and often, both) reach out to force women into submission. It is a fear which is well founded and with myriad historical examples, from the present Christian right's attacks on women's bodies through limiting access to birth control and abortion in the United States, to the biblical Ephesians 5:22: "Wives, submit yourselves to your own husbands as you do to the Lord." The vast majority of these novels— eight out of ten—have pregnancy and children at the heart of their narrative: having babies or not having babies, getting abortions or not getting abortions, wanting children and not having them, having them and not wanting them.

Overall, these are novels in which women are afraid of men because men do bad things to women—dystopias rooted firmly in reality, because men, empowered by the holy trinity of capitalism (the state, the patriarchy, and religion) do bad things to women (and non-binary people) all the fucking time.

For the purposes of this essay, for a novel to be counted as a work of feminist dystopian fiction, the story's events and society must be fictional and focus on women (or assigned female at birth, AFAB) bodies as a whole. For example, I could have counted Miriam Toews's *Women Talking*—in which the women of a Mennonite community debate whether or not they wish to remain after a handful of men in the community drug and rape several of them in their sleep, only for their leaders to admonish them into forgiving them, with no repercussions for the perpetrators—but I didn't, because although it is both decidedly feminist and decidedly dystopian, the novel is based on real (if fictionalized) events and societies. Likewise, I could have included Ling Ma's superb anti-capitalist novel *Severance*—in which a fungal infection turns people into hollowed-out zombies, and a young woman is held captive by a middle-aged man because he believes her child will be the start of a new world—but I chose to omit that as well, as the bodily oppression is happening to only *one* woman, not *all* women.

These works and, more broadly, the women who write them, as well as those who read them without a critical eye (in every single review I read of every single one of these books, none mentioned the absence of queer people in the narrative, nor the fitness of their representation in the scant instances they did appear), seem to quite mistakenly believe that the problems of cis-heterosexual women are *exclusive* to cis-heterosexual women.

They are not.

As any dyke will tell you, being in a relationship with another woman does not preclude you from being objectified by some Kyle at the end of the bar who won't quit staring at your tits.

As any enby will tell you, presenting androgynously (or masc or femme of centre) does not preclude you from being sexually assaulted.

As any trans woman will tell you, being trans does not protect you from male violence.

That's not simply my opinion, nor is it merely anecdotal—the stats bear it out. Bisexual and trans women (including bisexual trans women) experience significantly higher rates of sexual and intimate partner violence,[21] with more barriers to access than cis-heterosexual and even cis lesbian women. The numbers rise again for people of colour, especially Black bisexual women. For reasons that aren't entirely clear (stigma is believed to play a role), bisexual and, in some cases, lesbian-identifying girls are more likely than their heterosexual peers to have an unwanted teen pregnancy[22] in both Canada and the United States, and transgender youth are as likely to be involved in a pregnancy as their cis peers. The rates of same-sex couples raising children—pregnancy and child-rearing are an overwhelmingly common theme in these books—are rising dramatically.[23] Almost half of all trans women report having been sexually assaulted at some point in their lives, and if they've done and/or do sex work, that number jumps to 72 percent.[24]

Being a queer woman or trans or non-binary person doesn't mean being immune from the problems of misogyny and patriarchy. It actually means dealing with all the socially ingrained misogyny all women deal with under the capitalist patriarchy, *plus* a whole bunch of other shit that comes with being queer and/or gender non-conforming. Add in being a person of colour, or neurodivergent, or disabled, or working class, and you've got yourself a pretty fucking potent cocktail of oppression—one that these gin-and-diet-tonic, middle-class, cishet white "feminists" probably couldn't even pronounce to properly order, never mind choke down.

Personally, as a queer, non-binary person with a female-coded body who (very) occasionally sleeps with men, I've been sexually assaulted twice. I frequently get catcalled and shouted at—calls for sexual favours, questions about my gender when I walk home alone at night; even in my small community, I carry a knife, because I know men cannot be entirely trusted even at the best of times.

Does that not sound like the life of someone who lives under the weight of misogyny and patriarchy? And yet, not one of these books contains someone who looks like me, who exists as I exist; there's not a single person in all ten of these so-called feminist novels who I could relate to.

Excluding queer women and non-binary people from these conversations, as they are excluded from these books, effectively erases and invalidates their experiences. It's not as if I and people like me don't fight and suffer alongside cis-heterosexual, even cis-bisexual women. We do; queer women and non-binary people have been leaders in the women's rights movement since the days of suffragettes. It's as if these novels are saying the part about you that matters most is whether or not you relate in a daily romantic, sexual way to men. Curious criterion for supposedly feminist novels.

To say the quiet part out loud, our exclusion from these "feminist" books says: *you are not one of us.*

———

So, if most of these books function as if queer people don't exist, effectively erasing us from the feminist conversation, where *do* we exist and what does it mean when we appear?

Sedgwick's *The Growing Season* has one gay male couple, written with emotional depth and sensitivity, even if it doesn't really address the problem of representing queer women in the work. One side character is an admitted bisexual, although she appears only briefly, is not depicted with a partner, and has no real impact on the story. Likewise, in *Season*, there is the possibility—if you squint *super hard*—that one of the women executives of FullLife, the company that controls "the pouch" (the device that allows pregnancies to take place outside the body), might be a trans woman. She says she always wanted children, but didn't have the "biology" for it without the pouch, which suggests she's trans but could just as easily mean she's infertile (which is why, for the thousandth time, the ability to have children is a piss-poor way to define womanhood).

Vox—which involves a secret government plot to permanently silence women with a genetically engineered virus designed to destroy a specific part of the brain essential to speech, plus shock collars and a berserk lab monkey (yes, you read that correctly)—is just an absolute clusterfuck of a book. To her credit, Dalcher is the only writer who bothered to construct a horrific near-contemporary misogynist dystopian future and wonder what would happen to the queers in a Christian-right-zealots-seize-control-type situation: they get sent off to re-education camps, so everyone who can goes back in the closet, which is probably exactly what would really happen. Ten points for Dalcher. Her lesbian characters, however, are clearly tacked on, thin, two-dimensional representations of how Dalcher, a straight person, imagines lesbians, which is as clearly secondary to and in the service of cis-straight relationships. Jackie, a lesbian feminist activist, and Lin, a lesbian scientist, appear and disappear as Dalcher needs them, and we know very little about either except her profession and sexuality. Moreover, neither woman is ever shown with her partner, nor engaging in even the most banal expression of her hypothetical sexuality—not so much as a chaste kiss. This is especially notable, as Dalcher spends an absolutely wild amount of time on the novel's (totally unnecessary) romantic side plot, in which the main character, Jean, a middle-aged neurolinguistics professor (who sounds astoundingly similar to Dalcher, who herself holds a degree in neurolinguistics *cough cough*), has a torrid sexual affair—albeit described in PG-13 detail—with a wildly attractive, swarthy Italian colleague named Lorenzo (again, yes, you read that right).

Reading the book, I had to wonder whether Dalcher has ever *met* a lesbian; Jackie and Lin are both not only traditionally femme (Dalcher goes to great pains, actually, to let readers know how pretty Lin is), but totally freaking helpless in pretty much every situation they're placed in, content to wait on the sidelines while Lorenzo and, to a lesser extent, Jean, try to find a way to save them. Honey, trust me, if you're going to take down a fascist regime, you're gonna wanna call the butches in, too—they've got the best boots for the job.

Vox, in short, is a great example of a straight, white, middle-aged, upper-middle-class writer affecting "diversity" in order to further the sort of feminism which excludes the very bodies she's adopted for the cause.

So, what do I want, exactly? I'm pissed off when queer people aren't included and then I'm pissed off when they are. Typical lippy queer, eh?

What I want is for queer people to be included as part of the feminist agenda, not used only to further a feminism which excludes the validity of our lives, bodies, and experiences. What I want is for the straights to not only include us in that feminist agenda, but to think of us—and to write about us—as we are: your legitimate siblings-in-arms in the war on patriarchy.

There is one novel, however, and only one, in which important, fully realized female characters engage in same-sex relationships. The most recent novel on the list, published in 2020 and written by one of the two authors under forty-five, Mackintosh's *Blue Ticket* has at its heart if not a queer love story, then a story of queer desire, of the way that desire is shaped in the context of patriarchy, misogyny, and the male gaze.

And it's absolutely fucking *damning*.

—

Full disclosure: I hated *Blue Ticket*. Despite its masterful use of language and a layer of unapologetic eroticism spread thick as buttercream icing, it was a slog to get through. Specifically, I hated—despised, loathed, wanted to punch in the throat—the book's absolutely unlikeable, selfish, manipulative, greedy, shallow, narcissistic, possibly even borderline psychopathic first-person narrator, Calla.

Calla is only ever interested in her own wants and needs and never seems to think, even for a moment, about the ways her actions impact others—not when she tricks a guy she supposedly loves into impregnating her against both his consent and his will; not when she disappears on the run, never once thinking of her father or her friends; not when she breaks into a nursing mother's house and threatens her at gunpoint while the baby sleeps in her arms.

Moreover, Calla's infuriating obsessiveness and unfocused navel-gazing is a problem that spills over into the novel itself, the premise of which revolves around the idea that the state decides which women get to have husbands and families and babies—"white ticket women"—and which ones get to have professional careers and never have babies—"blue ticket women." *Why* is never made clear. In an interview with *The Guardian*, Mackintosh herself admits there's "not really much world building" going on.[25] The focus is on what happens when you disobey, which is apparently this: if you go and get yourself knocked up as a blue ticket woman, a shadowy state cabal will let you run like a hare all over an unnamed but very UK-like countryside so they can hunt you and catch you and drag you in for an unknowable punishment.

Look. I'm gay and non-binary, but I have all the same hormones straight cis women do; I have a biological clock, too. I sometimes want a baby—*desperately*, against all reason and desire. I actually love kids, and, being in my thirties, I know there's a ton of pressure on women to have kids *now now now* while you still can, and being single, especially, coupled with this social imperative can be frustrating, even make you feel like a failure—but this book is patently ridiculous.

No one—and I mean absolutely fucking *no one*—is telling straight, white, middle-class cis-heterosexual women not to have babies.

In fact, you could make some pretty good arguments that exactly the opposite of that is true. It seems a wildly self-serving and narrow-minded position to be taking at a time when Latina women have been held and forcibly sterilized against their will in Trump-era border internment camps,[26] Canadian doctors have been forcing Indigenous girls as young as ten to have IUDs implanted,[27] and waves of anti-trans legislation are rolling out across the globe,[28] including calls for the forced sterilization of trans people, a practice which many in the United States and the United Kingdom would like to see implemented and which was a requirement for gender-affirming surgery in the Netherlands until 2014 and *still is* a requirement in some countries today, including Japan.

This novel, like its narrator, needs to take itself firmly by the shoulders and pull its head out of its own ass, because *pay the fuck attention*.

Calla, on the run from the nebulous forces that for inexplicable reasons are chasing her in an attempt to keep her from motherhood, falls, albeit briefly, for dark-haired Marisol, also pregnant and on the run. Together, the two women begin an intense sexual relationship, although from the very beginning, this femme-femme erotic attraction is rooted in their shared pregnancies—an obviously heterosexual act—and their abandonment by their preferred previous male partners, in Calla's case, "R," whom she obsesses about even when she's with Marisol.

Calla is fixated by the idea of motherhood, not only as a biological function, but as a cis-heterosexual value system. She wants to be protected, cared for, looked after, with a husband and a house and babies and a yard: domesticity. In the end, Calla abandons Marisol—leaves her alone and sleeping on the beach, still on the run, heavily pregnant—and doesn't even know *why*. She just *does* it, as if leaving Marisol will somehow grant her access to the white ticket life she so covets.

The abandonment, a disgusting betrayal, doesn't really matter, though, because Marisol has *also* been playing Calla. Even as Calla tries to plot her way into escaping with her baby across the border without her, Marisol is really a double agent working for the state who plans from the beginning to sell Calla out in order to save her own skin and her own baby—a moot point, since Marisol's baby ends up stillborn.

Although the women are bisexual, their queerness—their love for each other and for other women, be it sexual, platonic, romantic, or otherwise—is always *secondary* to their heterosexual desires. Women can be lovers and co-conspirators, but their loyalties are often suspect, and more often than not they are outright enemies, trying to step over each other to get what they want—or even to hurt each other just because they're both woman and, therefore, rivals for this desired domestic life. Their allegiances are always to themselves, to equalizing and attaining the cis-heterosexual dream of a man and a woman and a baby, first and foremost. Everyone and everything else is not only *secondary*, but *expendable* to those concerns.

And if you don't want that—if you don't meet the criteria for that—*fuck you*. You don't matter.

If I could meet Sophie Mackintosh, I'd buy her a beer and shake her hand and say *Thank you, Ms Mackintosh, for this absolutely perfect metaphor of what white, straight feminism is about today.*

———

So, to return to my initial question: what the fuck is going on here? It's not like there's a sinister rouged cabal of women sitting around in power pantsuits and drinking chilled rosé, conspiring to keep queers out of feminist dystopian novels and the feminist conversation at large—although, if there were, they'd be doing a remarkably good job of it.

To understand the *why* of this, we need to ask two questions: *what* else is missing from these novels besides queer people, and *who* is writing them?

What is missing, largely, is people of colour and working-class people.

There is an absolute *stunning* lack of racial diversity in these novels, both among leading and secondary characters. Only *Future Home of the Living God* features a consistent BIPOC perspective, although *Red Clocks* and *The Power* also feature secondary of-colour narrators. Alderman's portrayal of Allie as the multiracial "Mother Eve" falls back on a troubling trope, however. Allie, an orphan, is adopted by wealthy white parents who sexually and physically assault her, and both she and Roxy, whose mother was murdered before her eyes, attain their power through male-induced trauma. *Gather the Daughters, The Water Cure, Red Clocks, The Handmaid's Tale*, and *The Testaments* are all basically white paint swatches—pearl, lily of the valley, or ivory, I'll be damned if I can tell the difference once it's on the wall.

There are also virtually no working-class people in these books. Few, if any, of these women want for anything; everyone seems to be comfortably middle, if not upper-middle, class, at least where these class structures still exist. I found this the most galling in *Blue Ticket*, where Calla, perpetually miserable and neurotic, can afford to pour a bottle of excellent Beaujolais down the sink, and still bitch about how unhappy she is and how terrible she feels because she can't have *exactly what she wants right now, stat.* Everyone always has housing, a job where jobs are permitted—many main characters work in academia or as teachers—and are clothed and properly fed, except toward the end of *Gather the Daughters*, when a plague disrupts food production on the island everyone lives on. The day-to-day struggles of working-class people—employment, rent, bills—do not seem to concern anyone in these novels. Even under totalitarian regimes, the only real lives are middle- and upper-class lives, apparently.

Of the eight women who wrote these ten novels, only one is a person of colour: Erdrich, who is Ojibwe American. Only one of the writers, Sophie Mackintosh, is verifiably under forty-five (I suspect Jennie Melamed[29] also is, but could not confirm this, as her website no longer exists). All of them have been to university, all have graduate degrees, and five of the eight hold doctorates or are PhD candidates. All of the writers—with the exception of Atwood, who is Canadian—are from the United States or the United Kingdom; both nations are presently home to *vicious* anti-trans sentiments and political policies. Only Alderman is a confirmed bisexual; five are confirmed heterosexuals and two have not made public statements either way.

Basically, it's largely a bunch of white, well-off, university-educated British and American women yammering away about how hard it is to be white, well off, university-educated British and American women and who, quite mistakenly, seem to believe theirs take is the definitive take in the gender war—which, by the way, is the *gender* war, not the assigned-sex-at-birth war.

There's also one other, perhaps surprising, common thread: the involvement of, comparison to, or inspiration by Margaret Atwood's Handmaid duology.

Atwood's name came up again and again, sometimes directly from the authors themselves, sometimes in comparisons by various reviewers, and at other times when discussing the feminist dystopian genre generally. Alderman's *The Power*—so different from her earlier work, *Disobedience*, which focuses on a bisexual Orthodox Jewish woman—has Atwood's own hand in it, as the elder author mentored the younger while writing it. Atwood is the originator of the "angry feminist" trope in North American literature, and among the first (especially female) writers of speculative fiction to have their work taken seriously as *literature*, not merely pop entertainment. As far as feminist dystopian fiction goes, Atwood is considered both the mother and the expert of the genre.

Which is a bit of a problem, because Atwood has proven herself, both in her work and in her actions, to be a feminist of a certain stripe. The feminism of her novels concerns straight, white, middle-class women, and straight, white, middle-class women exclusively. Many women—especially young women—were dismayed by her support of Stephen Galloway during the now-infamous sexual assault allegation scandal at the University of British Columbia. She is, at best, a champagne feminist. Likewise, her support of columnist and all-around jerk-on-main Rosie DiManno's abhorrent anti-trans "defence"[30] of the word "woman" proves what many in the queer community have long suspected: Atwood is not only a bad feminist, but a big ol' unapologetic TERF. Despite whatever protestations she might make to the contrary, the proof is in the rich old white lady pudding.

With that said, I don't mean to detract from Atwood's work, which I personally think has about as much colour and personality as an old plastic bag; she has her fans, though her work clearly isn't for me (I vote for the much more talented and good-hearted Alice Munro to usurp Atwood as Canada's Literary Queen). There's no denying that Atwood has made huge strides for women writers, just as there's no denying *The Handmaid's Tale* is a masterpiece of dystopian fiction, one that's possibly even more relevant today that when it was released in 1985. All I'm saying is, we aren't getting anywhere by copycatting the same model, in literature or in feminism, over and over when that model applies to only a fraction of the bodies it's supposed to represent.

Atwood may at one time have been the mother of feminist dystopian literature. These days, however, she is at best the crotchety, sometimes embarrassing aunt whose outspoken "traditional" views you might warn a friend or lover about before inviting them over for a family dinner.

—

Once, several years ago, when I was working on Salt Spring Island as a farmhand, I was invited to an evening at a women's circle.

It was a very thoughtful and well-intentioned invite; I was new to the island and didn't really know anyone, and, moreover, I was finding it a bit of a challenge being single and gay there, especially because I was working twelve to fifteen hours a day. I happily accepted, made a batch of fish cakes—it was a potluck, and I make very nice fish cakes—and bobbed over to the house where it was being held. What I *thought* I was going to was a casual, women-only potluck with maybe some wine and some light conversation about how we need to burn down the patriarchy and piss on the ashes.

What *actually* happened was, frankly, fucking weird.

We sat in a circle on the floor, where we were instructed to hold hands and close our eyes. The group leader—a white woman in her thirties with dreads and a hand drum—began to sing and chant softly. After a moment, we asked to raise our voices and *sing a song of thanks to our wombs*.

God fucking help me, I thought it was a joke, and I *laughed*.

I mean, I giggled—the start of a laugh, which just barely slipped out, mostly smothered by the song everyone but me seemed to know—because I peeked out of one eye and caught the reverent, beatific faces of the women around me and realized it was *not*, in fact, at all a joke and shut my mouth.

We gave thanks to our wombs and to our "yonis" (apparently, one does not say "cunt" in this context) and to the "divine life-giving essence of our femininity." We went around the circle, and women were invited to share things that were troubling them. These were largely issues around parenting, male partners, and pregnancy. Everyone there, I realized, either had children or was actively trying to have children or just *really* wanted children. There was a lot of talk about our "inner goddesses" and the importance of welcoming the power of new life into our bodies. Notably, the only sex-specific part of our bodies we didn't thank was our clits, which seemed a strange omission, given its potential for boundless and specifically biological female pleasure that does not require any interaction with men at all (well, not necessarily—you do you).

I was incredibly uncomfortable. I felt I did not belong, that this wasn't a safe place for me. That wasn't what the group had intended; they weren't malicious at all. It was simply that they assumed their world view of what it meant to exist in an assigned-female body was a view that *everyone* shared, and that their experience was the true and universal experience of living in that body. It simply didn't occur to them that their narrow definitions might be alienating to other people who lived very differently, in bodies that were a lot like theirs—or that people in bodies different from theirs might also identify as women. They assumed experiential authority and reinforced it by surrounding themselves with people with the same biases—same class, same race, same sexuality, same beliefs— to such a degree that it appeared as if it *was* a universal viewpoint (to them).

I am not a woman—although I was not out as a non-binary person at the time—but that's not the reason I didn't belong in that room. I didn't belong in that room because the idea of "woman" was tied up not only in the body, but in the *function* of the body as it related to heterosexuality—specifically, to heterosexual reproduction and traditional gender binary and sexual roles. If you are a *woman*, you are a caregiver, you create life, you *thank your womb*. The idea was function over form—an idea that naturally excludes queer and trans women, along with women who are infertile. If you feel this way about yourself and femininity, cool—I'm just saying there's a dangerous knot in there that needs to be carefully thought about. It seems a narrow definition of womanhood, and a perilous position to place oneself as a woman.

This is precisely what is happening in many of these novels, and what has happened to mainstream feminism in general; it becomes self-referential, a cultural circle jerk. A lot of these books are good books, but it's incorrect to call them feminist dystopias. You could, perhaps, call them more specifically cis-heterosexual, white, middle-class feminist dystopias. It's not a problem to have these voices—it's just that they overwhelmingly populate the literary and cultural feminist landscape to such a degree that they appear to be the authority, as opposed to the minority.

A handful of novelists *have* subverted and reshaped the feminist dystopian genre, of course: Octavia E. Butler's anti-capitalist *Parable of the Sower* has long been considered a masterwork; Bina Shah's

Before She Sleeps reappropriates the story of *Romeo and Juliet* to comment on both Western and Middle Eastern expectations of womanhood, motherhood, love, and sexuality; and the feminist dystopia painted in Larissa Lai's brilliant, Lambda Literary Award–winning *The Tiger Flu* flips a very intentional middle finger at everything we expect of the genre. These sorts of books, written by women of colour (and Lai's work is *exquisitely* queer, too), are fewer and farther between—and get much less press—than their counterparts, likely precisely because they deviate from what we have come to consider the "standard" for feminist dystopian fiction, namely that it be geared toward a white, cis-heterosexual, middle-class experience. Most of the novels I've mentioned, for example, were reviewed by *The Guardian*, but I could find no mention of either Lai's or Shah's work in that publication. Butler, inarguably the most famous of the three, was referenced by *The Guardian* first in her obituary and then in several other stories about science fiction. One in particular stood out: a piece on "feminist dystopian fiction" which briefly mentions Butler midway through. The article revolves around and opens with a direct mention of Atwood's *The Handmaid's Tale*. Unsurprisingly, this piece was written by Atwood's aforementioned acolyte Alderman.[31]

We need new ideas and new voices, and to do that, we need to take the old idols like Atwood down off their pedestals and start thinking critically about what they represent—and whether or not those values serve the all people they're supposed to.

Feminism which excludes queer and trans bodies—and working-class bodies, and non-white bodies—is not feminism at all. It's oppression musical chairs, a game that leaves the majority of women and female bodies standing outside the circle.

The only true feminism is intersectional. That doesn't mean you can't have novels about white, middle-class, straight cis women struggling through patriarchal dystopias written by white, middle-class, straight cis women struggling through a patriarchy on its way to being dystopian.

It just means that shouldn't be the *only* story we tell.

Other People's Houses

AT THE FIRST APARTMENT BUILDING I LIVED IN—I was eighteen, it was 2004—a tremendous raccoon made a den under our porch. At night he would crawl out from underneath it and up the long set of stairs to stand at the screen door with his paw-hands pressed against the wire mesh and scream at my cat, this high-pitched, furious shriek, whenever he walked by. The raccoon was easily thirty pounds of fur, froth, and misplaced rage. I called him Bugsy.

In this apartment, there were no screens on the windows, so we had to keep them shut all the time, even in the summer. Once, sweltering and desperate in our beds during a July heat wave, my roommates and I threw the windows open, mosquitoes be damned, but a bat flew in, darting around the apartment and squeaking with terror until we killed it with a broom out of fear of rabies. We never opened the windows again after that.

Set into the side of a hill, the building was on Cedar Street, one of the oldest and poorest parts of Belleville, that strange, working-class town in the no man's land of the other strange, working-class towns that run the 401 to 417 highway heartline between the bourgeois cities of Toronto and Ottawa. At night, when you went out on the stoop, you were close enough to smell the Moira River, which in the summer heat got very low and stank.

The apartment building had once been a house, but the owner had subdivided it into two equally shabby apartments, which he took little care of. The caulking in the bathroom peeled like old toothpaste, the yellow paint on the exterior was flaking, and the carpets were ripped and shabby. The fridge didn't work properly, so I ate most of my meals at the bar where I worked because groceries quickly spoiled. There was no place to put the trash—no bins, no Dumpster—and pickup was every other week. If you put trash outside, Bugsy got into it, so there was just an industrial-sized communal bag in the kitchen that I'd taken from work. With three people living there—sometimes four or five, as there was always a rotating cast of girlfriends and buddies and other persons of various origins washing up on our couch or on the floor—it piled up quickly, and the house often had the wet, rotten smell of hot garbage.

One night I took the trash out, but the bag was too full and too heavy; it ripped as I tried to take it down the porch stairs, spilling garbage down over the steps. I ran inside, cursing, to get a broom and a dustpan, but when I came back out I stopped, confused; there appeared to be mounds of white rice all over, cups and cups of it.

I leaned in closer to examine it. It wasn't rice—it was maggots. Thousands and thousands of writhing, fat, white maggots which, disturbed from the warm, edible loam of the trash, were now wriggling all over the deck and down the stairs.

Horrified, I raced inside, grabbed a bottle of bleach and poured it, raw, over the mess; the larvae writhed in agony as they died, and the smell of bleach and garbage was so unbearable I staggered back into the apartment and vomited in the kitchen sink. After that we started sneaking our garbage, one household bag at a time, into the unlocked Dumpster behind the Tim Hortons several blocks away, disposing of it at night when no one was around.

For the pleasure of living in this hot, stinking, raccoon-besieged two-bedroom apartment, my roommate and I paid around $375 each—$750 in total, plus internet and hydro.

As of 2021, the average price of a two-bedroom apartment in Belleville, Ontario, was $1,700 a month before utilities.[32]

———

We moved out of the Cedar Street house in the fall of 2005—I'm a September baby, I had just turned nineteen—because my roommate decided to move back in with his parents. He just came home one day and said the lease was up, and he wasn't going to renew it. The lease was in his name, and the landlord wouldn't transfer it over to me because of Bob, my orange tomcat. The lease specified that pets were allowed, but the landlord was nonetheless very upset that I refused to get rid of him. He tried to make me, and when presented with the details of our contract, clenched his jaw and told me he would make sure I never got an apartment in that town again if I ever tried to use him for a reference. I found myself in need of a place in a hurry, preferably close to a bus stop, because I was enrolled in a trade program for journalists at Loyalist College and had to be in class every morning at eight a.m.

I took an apartment on Ann Street, on the other side of town. It was a strange apartment. So many of the houses in that part of the city were the kind of beautiful old ivy-covered houses that rich people with a taste for the white, Protestant, colonial past live in because they are interested in "heritage"; it was, in fact, the same neighborhood Susanna Moodie once lived in. My apartment, a one-room bachelor, seemed an anomaly, stuffed into a squat two-storey building on the corner of the street, not far from a Victorian-style rose garden; its address could not be found on any of the city maps, nor did the phone, electricity, or internet companies have any record of it. When I had the utilities put in, I had to meet the installer on the corner because they couldn't find it in their system and the building had no numbers on the outside.

I got a discount on my first month of rent because the landlord didn't want to be bothered cleaning it out after the last tenants. There was rotten food in the fridge, old eggs and meat and something pickled that had turned an offish colour, floating in miserable-looking brine. The carpets were old and dirty. It was partly furnished, and in the nightstand there was a bottle of K-Y Jelly and a pair of edible underpants with a bite taken out of the crotch. The bathroom had no door and was curiously exposed—you could see the toilet from anywhere in the apartment—but I liked that it had a little breakfast island, where I drank coffee and read the *Toronto Star* in the mornings, who I dreamed of working for. I found that I enjoyed living alone. I still do.

My upstairs neighbour was a drug dealer. Working in restaurants, I knew many people who made extra cash as small-time weed and coke dealers, but my upstairs neighbour trafficked in harder, more serious stuff, which was unfortunate, because he was also a complete fucking idiot. A white guy in his early twenties, he referred to his friends as his "N-words," wore his hair in greasy dreads, left his beer bottles in the hall, and played Shaggy's "It Wasn't Me" on repeat at a volume sufficient to make even the most mild-mannered and forgiving human contemplate sneaking in through his window and bludgeoning him to death with two dozen navel oranges stuffed into a pillowcase.

One night, shortly after Christmas, somebody almost did, although the beating was with a baseball bat, not fruit. There was a terrifying, terrible row in the night: screaming, swearing, thumping, someone thrown against my front door over and over and over so hard the chain rattled. When I came out for school in the morning, there was blood on the floor and the walls, the windows and rails of the porch were broken, and a single high-heeled shoe, bright yellow, lay discarded at the bottom of the stairs.

At the time that I lived there, I paid around $600 a month, plus utilities.

In 2021, there were so few bachelor apartments available for rent in Belleville that standardized information was not available on their cost, but the cheapest I could find on Kijiji was $1,000, plus utilities.

—

When I graduated from college, I left the Ann Street apartment to do a monthlong internship as a municipal reporter for the *Ottawa Citizen*. At the end of the term, they offered me a job. I turned it down, in part because I wasn't even yet twenty, in part because I didn't understand I was being offered a *job* job, and in part because everyone at the paper seemed so stressed out and angry and miserable that working there didn't seem like a good idea. Now, of course, being a journalist, I realize that's just how most of us are—perpetually stressed, chain-smoking anxious-depressives constantly shivering under the gun of unreasonable deadlines in a dying industry rotten to its guts—but there was no way for me to know that then.

In any case, I turned it down and, after briefly moving back to Belleville to live (disastrously) with an older woman with whom I was having quasi-romantic, quasi-platonic love affair (I believe this to be a specifically lesbian rite of passage), I moved to Ottawa in the fall of 2006 to attend university. I believed—because I had been led to believe all my life—that going to university was the path toward a successful, well-paying career.

I rented an apartment on Dalhousie Street, on the top of a century-old three-floor walk-up. The house had belonged to rich people in the city's colonial past (my apartment had once been servants' quarters) but now it was designated a "heritage" building, which seemed to mean little except that it could operate in a wild state of disrepair, irrespective of safety codes. The bathroom was in the kitchen and had a beautiful claw-foot tub I adored. A metal pipe had been crudely bent over it to make a shower, and the water pressure was finicky and unreliable, the hot water sparse—the only way to ensure I got a shower that wasn't the temperature of a forgotten cup of tea was to use it after ten p.m., when everyone else had gone to sleep. I had to be quite careful when I did, because there was a gap all the way around the uncaulked pipe that came up through the floor wide enough to put your fingers in; the floor wasn't level, so any kind of overflow ran directly into the gap, causing my dirty bathwater to rain down into the apartment below me.

Most curious of all was the gap between the interior wall and the exterior wall. Supposedly, this was the "fire escape," which led to a rickety set of spiral stairs, letting you out on the roof and then down a rusty ladder on the side of the building onto the street. The space, however, was so narrow that you couldn't raise your arms to your chest and extend your elbows without hitting the wall. One larger woman who came to inquire about the apartment next to mine remarked when she caught me in the hall that she had decided to turn it down because she didn't think she could get in and out of there in an emergency without becoming stuck.

Regardless of its quirks, it was and remains to this day my favourite apartment that I have ever rented. On the days I had classes, I walked to school through Ottawa's ByWard Market, past the smell of bakeries making baguettes and BeaverTails, often buying a newspaper to read over coffee between my courses. In the evenings, I went to work, also on foot, and worked in the lively bars and restaurants to put myself through school. It was within walking distance of Major's Hill Park, near the parliament buildings, and in the summers I would bring books and sit under an old, gnarled tree facing the National Gallery of Canada, reading and drinking coffee or beer from a Thermos. Later, after I graduated university—I took overloaded semesters of six classes at a time, because six cost as much as five if I kept up my GPA—I bought my dog, Herman, who I trained to wear a backpack and come to the ByWard Market with me in the afternoons. I would bargain for leftover produce from the vendors and Herman carried them home for me in his little backpack. In the evenings, as he grew, we would curl up together and watch movies on the ragged old couch I had pulled from the street corner.

I lived at the Dalhousie Street apartment for five years, the longest I've ever lived anywhere as an adult. It is often true that we know we are happy, fortunate people only in hindsight, when we are no longer so happy or so fortunate.

For this apartment, I paid $750 a month, plus utilities and internet.

In 2021, a one-bedroom apartment in Ottawa was, on average, $1,500 a month.[33] In the neighborhood where I'd once lived, which has now been gentrified, it would probably be significantly more.

—

In the summer of 2010, having graduated university and finding myself still waiting tables at a downtown bar, unsure what I wanted to do with myself, I grew restless. I had been freelancing for what was then *Xtra Magazine*'s Ottawa print edition, *Capital Xtra*, and writing reviews for *Arc Poetry Magazine*, but work of any meaningful kind with any sort of stability escaped me. I knew I wanted to be a writer, but with the exception of a handful of poems in very small magazines (yes, I once wrote poetry, terrible, terrible poetry; we all make mistakes) I couldn't seem to get anything published.

Like many young would-be artists, I assumed the problem lay in my surroundings, in not having enough time and mental space to create, and not at all in my youth, inexperience, or lack of disciplined artistic practice. I took a job in the Alberta Badlands as a ranch hand, imagining myself in the romantic prairies, working hard by day— sweating as I built fences, corralled cattle, rubbed down horses—and writing novels by night. This is a way of saying I was twenty-three and a fucking idiot.

I gave up the apartment and my serving job, got in my rusty 1999 Honda stick-shift CR-V and drove 3,000 kilometres west, where I was supposed to manage a small herd of free-range pigs, for which I would receive a small stipend, meals, and a place to live that had been described to me as a "quaint heritage farmhouse."

It was, predictably, a tremendous disaster, for a variety of reasons, not the least of which being that the house I lived in, alone, forty-five kilometres away from the main farmhouse in the dark, endless, yawning existential horror of the prairie night, was *haunted as shit*. By November I had quit and was hightailing it back through Northern Ontario, broke and exhausted and heartsick at the failure, sleeping in the back of the car with Herman, with whom I subsisted on shared Subway sandwiches and instant ramen.

It wasn't until I got to Toronto that I realized just how dearly my adventurous mistake had cost me. For an upper-class kid with parents and money and connections to fall back on, a four-month-long fuck-up of the calibre I had committed would have been, at worst, an embarrassing blunder their relatives would remind them of each year at Christmas dinner until they died, but not a *disaster*, as it was for me. Being working class, this bad move left me broke, in debt, without a place to live or a job. I crashed-landed on my brother's couch in Scarborough for a while, and he more-or-less patiently put up with me. I had long been the eccentric fuck-up of the family, so my failing in such a ridiculous way probably did not surprise anyone.

Desperate for a job, for weeks I took the bus to the subway, then took the subway to various sections of Toronto, where I would emerge from the tunnels, resumé in hand, to stalk up and down the streets, stopping at each restaurant and café to ask to see the manager and enquire about work. By mid-November, it was snowing, and I did not have proper shoes; trudging through the slush, my sneakers quickly soaked through and froze, and the salt stained and hardened on the hems of my pants; none of this was doing me any favours, employment-wise. I would walk as far as I could, sometimes all day, stopping once in a while to spend a few precious dollars in a coffee shop so I could sit long enough feel my toes again before pressing on.

I had a series of failed job offers—a sales rep for what turned out to be a pyramid scheme; an interview I never went to for a position as a phone-sex operator; a bartender at a now-defunct gay bar where the owner made me work until three a.m. while they drank with their friends, took all my tips save a twenty, and then told me to come back the next day for another "trial" shift—before I finally found work as a server in the financial district. The commute from Scarberia, however, was brutal, taking hours out of every day, and so I set about trying to find someplace closer to work (and not a loveseat) to live.

I was, unsurprisingly, immediately dismayed by the cost, but even more so by the scarcity of apartments and the unreasonable demands of landlords: references, statements of employment, first and last and damage deposit, credit checks and interviews, as if they were going to be paying *me*, and not the other way around. I was stunned, especially, by the bald-faced lies told to me by my would-be landlords: that the hot water worked when I could see that it didn't, that the exposed wiring wasn't a fire issue, that a basement apartment with a ceiling so low that I, barely five foot four, had to stoop to enter the doorway was "a legal suite." One woman, opening the cupboard drawer in a shabby one-bedroom for which she wanted $1,100 a month in the

Annex, tried to tell me the scuttling brown beetles within were not cockroaches, but *ladybugs*, as if I had never seen either before.

Eventually, I found a room in a house between the Danforth and Little India shortly before Christmas. When I went to look at the place, I was met by a scruffy, thin man in slippers, the owner of the house, who lived in the master bedroom. While we talked, he served me a very strange cup of tea—weak and watery, with milk that was obviously curdled—which I took out of politeness but did not drink.

It turned out the tea was weak because he reused his tea bags and the milk was curdled because, in the name of frugality, he kept the refrigerator turned down so low that perishables—meat, cream, leftovers—went rancid much faster than normal. He had an app for the thermostat that ensured he would receive a notification were it turned up in his absence. The house was unfinished and poorly insulated, and the room I rented in the topmost corner, farthest from the furnace, was extremely cold and drafty. I had to sneak in a space heater by hiding it in my backpack, and I only turned it on late at night, after he had gone to bed, because he fretted about the additional hydro costs.

In 2012, for this single room in a house which I shared with three to four other people, I paid $750 a month—the same price I had paid for an entire apartment in Ottawa in 2005.

As of 2021, a one-bedroom apartment in Toronto cost around $1,800 a month[34]—an amount which had actually fallen nearly 20 percent from pre-pandemic prices.

———

I hated Toronto. Fuck Toronto. Never have I lived anywhere so pretentious and silly, so preposterously obsessed with its own self-image.

To be working poor in Toronto is to have your nose pressed against the window of a fabulous party where beautiful people wear posh clothes and eat delicious food and drink fancy cocktails, a party where there are cut flowers on the table and people are laughing and music is playing, a party to which you are not only not invited but, it is implied, neither do you *deserve* to be, having little money. To live in Toronto as a working-class person means the only way you'll even get to be in the same room as that party is to come in through the back door as the help.

I was working at a fancy restaurant, serving fifteen-dollar cocktails and forty-dollar plates, when I moved into the room near the Danforth, but about a month later I lost my job. When the two obscenely rich white male owners of the restaurant came in, I did not immediately recognize them and called one by the other's name, and for this grievous error, I was canned. After some scrambling, I found another job serving at a diner in the Beaches—the rats, the impossible size of the rats in the kitchen in the morning, like miniature poodles!—but I was overcome with a growing certainty that Toronto wasn't for me. A friend I had worked with at a restaurant in Ottawa had just taken a job up in Whitehorse, said she loved it, and encouraged me to come up and join her for the summer, but I was dubious, partly because I had already moved three times in the last year and partly because I had only a faint idea of where the Yukon actually was.

Then, someone tried to poison a bunch of dogs at park near my house, and I had to get my dog's stomach pumped because he ate some of the bait. A week later, my roommate had a severe schizophrenic episode and became obsessed with the idea that I was trying to get her arrested. The landlord, not I, finally did just that—the catalyst was her running around the house with a knife demanding to know where I was while I hid out at The Only Cafe. Toss in a sudden breakup with the beautiful but flighty bisexual burlesque dancer I had fallen hard for, and bang, there you had it—I was *done* with Toronto.

I said *fuck it, yes* to the Yukon, quit my job, loaded up the car again, and drove 5,500 kilometres north and west with Herman riding shotgun, his tongue flapping against the window, off for greener (albeit much colder) pastures, just after Mother's Day weekend, 2012. I was twenty-six.

Work in Whitehorse was plentiful, and I quickly found a job as a server. The housing situation, however, was dire. Housing in Canada's North has been some of the scarcest, lowest quality, and most expensive for decades, not that I knew that when I moved. Honestly, when I first drove out there, I had to stop in Edmonton to check the map and remind myself if I was headed to the Yukon or the Northwest Territories, so you can see my university education was money well spent.

It wouldn't have mattered, ultimately, as housing in the North is universally terrible and wildly expensive, although the crisis has long been the most acute in roadless Nunavut. You'd think that, in a climate where you can literally freeze the fuck to death nine months out of the year, governments would invest in livable housing that people could actually afford, but evidentially landlords, developers, and property owners (most of whom work in said government) making money hand over fist is a more tantalizing proposition than dignity and human rights.

In the beginning, I took a room in what is locally known as "the Bicycle House"; the owner, an eccentric but kind mad-inventor-type who ran a bike repair business, had built a geodesic dome out of bike rims, making the house a local landmark. Heated by a wood stove, the house was warm and my roommates kind, but it was always packed with boarders coming and going, bike tourists stopping by, strangers stepping in through the unlocked door to ask for the well-known owner—too many people. I spent the winter of 2012–13—it was -40 degrees Celsius for two solid weeks—in such tight quarters that I could hear the *thwap thwap thwap* of my nearest roommate's balls slapping against his girlfriend's ass when he fucked her.

One afternoon in early February, the chaos just became too much for me. I came home to find that the homeowner, drunk, had built a hydrogen still in the kitchen (when I say "mad-inventor-type," I mean it), which he was using to fill balloons, then explode them with a Zippo in apocalyptic balls of flame, an activity that cost him his eyebrows. I moved into a townhouse up the street with a friend.

The townhouse belonged to my boss at the bar, who had bought it when she was a single parent and had since moved into a larger house with her two kids and her new wife. It had been built by a southern company with no real understanding of the northern climate and, because they had neglected to insulate the drainpipes on the outside of the building, they often froze, backed up, and flooded the bathroom. We'd lived there less than a year when, with a month's notice, my boss demanded the apartment back; her kids were going off to university, and her own landlords had demanded *their* house back because *their* kids were coming home, a frustrating game of musical apartments that left us the ones outside the circle.

Scrambling, my friend and I found a similar townhouse at an inflated rate; we didn't have time to quibble because it was April, when all the Southerners snap up what housing is left over from the winter, and the market gets tighter than ever before. The previous tenant had a pair of huskies who shat in huge piles on the paved patio; when spring came and the snow melted, they were revealed like unmarked land mines, stinking and melting into a brown slurry we hosed down as they thawed. The dishwasher never worked, and the landlord refused to fix it, because it was not listed as an appliance on the lease. The house was heated by oil, which was not included in the rent, and it wasn't until September that we discovered the previous tenant had run the regulator on nothing for so long that it had messed up the unit. It had to be serviced multiple times before it worked again, and then never very well, so the house was perpetually cold. The landlord never paid the service technician, who left me an increasing number of angry, accusing voice mails.

For the room I first lived in, I paid $750 a month—exactly what I had paid in Toronto.

For the first townhouse I lived in, I paid $1,800 a month split two ways, plus heating, hydro, and internet.

For the third, I paid $2,400 a month split two ways—half my monthly income—plus heating oil, hydro, and internet.

In 2021, the average price of a one-bedroom apartment was reported at around $1,100 per month, an inaccurate number reduced by the small population size (40,000 in the Yukon, 30,000 living in Whitehorse) in which outlier statistics cause dramatic shifts in the reported data—an issue which, as a reporter, I've written about extensively, especially as it pertains to housing. The real cost was closer to $1,500 per month, before utilities.

In early 2014, I began seeing a beautiful young Québécois dancer who had moved up to teach at a French language program in Whitehorse. I fell wildly in love with her, which was a problem for my roommate, who harboured mild homophobic tendencies—previously, she had been extremely insulted when people mistook her for my girlfriend, because she resented being thought queer. She was also an incurable prude (the WASPs are not okay) and became upset if we had sex while she was at home, in turn demanding I leave the apartment when she had gentleman callers. Our apartment was costing me more than half my monthly income—I was working, at this time, as the editor of a small, shabby weekly newspaper—and the high cost of utilities, internet, and food ate what was left of it.

Tensions mounting, my roommate and I agreed that we didn't want to renew the lease, and I moved in, briefly, with my girlfriend, who had a room in a shared house. I managed to scrounge up enough money through extra freelancing and not having my own place for a month to purchase a 1991 GMC 2500 long-box truck, on which I put a 1987 camper I had gotten free from a friend. The cost of housing, utilities, and food was getting higher and higher, and the plan was for me to live in the camper over the summer. My girlfriend's roommates were vacating the house at the end of July, and I had arranged a house-sit for her and me through August and September, at which point the two of us planned to move to Montreal, where things were cheaper and my girlfriend had family.

Except that, in June of that year, she cheated on me. And then we broke up. And then she took the house-sit.

And, just like that, I was homeless.

As I've said, a big difference between middle class and working class is the cushion to fuck up.

———

Heartbroken, without a place to live, I couldn't maintain my job. I had been working on and off as professional wild food forager, making extra money in the backcountry picking mushrooms and berries and herbs, for a couple years at this point. It was a good morel season. It was the North. I had a camper.

In the summer of 2016, I simply disappeared into the bush.

I drank a lot. I did a bunch of drugs. I met a man and, for the first time in twenty years, had a boyfriend. He was a bum and I was a bum. We drank and smoked through our money. Some bad things happened, and then he became one of those bad things.

By October we were living in my camper, the two of us and the dog, in Whistler, working construction jobs for cash. We lived in Municipal Day Lot 4. In November, it rained twenty-eight out of thirty days. The propane heat in the camper did nothing to draw out the moisture. The walls blossomed with puffs of mould that flowered like dandelion fluff, sporing out. My books mildewed, turned wild colours. It grew colder and colder, but it did not snow. We pissed and shit in a coffee tin, or else in a ditch. I got very sick from the wet and the constant cold and the toxins from the mildew. My man developed a temper and a taste for Fireball Cinnamon Whisky.

I told myself it was a choice, that it was an adventure, to be living this way, but it wasn't a choice, and it wasn't an adventure. It was horrible.

I'd asked my boyfriend to leave several times, but he always just laughed at me, or else became furious. He didn't want to be with me any more than I wanted to be with him, but I had the truck and camper; if he left me, he'd be out with nothing but the clothes on his back. He hurt me, more and more, to control me—he took the credit card, he took my PIN. I thought about just packing up, driving away one day while he was out, but I was afraid he would find me, afraid of what he would do to me if I left him there, alone, in the cold and the rain.

When he wasn't around, I would go to cafés and use the Wi-Fi to look for apartments, for rooms in houses. I had a friend in the area, but I didn't—couldn't—tell her how bad things had gotten. I was ashamed. She told me, though, that she knew of no pet-friendly housing, that everyone she knew in Whistler who was not rich lived in shared housing, that at that time of year—the start of the ski season—there was no shared housing to be had. There were many people, like me, she said, who lived at the Owl Creek Campground, or at Lot 4, and I knew that was true, because I saw them there, camped out at night in their vehicles. Some of them were single. Some of them were couples. A few had children.

The construction project we were working on was building a mansion. It had three floors, an indoor waterfall, and a parking garage larger than the house I grew up in. It was a second home for a rich person who would live there only a few months a year while they took in Whistler's coveted ski season.

In 2021, a one-bedroom apartment in Whistler went for around $2,000 a month[35]—if you could find one.

—

I talked my way out of things with my man. It was complicated. I said we were parting for a while. We planned to meet up again in the spring. I put him on a ferry to one of the Southern Gulf Islands and fled.

I went east, first through rain and wind, then through ice and snow. I was in a terrible car accident on an icy December highway near Saskatoon. I lost the truck and camper, pulled a car out of a junkyard. It ran. I paid whatever I had for it, put as much as would fit into it, and drove away, abandoning the rest. I arrived in Montreal with my dog, thirty dollars in my wallet, and what was left of my possessions in tow. I stayed a brutal, miserable, drunken three months there, struggling to find work in a city whose language I did not speak, racked with mental health problems which would later be diagnosed as PTSD. In March, I was offered a short-term contract at *Yukon News*, for whom I had been freelancing. I scrounged up a few dollars—I collected and cashed beer cans, took odd jobs, borrowed money from anyone who would lend it to me—and drove back across the country to Whitehorse.

I was a mess. Depressed, broken, exhausted, skinny, and sick from uncertainty and homelessness, from the indignity of poverty and hunger and sexual abuse. I stayed at a friend's place in Mount Lorne—no running water, no power, no cell service—but the fifty-minute drive into town every day on dirt roads to get to the newsroom was untenable, and after I blew through three tires, I found a cabin thirty minutes out of town, on Burma Road, ten minutes south of Lake Laberge.

My landlords were kind. There were cows, whose noses I liked to scratch. There were chickens, and I liked the soft, cooing sounds they made. I had a garden and grew vegetables, which I tended with dedication and care, but no running water; I showered at the Takhini gas station twice a week, an occasion for which I would buy a tallboy to drink while I washed my hair and listened to the person in the stall next to me take a shit. I had a wood stove to keep the place warm, but they didn't plow the roads as far out of town as I lived, so in the winter I drove, white-knuckling, in the pitch-fucking-black, in my tiny Suzuki hatchback through storm after storm.

More than anything else, though, I was alone. Terrible, awfully, totally alone, out there with no one to talk to, no one to call, only the dog and the sound of the cattle and, sometimes, the flickering-candle eyes of the coyotes running the fencelines at night.

For this, I paid $750 a month—what I had paid twelve years previously for a full apartment in downtown Ottawa, plus the eighty dollars a week ($320 a month) in gas it took to get in and out of town every day for work, making it closer to $1,400. I had no internet, because I couldn't afford to have it installed. It had been the only place I could find that would take pets. I refused to be separated from Herman. He was all I had left. He was the only creature alive who loved me.

He was the only creature alive who knew me before I was a disgrace.

———

By January, the long commute, the cold, the poverty, the stress of work had broken me. I was making about sixteen dollars an hour working for *Yukon News*, which is owned by Black Press, a company that notoriously overworks and underpays their journalists (a living wage was and is around nineteen to twenty-one dollars an hour in the

Yukon). It simply wasn't tenable to live that way anymore, so I quit the paper, scrounged together some money, left my cabin, and drove once again to Montreal, where I had found a sublet and a friend had promised me a job working at a burlesque club.

It was -47 degrees the morning I drove out of Whitehorse, the roads a slick sheet of ice as clear as resin, once again in search of housing I could afford, of a better, more dignified life.

The promised job, however, did not appear. I hadn't realized that my friend was herself barely making her rent, caught in the throes of severe alcoholism and a cocaine addiction that, later, would nearly destroy her. The job didn't materialize because it had never existed. For a while I subsisted on a grant, using it to write and freelance, then later on odd jobs and, again, collecting cans. I looked and looked for work, but what I could get was deeply limited by my poor and patchy French. I was living in an apartment sublet in Saint-Henri, near the infamous Fattal lofts. I lived along the tracks, and at night, I heard the trains and loved them.

One morning at about eight, a month into my sublet, there was a tremendous noise: crashing and banging, the sound of heavy machinery, men shouting. I staggered out of bed and into my clothes and threw open the back door. Where, the day before, there had been a townhouse just like the one I lived in, there was now a growing pile of scrap and rubble. They had torn it down. Later, I asked a workman why, and he told me the property had been sold and they were going to build condos there instead. Broke, I spent much of my time walking around the neighbourhood and had seen many other condos going up. People told me it was because the neighbourhood was becoming trendy, and wealthy people were moving there from the West End. Rents, people said, were already rising.

This was 2017. I paid $1,100 a month for an entire flat, all inclusive, with internet, hot running water, a kitchen, and a bright, sunny backyard.

In 2021, the average cost of a one-bedroom apartment in Montreal was about $1,400 a month.[36]

———

By spring, I was running out of money.

I couldn't find work, and I couldn't afford the sublet anymore, so I took a job on Salt Spring Island as a farmhand. I piled back into the car with my things and my dog, thinking once again that I was headed, if not for something better, then something stable. In my head, I thought the warmer climate would make things a little easier. At least, I reasoned, if things didn't work out, I could sleep in the car or camp for far longer than I could in the East or the North.

I drove through the upper United States in March. There was wind and rain. There was snow. There was ice and impossible mountain passes. I was to start the first of April and, finding myself held up in the Bitterroot Pass of Montana in a terrible ice storm, sleeping in a tent, I waited for a break in the weather before driving from Butte, Montana, to Vancouver, British Columbia, some 1,000 miles straight, on nothing but ramen, truck stop coffee, a pack of Marlboro reds, and a beer every 300 kilometres.

I was thirty-one when I arrived on Salt Spring Island. In many ways it was a repeat of the Alberta fiasco eight years before. Although the farmers were kind and the food excellent—fresh greens and fruit, after being in the North for so many years, seemed a delicacy—there was no running water or electricity in the cabin I was provided. There was an old futon mattress, which was mildewed and damp. The wood stove, improperly installed, leaked smoke dangerously. The work was gruelling—one week, I did nothing but pull weeds from a blueberry field in which nests of hornets and mildew had taken root, tearing out piles and piles and piles of what locals call "cooch grass." I would wake in the morning with my hands so stiff and swollen I couldn't make a fist. My friends tried to heal them by wrapping them in plantain and mullein overnight.

My first week on the farm, seeing how little my $500 a month stipend bought me, I started a side business. I had always been resourceful and good with my hands, traits that my time in the bush and working construction had only refined, so I advertised myself as a handyperson for twenty dollars an hour. In a week, I had more clients than I could handle and had to pull the ad. Soon, I was working eight- to ten-hour days on the farm—hauling irrigation lines, picking fruit, pulling weeds—and another three to five hours of manual labour in the evenings—building fences, splitting wood, moving furniture. All the while, I continued to write news stories and essays periodically for *VICE* online. I grew thin, wiry. I was hungry all the time, but when I came home at night and lay down, tired down to my bones, lips sunburned and peeling, I was often too exhausted to cook, let alone eat. More than once I ate fresh, raw duck eggs just for the calories.

It was during this time, however, as I roved the island, that I noticed something strange. There were all these big, beautiful houses—so many windows! So many bathrooms! Such gardens!—but only two, three, four people living in them. There were few apartments, and people rented anything and everything in their desperation—unheated cabins, RV campers, shipping container "houses." One person I knew even rented an old van propped up on cinder blocks in someone's backyard. I met people who lived on sailboats and people who lived in their cars year-round—not only the usual roamers, but people with jobs, people who had dogs, even kids.

Most people I knew—mostly people of my caste—worked on farms, which rarely paid full price for their labour, instead offering room and board and a stipend, which meant if you wanted to quit you usually had to leave the island, because there was nowhere else to live that poor people could afford. There were homeowner associations and community groups that tightly controlled what kind of housing could be built, and where, and how many people could live there, in order to maintain the "character" of the island—code, of course, for keeping the trash out. There were secret, quasi-legal housing units which, when they came on the market, were advertised only by word of mouth. There were innumerable houses in which no one actually lived, instead hosting a rotating cast of off-islanders paying a premium for their luxury accommodations through Airbnb.[37]

Basically, if you lived wanted to live on Salt Spring and were not rich, you had to work for someone who was. They'd give you a place to stay so that they could make money from you, either by your direct labour, or by renting something to you that, elsewhere, would not be thought fit to live in. You didn't have a place to live unless you lived to take care of other people's property, paid for other people's mortgages. It was an island of the rich and their servants.

In 2021, a one-bedroom apartment on Salt Spring went for around $1,500 a month. The vacancy rate, however, remains as it has for the last five years: at or around zero.

—

By June on Salt Spring, I saw the trouble I was in; at the end of September, as the growing season ended, my contract with the farm would finish up, at which time they would require me to either move out or begin to pay for lodging. Locals had told me that work was scarce in the winter—the tourists were all gone, many shops were closed—so it would get even harder to make a living. My meagre stipend barely covered the insurance on the car and groceries each month, so if I wanted to save money, I'd have to keep freelancing and keep up the handyperson business, which, compounded with the work I was already doing, meant maintaining an absolutely brutal pace. As the cafés closed in the fall and winter, I'd have fewer places to work out of; writing would become harder, and the ferry off island was expensive.

If I stayed, I would likely be trapped until spring, unable to afford to leave.

I knew there were good burns from the year before in the BC interior, where forest fires had summoned morels. The price, I knew, was low that year, but I was a seasoned picker; working alone, I could make a go of it.

A younger, less-cautious me might have waited it out—I liked the climate, I liked the people—but I saw it coming, the cold, wet winter alone in the cabin or in my car, in either case without power or water or internet. I went, not because I wanted to, but because it felt like the only way to survive long term. I quit the farm, left the island, with its smooth-skinned arbutus trees and its blackberries growing in fist-sized clusters and its tiny Sitka deer, tame as chickens, and went back out into the bush.

And there I was a second time. Homeless.

I worked the burns, first the Elephant Hill fire, and then, when that dried up, the Whiteswan fire, near Canal Flats in the Kootenays. When the season ended, I worked on farms in the Okanagan picking fruit, then in Salmon Arm, picking prickly lodgepole pine cones, which would be used to start seedlings for tree planters. Often paid in cash, I saved my money in a coffee can hidden in the back of the car—bills bound together with a paper clip in a President's Choice Dark Roast coffee tin.

When the season ended and it grew cold, I turned the car north and went up the highway again, back to the last place I had been safe or stable, the last place that had felt like home: Whitehorse. There was nothing else to hope for, but also nothing else to lose.

When I arrived, the housing crisis had grown even more intense, the prices even higher. I slept on couches and house-sat. I kept freelancing, slowly building my portfolio writing news stories for VICE and features for magazines like *Up Here* and *North of Ordinary*. I hopped from house to house, from situation to situation; I slept in the car until it froze; I snuck in at night and slept on the couch of the writer's residency I was attending in November; I house-sat for December. In January I found a sublet from a woman who wrote me a twenty-page set of instructions that included a daily check around the perimeter of the house for fingerprints in the snow on the windows;

she charged me $700 a month plus internet and a portion of the utilities, then left for a four-month road trip.

While she was gone, I found work as a server, took a short-term contract as a reporter, and kept building my freelance business. In April, when the owner returned, she accused me of breaking a single glass, using all the ink in her printer, and misplacing two salad forks. I rolled my eyes and moved into my van—a 2000 Dodge Caravan I had torn the seats out of, a gift from a friend after the transmission in my last junkyard vehicle had given out—and slept in the 0 degree chill overnight along the river.

During this time, I wrote many news stories and op-eds about the housing crisis in the territory. When I interviewed Pauline Frost, the minister then in charge of housing for the territory, about the brutal shortage, the high cost, and the low quality of housing in Yukon, I had been without an adequate, permanent place to live for over a year. I had been underhoused or housing insecure for nearly three.

———

In the place where I live now, there is a drop sheet which covers a portion of the ceiling where a pipe from the upstairs apartment runs through my basement suite. There are lots of windows, so it's not as dark as you might think it would be, which is important in the North, when mid-winter days are so short.

Like my first apartment on Cedar Street, it too was once a house, now broken into apartments. Nestled downtown, close to the clay cliffs that overlook the city, I can walk to work, which I love, and it's not far from the river where I go fishing for grayling on summer evenings. There's a yard, which Herman—now twelve, my lifelong partner in crime, well deserving of retirement—loves more than anything, dozing in the sun, chasing red squirrels, watching Whitebelly and Blackears, our neighbourhood foxes, come and go up and down the alleyways. I have a small garden.

The apartment itself is worn and ragged and outdated. It needs painting. Over the last five years, it has been passed down through three successive lines of journalists, without any cleaning in between, and sometimes I still find strange and lovely items left behind by former tenants: a bag of leather-working materials, an old dog leash, a flat of expired mac and cheese, an upturned baby carriage.

I love it. It's home. I've been here now for two years—the longest I have been fully housed in the same place since I left Ottawa in 2010 more than a decade ago.

Even if I wanted to move, though, there would be nowhere to go. The housing crisis in the territory has only gotten worse, and finding something similar—even downgrading—would present a serious challenge. People sometimes live in their cars when they can't afford housing, as I have done. In the winters, too, I've seen the hardiest (or most desperate) people living in camper vans they have fitted with small wood stoves, squatting in parking lots, smoke churning in black curls from a pipe cut into the roof of the vehicle.

I often think, too, of moving somewhere else, a place where the climate is better and life is a bit easier, where Herman doesn't get frostbite on his tail, as he did last winter, where the queer community is larger and there are more opportunities for me as writer and journalist. I love Whitehorse, and it will always be home, but in many ways I know I am outgrowing it—except that I am terribly afraid to move. I look at the prices of apartments in major cities—Toronto,

Victoria, Ottawa, Halifax, and Vancouver—and wonder how I would afford to live there, if I could even find a place. All the smaller towns—Hamilton and London, Nanaimo and Surrey, Kelowna, even Kingston—all seem equally difficult to make a leap to, for all the same reasons. At this point, I couldn't even afford to move back to my hometown of Belleville if I wanted to, where rents have increased 20 percent[38] since the pandemic and are on par with prices in Victoria— or here.

I look back on where I have been and I can see that, for working-class people, for young people especially, things have gotten worse, not better. We live in other people's houses without much prospect of ever having our own.

I often think of the house I grew up in—a red-brick bungalow on Harrington Road, somewhere between Belleville and Tweed in Southern Ontario. Four acres of land, farms on one side, and forest on the other. I left home when I was seventeen. I'm thirty-five now. That place is gone, literally and metaphorically. My parents sold it years ago, but it's the idea of the thing that I can never return to. Most likely, I will never live in a home—in a house—like that again, in all the rest of my days. It's out of reach for my generation, out of reach for working-class people, and out of reach for single people, either to rent and certainly to own.

Out of reach, but still within memory.

The Hour You Are Most Alone

TWO YOUNG BLACK BULLS stormed up out of the ditch and began to fight in the middle of the road.

Their muscles strained as they bludgeoned one another with their flat, heavy skulls, and the red dust they kicked up clung to their sweat-dampened flanks like old blood. On either side and behind them, the cows and their calves—red-spotted, fawn, and black— boiled with anxiety, lashing their tails, further blocking my path.

Deciding against driving through a herd of cattle, I turned the truck around and took the next side trail into a field and parked— nose out, in case I had to leave in a hurry—next to a man-high pile of cut brush. It was past dusk now, verging on dark. I had been looking for a campground that was flagged by a sign on the side of the highway, but I hadn't been able to find it. Later I'd find out that this was because it no longer existed; when the fires had swept through the year before, they had taken the park with them.

I fished my headlamp from the glovebox. It was getting cold already; the air had bite. Moving quickly, I scrounged the field for wood, gathering branches, tree roots pushed up by a plow, and made a pile by the truck. As I worked, I could hear Herman, my dog, snuffling in the brush, moving in widening circles around our campsite, patrolling for both other people and other animals. I built a fire and, once it was going, put on a pot of water. While it came to a boil I laid out my bed in the back of the truck: sleeping pad, wool blanket, down bag and a duffle of clothes for a pillow. I could hear a coyote singing in the far distance. I made a mental note to be careful not to leave any food scraps out, to make sure I brought in Herman's bowl before I slept.

Beyond the fire, true night had set in, blue-black as a bruise, stretching over the steppe and sagebrush country of the southern British Columbia interior. When the water had boiled, I threw a pack of ramen and cracked a couple of eggs directly into it, whisking everything around with an old set of takeout chopsticks. When it was ready, I ate the mess straight from the pot without relish, and when I was full I threw in several handfuls of dog food and put the pot on the ground. I whistled and Herman came back from his scouting, wagged his tail, bowed his head, and ate too. He licked the bowl clean, his teeth clattering on the rim.

I produced a tin mug from a carabiner clipped to a rope running across the ceiling of the truck and poured myself a generous cup from a box of wine. It had a cheap, tinny taste, but I took a greedy sip as I reached for my phone. I had dozens of unread messages.

Happy Birthday, Lori!

Lori, it's your birthday!

Hope you're having a great birthday!

It was September 13, 2018. I had just turned thirty-two.

The ship which keeps a life afloat is constructed of surprisingly flimsy material. Not all shipwrecks are physical; there are things that can swallow up what's inside you as easily as the sea.

At the time I was setting up camp in that field, I had been living in poverty, either homeless or housing insecure, for over two years. I had been severely, cripplingly, depressed for just as long.

The demise of my old life began with a single, tiny mistake: my then partner, making a left-hand turn, forgot to signal.

The car accident shattered our lives. My partner incurred a concussion that left her in need of near-constant care. I maxed myself out physically, emotionally, mentally, financially, only to be met with another blow: when my partner recovered, she cheated on me, quite publicly, ending our relationship. This emotional *coup d'état* was worsened by a practical one; I had given up my apartment just weeks before the breakup because we had intended to move in together. Now I was reeling, one-two gut-punched by the financial and emotional distress of the situation.

Studies have shown that depression and anxiety can impair the decision-making process; anxiety, in particular, can disrupt action in the prefrontal cortex, the seat of rational decision making.[39] Poverty likewise affects the decision-making process, negatively impacting cognition.[40] Essentially, poor or unwell people make choices with short-term payoffs, rather than looking at long-term goals.

You don't make good choices in a crisis, and I had been bouncing from frying pan to fire for months.

I soon began to make decisions based on what I could tolerate, not on the wisest and most logical outcome. I quit my job and fled into the bush, where I worked as a professional forager. I lived in an old truck and camper without running water, electricity, proper food, sanitation, or internet.

Naturally, this only further strained my precarious finances, which in turn required more and more mental energy to handle. Soon, I was living hand-to-mouth in the bush, so profoundly depressed that getting out of bed without a drink was impossible.

The *coup de grâce* was not so much a blow as a blade upon which I fell willingly.

I began a relationship with a man who quickly took what little control I had left. Charming and manipulative, he threatened and abused me physically and emotionally, assuming control of my money, curating where I went and who I spoke to. When I had the strength to protest, he battered me down. No one else would have me; my ex had cheated on me because there was something wrong with me. I was crazy, he said, and I was lucky to have him, because no one else would put up with me. I needed him to make the choices, to be in charge, to be in control. I had to trust him. I literally stopped being able to say no, because the word "no" lost all meaning; anything I said or did, especially if it was about the way he treated me, was a result of this instability. I was unfit, he said, to make choices.

When the relationship reached its bitter, violent crescendo—a drunken sexual assault—I was so convinced of my own insanity that, the next day, when he told me he had not raped me, but "punished" me for the way I had treated him so that he could forgive me, I believed him.

I believed him so much that, with my body still bruised and aching, with his hand marks still red on the small of my back, I apologized to him.

After that, there wasn't very much left of me for a long, long time.

—

In the back of the truck, hunched over my phone, I had begun to cry, and the jag threatened to turn into a panic attack, which I pushed back with wine. I forced myself to breathe deeply and reached for the empty coffee can I kept my money in.

Earlier in the year, my credit card had been closed, and the meagre contents of my bank account—$86.32—seized. What little money I made now I kept in cash, which I counted daily, a soothing act. Money is power in that it determines the range of your choices—what you can eat, wear, and do. Counting it was like holding that power in my hands, a physical tabulation of my ability to survive.

I opened the tin and, under the light of my headlamp, counted out the contents. I had $3,000 in crumpled five-, ten-, and twenty-dollar bills.

That money had been painstakingly earned over the spring and summer, which I had spent as a farmhand, fruit-picker, and vineyard worker, hustling from town to town as the work came and went.

I was 2,000 kilometres from my destination—home—in Whitehorse, Yukon Territory. Eating as little as I could, sleeping in my truck, if nothing went wrong—if I didn't get into an accident, if I didn't hit bad weather, if another bearing didn't go, as the left front one had a week ago—then I would get to Whitehorse with around $2,300.

I had no job or housing arranged and winter was coming, but I had the money to get home.

——

When I left my boyfriend—when I escaped from him—I drove 4,500 kilometres east in late November. My truck, a 1991 GMC 2500 I had long neglected, not out of carelessness but because I was too poor to have it repaired, had a set of improbable and ever-increasing mechanical problems. The transmission was faulty; second gear was gone, so when I stopped at lights I had to floor the accelerator and jump straight into third, or it would get stuck there, the engine revving to a humming redline. The dash lights didn't work, so I superglued a hockey puck LED to the console so I could see how fast I was driving after dark. There was a hole in the muffler. The high beams didn't work. None of it mattered. Both my truck and camper, which I had been living out of for nearly a year, were destroyed when I spun out in an ice storm just past Saskatoon; the roads were so slick you could take a little run and slide from one shoulder to the other. I kept the truck from flipping, but slipped into the passing lane, where a semi was gearing up to pass me. Hit me so hard the camper flew through the back window into the crew cab. The sound was so loud—the glass breaking, the truck frame bending—that in the long brevity of terror I thought someone had shot out the back window.

I was okay, though. I had whiplash, but I was okay. Herman was okay, too—he'd been sitting in the front seat with me. Truck was a writeoff, though; when I went to see it at the tow yard, it had the air of roadkill, bulbous in all the wrong places, crushed and broken open. I bought a five-hundred-dollar junk hatchback from the yard owner—it ran, it had tires, that was enough—loaded whatever I could fit into the car, and moved on. I left a lot behind, just rotting there in the tow yard, clothes and keepsakes and books, but there wasn't enough room.

I white-knuckled it through Northern Ontario, where the ice storm turned into snow squalls on the other side of Thunder Bay, and washed up on a friend's couch in Montreal, thin and sick from stress and hunger.

In this new city, away from my boyfriend, I was supposed to be safe, but I didn't feel safe.

Anxiety coloured everything in neon hues of danger, made more real by the omnipresence of poverty. I had brutal panic attacks that petered into dissociative episodes, in which I felt as if some other person was playing the part of myself in a movie I had not seen. I drank copiously during the day, self-medicating. My nights were a blur of hot-wired, drunken insomnia.

My condition made me near unemployable. I eked by on a mixture of charity, odd jobs, and freelance work, which I was often late on, unable to maintain concentration. I did not know where to ask for help. What few clinics offered free therapy (when I had the energy to look) had long waitlists. I didn't speak French. My friend, although well intentioned, was herself a crippling alcoholic. She was often too drunk to talk to properly.

I was sick, so I was poor. I was poor, so I was sick. I was deeply, deeply ashamed of being both.

The cycle felt inescapable.

———

At camp that night, I returned the money to its hiding place.

Calmed, I went back to my phone and chose a podcast—*The Book Review Podcast* by the *New York Times*—using a spare cup as a speaker. It was the episode where they review Nico Walker's debut novel, *Cherry*.

I listened. I fed the fire, drank my wine, and thought about the books I wanted to write, what it would feel like to sit in a warm, clean room and write them. I imagined an apartment with a large bed covered by a dark-green down duvet, a desk, and a shelf full of books, a large, comfortable chair, a door without windows through which someone could peer at me while I slept, as they could with my truck. I imagined a refrigerator full of the foods I was denied without electricity: meat, yogourt, greens.

A good life, in which a person has enough to eat and a warm place to sleep and work that is meaningful, in which a person has the leisure to love and be loved, is such a small dream.

—

All that long, dark winter in Montreal, the thought of suicide, the relief of it, was with me.

I did try—and fail. Obviously.

I was so lucky, through all this, to have been blessed with so many good friends who loved me and stood with me through so much, even when I did not deserve it. I was not a good friend at that time, selfish and needy. To give to others a dollar or a minute of yourself, you need surpluses, and I had none. I am humbled that my friends saw this and forgave me.

I would like to write that it was this great love that saved me, but that's not true. In the hour you are most alone, all the love in the world is not enough.

—

In the morning, my breath had frosted over the inside of the windows, and the field was covered with a pall of wet snow. It was terribly cold in the back of the truck—a 1998 Chevy Blazer. Herman had crawled under the blankets in the night, curled in a ball at my side.

As I moved about in the chill and the gloom, making coffee and eating a slice of dry bread, I noted a pain in my right eye. It felt hot and swollen, like someone had put a grain of rice under my bottom eyelid as I slept. As I drove north, the pain worsened. By afternoon there was a visible pea-sized lump. That night I had a fever, sweating and tossing in my sleeping bag.

An ER doctor in Hazelton told me I had a severe stye—an infection caused by *Staphylococcus aureus* bacteria and worsened by my poor diet and dirty living conditions. He wrote a prescription for antibiotics even as he said they wouldn't work. It needed lancing, he said, but he refused to do it—I think he was too nervous. I didn't fill the prescription. Instead, I picked yarrow and plantain leaf, common medicinal plants in the North, crushed and wrapped them around tea bags soaked in cheap whisky, and taped the compress to the infected eye, hidden behind a pair of sunglasses. I drove home like that, 1,200 kilometres of twisting mountain passes, changing the concoction in gas station bathrooms. I don't know if it helped the infection, but it eased the pain.

I saw a better doctor the day I arrived in Whitehorse. Gently holding my head with one hand, she lanced the infection with a tiny silver needle she held impossibly steady. A thin trickle of yellow-white poison ran down my face as it drained, the colour of old tile grout. When it was over I felt better, but also empty, aching, as you do after you've cried for a long time when crying for a long time was what you needed.

In the following months, I lived on couches and house-sat, penniless in the brutal Yukon winter. I drove editors crazy chasing the money from freelancing assignments. I took cash jobs fixing houses. I shovelled sidewalks and fixed fences. I keenly felt my poverty and sometimes slipped back into depression.

Slowly, though, cheques and assignments came in. I filled the fridge with food, went to bed warm.

One cold day in February, I bought a package of wool socks. I threw out my old ones, full of holes. I wept when I put on the new ones.

For my birthday that year, my thirty-third, I went out with a few friends. We had drinks and pizza. When the evening was over I went home—in July, I'd found housing, a room in an apartment downtown.

I went inside and sat down in an armchair next to a shelf full of books and read for an hour.

Then I got undressed and got into bed—my own bed, in a house with water and electricity—and lay down, pulling up the cool, clean sheets.

I worry all the time, every day, that something someday will go wrong, that one day I will misstep, miscalculate, and everything will be taken away from me again. A part of me is always afraid of losing this tenuous safety, this uncertain warmth, of waking back up one morning in the back of my van, my water bottle frozen, trying to coax the chilled propane stove into boiling water, my knife hard and cool under my pillow. Counting bills in a coffee tin.

I'm probably always going to be afraid of that. Part of me—a small, frightened part of me—is never fully convinced that I deserve this, the certainty of running water, the safety of a full pantry, doors that lock. That will probably always stay with me, too.

Now, two years later, I still live in the same apartment. Sometimes I buy flowers, and I put them in vase so that when I come home, the room is brightened by the splash of colour. I have a green comforter, heavy and soft. The dog—the same dog—still sleeps at my side, curled in a ball.

After the Hungry Days

INSUFFICIENT FUNDS

That's what the card reader said each time I tried to pay for the thirty dollars' worth of groceries scattered across the frayed conveyor belt.

After the third try, the cashier, a dour middle-aged woman with heavy pancake makeup and her hair done up in a plasticky, crisp-fried perm, learned forward.

"Honey," she said, impatiently, "You don't have enough money."

What I didn't have enough money for was a box of Tuna Helper, two cans of off-brand tuna, butter, eggs, milk, and chocolate chips.

With a hot blush crawling up my throat and cheeks, I confessed to the cashier I did not know what to do. This was the first time in my life this had happened. I was nineteen.

This admission seemed to soften the cashier, who explained, more gently this time, that it was best if I took out everything I didn't think I needed, then try again.

I took out the chocolate chips and butter—I'd intended to make cookies for a friend who was feeling blue—and we ran it through again.

INSUFFICIENT FUNDS

The people in line behind began to murmur impatiently. I stared at the remaining five items. I took out the milk and one of the cans of tuna. We tried again. The transaction went through.

The cashier bagged my remaining three items without looking at me. When she handed me the receipt there was a message at the bottom that instructed me to *HAVE A NICE DAY*.

I took the bag from the cashier's hands and walked out of the store, into the street. It was early spring and the roads were a mess of salt and brown slush. I lived about an hour's walk away. I had taken the bus to get to the store, but in light of my recent humiliating reality check, the fare seemed too pricey now. The rolled-up bottoms of my jeans—both too long and too large for me—grew soggy and heavy as I walked, my sneakers squelching audibly with each step.

Earlier that week I had been fired from my job as a server. I was so angry at myself.

I was a student enrolled in a demanding journalism program. I had been having trouble balancing school and work and had started missing shifts and being rude or inattentive to customers, partly out of sheer exhaustion and partly because I was a young, dumb twit. I was drinking a lot, often at work; in lieu of above-table wages and paycheques delivered on time, the owner of restaurant had a (very) lax "self-serve" policy when it came to drinks, which I and many staff members often took advantage of, in quantity, after and during shifts. I did not come from a family who drank, and I rarely drank socially;

instead, I drank to offset the screaming, never-ending anxiety that dogged me all through my days and, often, into my sleep in the form of nightmares.

The anxiety was all-consuming, so I worked and studied compulsively, often late into the night, so I wouldn't have to think, pounding coffee or Red Bulls. Then I would be wound so tight I couldn't come down, so I'd drink. Then I'd get more anxious about school and work, so I'd work even harder and drink even more.

Repeat, ad nauseam, until collapse.

I suspected something was wrong with me—or, more specifically, that something was wrong *in* me, in my brain, maybe, or if not there, someplace deeper and even more untouchable—but was so embarrassed by this flaw that to speak of it seemed impossible, even if words could be found to do so.

As I slogged home that afternoon in the grey March light, my discouragingly light bag of groceries clutched tightly in my fist, I thought, *how is it possible to not have enough for so little?*

I was so ashamed.

———

A week after this incident, my relationship dissolved. As a result, I lost my housing.

School ended. I was jobless, homeless, and broke, bereft of an outlet—drinking or work—to shut the anxiety down.

By April, I would be admitted for a two-week stay in the psychiatric ward of the hospital.

This breakdown was as much about my economic health as it was about my mental health; without stable income, I was reduced not only in my capacity to care for myself, but in my stability, quality of life, and dignity. This resulted in further mental health issues, which then resulted in further money problems, spiralling, down down down, until finally there was no more *down* left to go. I had a nervous breakdown.

This pattern—poor mental health leading to being poor as fuck, being poor as fuck leading to even poorer mental health—has repeated itself over and over in my adult life. In its most severe instances, it has led to prolonged housing insecurity and homelessness. I would have a second nervous breakdown, this one much more prolonged, much more severe, with much more dire consequences, almost exactly ten years later, at age twenty-nine.

This crisis robbed me of two years of my adult life. It may well be that it set me so far back at such a pivotal time in my life that, combined with the other crises my generation has faced—two recessions, a global pandemic, a shattering housing crisis, and the slow-motion disaster that is climate change—I may never fully recover, financially or socially.

During this time in my life—this time and many others—money was an all-consuming, never-ending need that constantly occupied my thoughts. Those were hungry days, both literally and metaphorically.

I remember driving to a fruit-picking job in the Okanagan past the large houses of rich people in the summer night, lights burning in their kitchen windows as I smoked bummed cigarettes to blunt the ache in my empty gut.

I remember lying down at night in the back of my truck, my hands stiff from working a bottling line in wine country, with that same ache still in my stomach and a different ache in my chest, lonely and exhausted and so, so ashamed of myself and life.

I remember making a single pack of ramen, fleshing it out with eggs, pulling half the noodles and yolks out before I added the flavour packet, and letting them cool before adding them to my dog's food dish—splitting a pack of ramen was a way to stretch out our food budget.

No part of me was ever full in those days.

Now that I'm recovered, now that I have stable work, a place to live, enough to eat, friends, a regular doctor, I feel incredibly grateful for things many people take for granted. I always—still, even now—experience a moment of disbelief at night, when I lie down in my bed with my clean sheets and think, *Jesus Christ, this is my bed*. I am never not proud when I pay my rent and see there are a few dollars left over at the end. I will never, ever tire of the miracle—the goddamn, unbelievable *miracle*—of hot running water in the shower whenever I want it, as much of it as I want. Recently, I was on a work trip to Victoria, and when I arrived at the listed of address of my Airbnb, I had to stop and double-check that I was in the right place; it was too nice. It didn't seem to me that I would be allowed in there—a not totally unfounded suspicion, given that, three years before, I had nearly been refused entry to a posh hotel where I had a room, prepaid for as part of a journalism award I was up for, because the front desk clerk didn't believe I could be who I said I was, dressed the way I was.

And yet, with each small satisfaction and each small pleasure, there is the first-hand knowledge that it could all be taken away again. A missed assignment, a misstep in financial planning, an accident, or, worst of all, another mental health episode leaving me unable to work as hard as I'm working now—any one of these could be the end of this respite.

And that's what it feels like. A brief respite. A grace period. A chinook wind.

Something not meant to last. Something to distrust. Something I maybe don't deserve.

Now that I have my life back, losing it again is a fear I may never shake.

—

Prior to my institutionalization in 2006, I sought counselling through the college I was attending. The waitlist was long, and I could be seen only once every two weeks, at extremely specific times, which did not meet my schedule as a student and working-class person and which required an extensive commute. When I was institutionalized, that counsellor, an unprofessional, incompetent drunk, broke confidentiality by calling the home of my parents and informing them that she had been seeing me for issues surrounding my previous sexual assault. The call was received by my father, whom I had not told about my rape.

I was kept for two weeks at Belleville General Hospital in Ontario, where I saw a psychiatrist once every few days and was prescribed the antidepressant citalopram. During my "therapy" the psychiatrist repeatedly and persistently described my homosexuality as "problematic," insinuating during my sessions that my attraction to women was the result of my mental health condition, pathologizing my sexual orientation. Homosexuality was removed as a mental health condition from the DSM in 1973, but being a bigoted asshole is forever, bay-bee.

Upon discharge, I was given no prescription for refills from the hospital and told to seek care elsewhere. I was not scheduled for any follow-up care, was not given information on how to find or pay for counselling or a therapist. I had just had a severe nervous breakdown which required hospitalization, but somehow the system felt I would be well enough after two weeks to manage—and afford—my own care. This is like asking someone with a broken arm to sling a bale of hay the day they get their cast off.

It would be 2016 before I saw any kind of a therapist again. Following a sexual assault, I was granted a limited number of sessions through a sexual assault survivor program with a therapist from a for-profit agency to address the severe PTSD-related symptoms I was experiencing. The difference in the quality of care—and the benefit it gave me—compared to my first stab at counselling in 2006 was astounding.

Nevertheless, once my sessions were used up, I couldn't pay for more. I had to cease care.

I was able to receive a handful of sessions in 2019 from a free (Canadian Mental Health Association) clinic in my territory. My counsellor, by her own admission, was not professionally equipped to deal with the level of trauma I had experienced. When I ran out of my allotted sessions, she suggested I seek more intensive for-pay therapy elsewhere. In an attempt to take control of my own mental health options, after a series of lengthy interviews and sifting through the services of nearly a dozen potential mental health care providers, I obtained the services of a queer therapist via video session out of Victoria. She proceeded to discuss her own personal issues during our sessions, fail to show up on time for or be mentally present during appointments, and—most damningly—subjected me to EMDR (eye movement desensitization and reprocessing), a therapy I had never had before and did not understand and for which she was absolutely not licensed or trained, during a mental health crisis, without my consent, without explanation of what was happening to me. This caused severe and prolonged distress, and after trying to work with her for another few sessions, I didn't go back—not that she followed up.

Basically, my track record of experiences with mental health professionals is dismal at best, kind of horrifying at worst. I still don't have a therapist I can afford, so I'm back at the free clinic, taking another round of limited sessions with a different counsellor.

This isn't surprising, given the lax and in some cases nearly non-existent certifications for so-called counsellors, which can mean seeing anything from a "wellness" professional to a social worker to a certified mental health care provider with a master's degree, depending on where you are in Canada and, above all, what you're willing to pay. A lack of mental health care providers and a dramatic increase in demand on existing services (especially since the pandemic started), along with government outsourcing to not-for-profits for these services, has led to widespread failure when it comes to the availability of affordable mental health care services.

These experiences severely shaped how I handled my mental health, both in the years following my first breakdown and now. Largely, I just *wouldn't*, because I didn't trust the system to help me and because I couldn't afford the kind of professional help I needed. Mostly, I drank, and honestly, I still use alcohol to self-medicate. In the absence of affordable (and competent, properly licensed, and regulated) therapy, my only other option is medication, the side effects of which include weight gain and loss of libido. Gaining weight is unacceptable to me, as it causes me severe and very distressing body dysmorphia—the more weight I gain, the more my body looks like a "woman's body" and the more uncomfortable my non-binary self becomes. Loss of libido, likewise, is a no go—having been repressed, assaulted, censored for my sexuality, not to mentioned raped twice, I consider every act of good queer sex, every orgasm I give, every orgasm I receive, to be an act of joyful rebellion against the white-male-dominated capitalist patriarchy that has made controlling, containing, and crippling me at every opportunity its apparent mission.

That's not a knock against medication, nor an excuse for the amount I drink—medication is right for lots of people—nor is it a kick at legitimate mental health care professionals, the majority of whom work really hard for not nearly enough money and genuinely want to help their clients. I'm just saying that the mental health care system doesn't seem equipped to help me—a queer, non-binary, sex-positive, working-class person—so I do what I can with what's available to me.

If, as the old adage says, "health is wealth," then in this country, health—a full mind-body picture of health, in which care for the mentally ill is treated with the same seriousness as care for the physically ill—is for the wealthy only.

———

In January 2020, as sometimes happens to a freelancer, many of my cheques were late coming in. Concurrently, business fell off at the bar where I worked, and my hours were cut back.

With a reduced income, the money I desperately needed to pay rent delayed, and the territory gripped in a brutal cold snap that saw temperatures of -40 degrees Celsius for weeks on end, I found myself standing in front of the freezer in my basement apartment with the door open, counting Tupperware containers, overwhelmed with anxious desperation.

During the preceding months, I had built up a cache of meals by purchasing food when it was on sale, batch cooking, carefully portioning out the food, then freezing it into equally sized containers. I am not a polished cook, but I am a resourceful and inventive one, and there were a variety of meals to choose from: potato soup, caribou meatballs and rice, mac and cheese, and various casseroles.

What I was doing, in counting them, was trying to determine how long I could go without buying groceries if I did not get paid soon.

This was totally unnecessary; my cheques came in a week later, I made my rent and had money left over to buy groceries, even to make a minor repair to my vehicle. The fear of not having enough, however, the trauma of it, was so triggering that I suffered a major, although short-lived, anxiety episode that rattled my carefully sheltered, recently recovered mental health.

What will I do if I ever get sick again? Will I be able to get the help I need? Will I fall through the cracks again?

Am I ever really *safe*?

As a working-class person, for-profit therapy is so far out of my reach as to be laughable.

Even when I worked as a full-time journalist for *Yukon News* my salary was so low that I could not afford to pay the $125–$150 a for-profit therapist charges. Even at a sliding scale of seventy dollars an hour, if I were to see a for-pay therapist once a week, it would cost me an extra $280 a month—around 25 percent of what the average one-bedroom apartment costs in Whitehorse.[41]

It's worth noting, too, that in order to get care I've had to be mentally stable enough to advocate for it; I've had to be well enough to make follow-up phone calls, arrange appointments, and discuss my own care objectively, something that very unwell people can't reasonably do and that I certainly couldn't have done at certain points in my life. In order to be well enough for this, I've had to reach a state of not only emotional stability, but financial stability as well. As I've noted, for myself and many other working-class people, mental health is inherently tied to having enough money that you know you're not going to wake up and find the electricity has been cut, or knowing there's food in the fridge when you get home after work, or that you can pay your rent on time and aren't going to be evicted.

Prior to escaping my last cycle of mental health crisis and poverty in my early thirties, I'd spent my entire adult life unaware that my level of anxiety—my shaking hands and nausea, my hyper-aware, constant edginess, panic attacks that left me panting and crying and exhausted— is not normal. I'd thought *everyone* felt like they were drowning in a too-bright sea of never-ending noise and danger. I thought *everyone* was overwhelmed with the fear that the slightest misstep or most minor failure would send you careening toward unspeakable pain and an inevitable miserable death *all the goddamn time*.

If I had been able to access care, I firmly believe I would have had a very different, arguably better life, one that has been denied to me because care was economically always out of my reach. I would not only be healthier, but happier.

Both poverty and mental health are about lack—lack of money, lack of dignity, lack of work, lack of meaning, lack of stability, lack of love. Treating them as separate issues ignores the fact that something is wrong with the way our system currently functions to create these social, economic, and environmental problems in the first place.

A step to ensuring that I and other working-class people like me don't fall through the cracks again is to ensure that the same quality of mental health care is accessible to everyone, regardless of income.

I'm always going to be afraid of losing what I've gained, economically and mentally. The hungry days are never really over.

Call You by Your Name

I

Do you remember, Lucky, how fucked up I was when we first met?

Gabrielle had just left me. She'd been sick for months after the car accident, after the concussion; she couldn't drive or read from a screen, she didn't know what time it was or how much time had passed even when she looked at a clock, couldn't keep appointments, couldn't watch a movie or read a book, couldn't remember a conversation that happened twenty minutes ago, so I did those things for her: I became not only her lover, but her caretaker, timekeeper, appointment manager, transcriber, personal cook, and assistant.

She became, overnight, a confused and furious stranger with the face of the woman I loved. It changed her forever, and by the time I realized this, I had already resolved to love her, no matter what.

And then she got a little better. And then I took a breath, stepped back for a few weeks to take care of myself, head out into the backcountry.

And then she cheated on me, as carelessly and casually as one might cheat at a game of cards—publicly, sober, in front of all our friends. Like I didn't even exist.

Watching her struggle, watching her suffer and despair and try to climb back into herself, watching her disappear and reappear and disappear again and again and again, even as I put my own life on hold for months at a time to care for her while she recovered, had put a crack in me so deep down, so far inside myself I didn't even know it was there. When she cheated on me, that hairline fracture splintered and broke under the pressure of that hurt and humiliation. I didn't understand, then, that sometimes people do things when they are hurt and hurting and afraid that are not about you at all— sometimes people hurt other people just because they are in pain and afraid and don't have any other language, any other words, with which to express it.

Had I known that, maybe things would have turned out differently … maybe I would have been able to forgive her sooner, maybe I never would have met you, maybe I wouldn't be talking to you like this now, six years later. But I didn't know it.

Something in me broke that wouldn't heal for years, something essential. I couldn't stand it, so I ran away. I quit my job and disappeared into the bush with my truck and camper.

There was a good burn south of Watson Lake, and I went out there to make my living picking morels. Nothing seemed left alive in that blackened, harsh country, nothing except the ravens that turned slowly overhead like the rusted cogs of some great, ancient machine. It was good. I needed that place, with the smell of ash always in the air and the endless expanse of destruction and resurrection spreading out forever under the midnight sun. I picked morels all day and I drank all night and then I woke up hungover, had a beer and a couple cups of black coffee, and went out to pick mushrooms again.

Which is where I met you, of course: in the mushroom camps, trying to make your season's fortune, like everyone else.

I barely remember the first time I met you. I was drinking all the time then, was already on my way down. I think Patricia, my dear friend, my polar opposite, dark-haired and boyishly tall and impossibly feminine, pointed you out to me when I told her what I was looking for as a possible candidate.

I'd seen you around, but I'd never spoken to you before. You were handsome: dark hair, strong jaw, lean and wiry and muscular. You had *awful* tattoos though, a screaming clown with a lopsided face, words scratched into your forearm as if by a hand that had been shaking. You never wore shoes, so the soles of your feet were black and tough as a strip of rawhide. You had a red-plaid coat full of holes and pockets, from which I had seen you produce an apparently endless supply of Lucky Lager. You had a tattered Lucky Lager T-shirt, too, from some flat of long-since-drunk beer, and you were always trying to get me take pictures of you in it so I could post them to Instagram when we got back within cell service. You were sure one day Lucky Lager would see it and give us a sponsorship, and then we'd be *made*.

That's why I started calling you Lucky, remember? You always relied so heavily on luck. It was part of your brand, of the person you wanted people to see you as. I liked that about you. It felt like confidence and optimism at a time in my life when I was absolutely not confident and certainly not optimistic. I know now, of course, it was neither of those things—really, it was desperation—but I know a lot of things these days that I didn't know back then.

I'm not particularly attracted to men, and so what women probably have liked best about you was probably not what *I* liked about you. I was attracted to your smile, though. You smiled often, and the smile was easy and warm, but always a little sad. I liked that. I recognized that. I saw something of myself in it. That's why I picked you. Privately, too, I always thought you had a rather feminine mouth.

I can't imagine the impression I must have made on you then, a skinny, hungry-eyed creature with long red-blond hair in a wild braid, a shirt full of holes, and a hatchet on their belt. My left hand was still wrapped in a dirty bandage from a dog bite fracture, and a severed tendon. You told me later that it was this detail that made you like me best, that I was strange and wild and obviously hurt, walking around out there in the backcountry, where you definitely need two hands to have a shot at surviving, my one, bad hand sticking out from my shirt sleeve like a *fuck you* to god and my own thin mortality.

Do you remember—how could you not?—how brazen I was when I approached you? *I'm interested—are you?* Direct and to the point. Men and women aren't like this, I know that now; you heterosexuals make things so needlessly complicated, are so attached to your gender roles. I was sitting next to you at the fire, flirting a little, half-cut on a quart of Kraken, and everyone else was chattering away about something else, and I just leaned over and met your eyes and asked if you'd like to sleep with me.

I was hurting, I said. I'd been betrayed. I wanted some comfort, but the thought of letting a woman touch me filled me with revulsion. The wound was too fresh. I was too angry. I wanted something new in the meantime. I hadn't been with a man in nearly a decade—I was twenty-nine. If you wanted me, you could have me, provided I was in charge of how things went down.

I was curious. I was terribly lonely. I had a plan.

You sat there drinking Fireball—cheap-ass corn liquor like liquid cinnamon hearts—and listening intently. I had a hand on your thigh, was looking into your face. You were thirty-three, had the beginnings of lines around your mouth, around your eyes, which were dark brown, so dark they were nearly black. When I finished, you were a bit flustered, but you said *thank you*, of all things, like you were flattered by something thoughtful I had done for you. Thank you, you said, but no—you liked me and you didn't want to complicate things and you would be moving on soon, and besides which I was very drunk and it wouldn't be right.

I listened and shook my head. That all seemed very reasonable. I said I liked you, too. I seem to remember we shook hands, even. You had very broad, strong hands. I have very small, strong hands. We both had thick calluses on the pads of our fingers, across the tops of our palms.

Then we got absolutely shitbagged, and I got really sad about Gabrielle and tried to get in my truck to drive three hours into cell service so I could call her, and Patricia quite rightly slapped me in the face and took my keys.

The next day, when you saw me, we were both hung over. You smiled at me, chagrined, as if it had been you who'd made such a ridiculous drunken proposal, and I smiled back at you. It made me like you more, this good-natured shyness.

I thought that because you'd said no—because I'd been too drunk and you'd known that and didn't want to take advantage of me—you were a good guy. I thought it meant you had a sense of honour. I thought it meant you were *safe*.

Like I said. There were a lot of things I didn't know back then.

———

Bush time is so funny, eh, Lucky? An hour in the backcountry could feel like a year, a day could be twenty minutes. It feels like months passed after that, but really it couldn't have been more than a week or so. I was either half-cut all of the time or all-cut half of the time, depending on how you looked at it, so maybe that had something to do with it.

We were on good terms. I saw you around a bunch. You came over to hang out with us, have a drink sometimes with our picking crew: Patricia and her new fellow, a tall, bearded farm boy from the Shuswap; Patricia's sister Annie who was up from Ontario on an adventure, intending in the end to get away from her current boyfriend, who was still back in the central eastern time zone; and Clay, Patricia's boyfriend's friend, a big-hearted, cantankerous fiftysomething-year-old man who had worked in the bush all his life and would be found ten months later dead of a drug overdose in his trailer, struck down by fentanyl-laced crack cocaine.

Clay—five foot three if he was a foot, built like Popeye, who swore up and down whenever he got good and drunk (which was often) that one time he had seen a lady sasquatch "with big hairy titties"—tried to warn me about you, actually. With the solemnity only a serious alcoholic can affect, he'd say that you were no good, that there was a reason no one in camp wanted to team up with you, that you did bad things for money and couldn't be trusted. At first, I had half a mind to listen, but then it came out that Clay, who I called "Uncle," was going around behind my back telling everyone how he was going to fuck me, and I was so disappointed in him that I disregarded his advice as possessive jealously.

Which it was, it's just that it was also right.

The morels were petering out in the lowlands, so we all hauled up an old ATV trail to the high country. Burned as fuck, too burned and too dry for anything to grow. We called it "crunchy country" because of the sound the burned lichen made when you walked on it. I don't think we found a single goddamn thing up there, not one fucking basket. I can't remember if you came with us or if you went into the deep back, over to the other side of the mountain with Fred. Fred would, in short order, become Annie's new lover, but I think this was before that.

I was still stoned by grief over what Gabrielle had done, and so I remember only two things clearly from that time. The first is the terrible, tremendous thirst; we had been told there was water, but by "water" the buyer meant "stagnant pool of green slime with a beaver swimming in it." Someone had stolen my water purification pump, we had only one small cooking pot to boil water in, and fuel was limited—the fire hadn't left much left behind when it had torn through. I resisted drinking that beaver water for days, but eventually caved—there was no other choice. I remember it tasted like wet socks. Years later, I joked with a friend that drinking that water was what kept me healthy during the pandemic—if we had swallowed that and not died of giardia or tapeworms or dysentery, we must be immune to pretty much everything.

The second thing is your friend: tall, skinny as a hare and about half as bright, but I'll be fucked if I can recall his name now. I remember that he had come with you and Fred, that he had that old white beater car, the "bog buggy," all full of Chicken McNuggets boxes and empty beer cans stuffed full of cigarette butts. You could hear the muffler a mile off before you saw the car, and you could smell it—burning oil, stale smoke, the musky animal odour of unwashed male bodies—a mile after it was gone. I wasn't very attracted to him. I found him annoying and desperate, and I hated the way he tried to mansplain basic chores to me, like cutting wood or fishing for pike, all of which I was better at than him, that little city shit. It was the cheese incident that really turned me off him, though. He had hiked in with a litre of heavy cream and, finding no cold running water to keep it from spoiling, decided to leave it out in the hot sun to make "cheese." I came back late from a pick with Annie and there he was, sick as a dog, lying on his belly in the shade and moaning, the smell of sweat and puke and spoiled milk coming up off him in a stink that was almost tangible, like the cartoon wafts that follow Pepé Le Pew. The idiot had mixed the curdled mess of the "cheese" into his noodles and eaten it all. I know my entire sexual orientation isn't much geared for the survival of the species, but if you think milk left out at 30 degrees becomes cheese and then *eat it* despite the odour screaming *don't fucking eat this* at your entire olfactory system, your genes need to stay far, *far* away from mine, thank you very much.

I'd flirted with him for like, twenty minutes, then decided I didn't want anything to do with him, a casual choice which had much further-reaching consequences than I could possibly have guessed. I didn't understand that when someone perceived as a woman makes lightly flirtatious eyes at a man, he assumes this means that not only will he get to fuck her, but that all other men are now *forbidden* from fucking her. I know, I'm sorry, I'm getting off topic, but seriously, Lucky, have you ever stopped to think about how incredibly ridiculous your whole gender is? You people are fucked in the head if you think a soft smile and the admission of sexual curiosity translates to *you will, for sure, sire sons from my loins*, as your friend apparently believed.

Finding nothing more than a few spored out morels up there, the whole crew returned to the main camp, just in time to celebrate the solstice. We waited, the whole pack of us, all the camps together, there must have been a hundred of us, until ten or eleven at night, and then we invaded Liard Hot Springs. There was no one around. Honestly, I think when people, park operators included, saw this army of dirty, bushed mushroom pickers crawling out of their rickety Toyota Corollas and rusted-out pickups and school buses converted to run on vegetable oil with moose antlers tied to the front with snare wire, they said *fuck it* and ran.

We took that place over: dogs running around the edges of the pools, many of us stoned and naked, popping acid, shrooms, tabs of ecstasy, dancing and drinking. There was a boy on the stones between the hot upper pool and the tepid lower pool, spinning fire to music blasting out of speakers in the soft blueish half-dark that stood in for night that far North. Someone was banging on a set of bongos. The bus kids were handing out home-brewed mead in plastic pop bottles that tasted like soapy honey. Ravens gathered in the upper branches of the trees to see what all the fuss was about. In many ways it's a miracle no one drowned or fell back on the wet stones and cracked their head open, but in many ways it wasn't. We always expected things to work out, and they always did.

In those days, I think I was so used to the small miracles of the backcountry that I took them for granted and only knew I had seen miracles when they were all used up and gone.

I was drunk, but only a little. I was standing at the edge of the pool in my blue bikini, holding a can of beer when you came up behind me and put one hand on my hip. You leaned into my hair—I had long hair then, all the way down to my waist—and it was wet and smelled of sulphur and other minerals from the hot spring. With your lips hot against my ear and your cock pressing through your shorts against my ass—which seemed a bit presumptuous, I thought—you asked me if my earlier offer was still open.

And I thought for a minute and then *yes, maybe, we could talk about it?*

And then you were taking my hand and leading me into the water.

Your mouth was slack, and your eyes were bright, feverish. Later, I would come to know that look meant you were right liquored, and after that brightness, if you kept drinking, there would be a darkness, and then I needed to leave you alone, if I could.

You pulled me into the second pool—the cooler, deeper pool that flowed off down into the greenish loam of the forest that surrounds the spring. Someone had strung fairy lights all around, although I can't remember what they were using to power them, maybe a car battery—and the water seemed very dark and thicker somehow for being so dark. I thought we were going to talk but then you were kissing me, pushing me into a little alcove, away from the others. I didn't like your scratchy beard and you were using a lot of tongue. I didn't know what to say; this wasn't what I had meant and I tried to say so, but you weren't listening to me, you already had your dick out, hanging pale and fat in the pool like some tumescent sea creature.

Then you had me up against the earth of the pool and you pulled the bottoms of my bathing suit aside, banged up against me roughly, trying to get it, your cock, into me. I was saying *no, Lucky, you're not wearing a condom*, but you were just ignoring me and then it was in, and it *hurt* because I wasn't wet and because we were in the water and because, aside from some small toys, I didn't often let myself be penetrated.

Suddenly, I was scared. I said no. You didn't seem to hear me. You were pumping away in little short flexes of your thighs that reminded me of the mindless, stupid way goats fuck, eyes glazed and thick lips wet, like you were imagining eating something really, really good. I was trying to push you off me—I was confused, stunned by the speed with which this had escalated—I had wanted to sleep with you but I hadn't wanted it to be right now and I hadn't wanted it like this and everything was suddenly out of my control and I didn't know what to say or how to get out of this situation and then—

Well, then, as I'm sure you recall, your fucking girlfriend came around the corner and saw you standing there, waist deep in the water and balls deep in me.

My god, Lucky. All my fucking gods, you dumb fucking prick. I knew you had slept with her, but I didn't know she was your *girlfriend*. I didn't know fuck all about it, and anyway when I'd said *do you want to fuck me* more than two weeks ago I hadn't meant that you'd just decide out of the blue to try and plow me without so much as a *hey, what do you think about this* at a party where you'd come with your goddamn girlfriend, you asshole.

And then you were gone, pulling out of me, going after her. This poor girl, maybe twenty, twenty-one—you liked them young, I was the exception—and then you were gone, stuffing yourself back into your shorts and I was just ... floating there. Alone. Sore. Confused.

After a few minutes, I put myself back together and came back out into the main pool, where I was surprised to find everyone looking at me, whispering. Clay was there, standing shirtless with his hairy potbelly hanging over the lip of his pants, holding a can of Old Milwaukee. He wouldn't even speak to me, just shook his head and turned away.

Again, what the absolute fuck is wrong with men, Lucky? I mean, you're all entitled fucking pricks, sure, I get that, but what the fuck is wrong with men *generally*? Who the fuck do you dogs think you are, sighing and carrying on and passing judgment and being *disappointed* in what other people do with their bodies? You sanctimonious assholes would fuck a wet bag of flour if you thought no one was watching, and then blame the bag of flour if you were caught, pointing accusingly with one hand and shoving your flour-dusted cock back into your shorts with the other.

Your friend the milk-eater was standing there at the side of the pool, looking straight at me with black, angry eyes. I didn't see where you'd gone, and I felt like I needed to talk to you about what had just happened, but you'd disappeared. I walked up to the milk-eater and asked him if he'd seen which way you went. He called me a whore and turned his back to me.

Everyone was looking at me, whispering about me—I was confused. This hadn't been my idea; this was all a big misunderstanding. I felt empty and distant. My stomach hurt and my cunt ached, and I wanted to be alone.

I went back to my camper. I crawled up into the top bunk with my dog. I put my back to the door and I curled up around myself and I cried into his warm, hairy back, partly because I was hurt and partly because I was embarrassed. Mostly, though, I cried because I felt guilty, because having sex with you, even if I hadn't wanted to, felt like betraying Gabrielle, and because I had hurt that poor girl who was your girlfriend without meaning to, hurt her the way Gabrielle had hurt me.

I felt I was a terrible person. I felt violated.

I felt, above all, that this was how I deserved to feel.

God, Lucky. You're such an asshole.

——

You came to my camper the next day and you apologized—you had not been a gentleman, you said, nor had you been gentle. You were drunk, you said, you shouldn't have done that. You looked very sad, very sincere, pulled a very convincing hangdog expression of heartfelt regret.

You had a reddening bruise on your cheek, which only served to make you look more pathetic and open to sympathy. You'd run into the milk-eater, you said. He'd tried to start a fight with you over your having fucked me when it should have been him (*what is wrong with you people?*). He threw a punch that hit you in the face, and you cold-cocked him with your left. After a minute he came to, picked himself up, got into the car, dumped all your things out on the side of the road, and drove away. We never saw him again, which was fine with me, but you were pretty mad about it, because he owed you a lot of money.

You told me—you told everyone—that you hadn't known the other woman, now your *ex*-girlfriend, was so into you. You'd thought it was casual. You didn't think she'd mind. Actually, you'd thought there might even be room for a three-way, which even then I laughed at, because it was such a stupid stereotypically *male* thing to think you could have that so easily.

You apologized for the way you acted and for the embarrassment and confusion and the general ungodly mess you'd gotten us both into.

I chose to believe you were sorry, and I chose to believe this wasn't a pattern of behaviour from you, because I had never had very much to do with men romantically, sexually, and so I was silly and naive. I didn't realize one of the privileges patriarchy gives men is the right to pick and choose what they do and do not want to know. I didn't know how to feel about what had just happened, because I had wanted to have sex with you, just not right there and not like that, and I knew I didn't like what you had done, but I also didn't know how much of it was really my fault.

I was quiet while you apologized, but when you were done, I forgave you. I accepted these apologies, although I didn't feel very good about them.

I still do that, you know. Forgive people I shouldn't forgive. I believe people when they say they're sorry. I believe them when they say they won't do it again and then I forgive them and try to move on. I do this because I'm stupid, because I don't want other people to hurt, because not forgiving people sometimes means losing them forever. I do this, I did this with you, because I always want to believe I mean enough to someone that I'm worth not only *saying* sorry to, but *acting* on that regret.

And I'm always, always fucking wrong.

II

The morel season ended. It had been very wet at the start of the year. Now it was very dry, and the mushrooms had shrivelled and hardened like dark little worms on a sidewalk. By late June, much earlier than expected, they stopped coming up altogether, which meant it was time to move. The camp, led by the buyer Big Joe Bear—did you know he died a few years ago of a heart attack, or so I heard? Hard to imagine the mushroom camps without Big Joe—packed up and moved south and west to a place near Meziadin Junction on the Cassiar Highway, to switch from morels to berries.

None of us had ever picked berries before—usually I went south to work the orchards in the Okanagan—but the price of morels that year had been lousy, and we were all broke and hungry, and I wasn't yet ready to return to civilization. Patricia, Annie, and I took the far corner of the camp, away from the main cookfire, because we liked the quiet. I parked my camper the farthest away, tucked against the treeline, because it was growing hot and I wanted the shade.

And then we were just ... kind of together. I'm not sure how it happened, but it did. You started sitting closer to me at the communal fires, started dancing with me and the bus kids and coming by to eat with my crew at dinnertime. By the strange alchemy of lovers, we were a couple, sleeping together and holding hands and staying up late at night, talking. You started coming by my camper at night, first occasionally and then more often. We'd talk and have sex and then we'd go to sleep with the hatch open, bug screen pulled tight, because it would get so hot in there with the three of us in the sleeping cabin, you and me and the dog. You had a tent somewhere off in the brush, away from the rest of the camp, that I never went to, which is how you said you liked it—you liked to feel, you said, like an animal with a den, like you had someplace to retreat to that was only yours.

On the nights you stayed over, you liked to lie in bed in the mornings while I got up and made us breakfast in the narrow little kitchen of the old camper—bacon and eggs and coffee, naked—with the open door facing the bush that went on for miles and miles and miles.

Looking back, you know what I suspect? I suspect that in part you started sleeping with me because it meant you got a bed and a hot meal. I don't know if I'd fault you for that, necessarily.

One night you came by very late. We were a little farther south now, so there was a short hour around two or three when there was something that actually looked like night and the stars came out. It was during this uneasy blue hour that you appeared, drunk as hell and leaning on my camper door. There had been a party down at the main fire. I think it might have been Canada Day. I was tired, and I was getting tired of drinking, too, by then, so I had gone back to my tent and gone to bed, and I woke up around two to find you holding yourself up against the frame. I came over to the door—you were very pale—and opened it. I asked you if you were all right. I was slightly above you, because I was up on the top step of the camper and you were standing on the ground, and you looked up into my face and you were crying. You looked so sad with your long, dark, wavy hair all mussed about your shoulders and suntanned face; you looked like a little boy who had lost a toy and was afraid to report so to his parents, even as he grieved its loss.

I asked you again what was wrong, and in a small voice, you said *I killed him.*

I paused. The others had been doing mushrooms earlier in the evening. I wondered if you'd had some, but I moved out of the way to let you in. You sat down at the table, and I went over to the little propane fridge and got you a beer—a cold beer was a precious thing in those days—and one for myself and sat down next to you on the torn vinyl seats.

Do you remember the story you told me, Lucky? You said you stomped a man to death over a debt, a debt that wasn't even yours, but one you'd been hired to collect. You and a couple of other boys, you said. You were young and there were drugs involved. You had only meant to rough him up, but then there he was, dead, and you all panicked. You all panicked, and you tied his body to a big stone and threw him off the pier and into the sea. He sank down beneath the waves, this dead man, and the dark things that live on the ocean floor scuttled all over him and picked his bones clean. He was Native, you said. Like you.

You hadn't meant to kill him, and you cried and cried and cried as you insisted this point. I stroked your hair and kissed your cheek and nodded my head, listening. When you finished telling this story you crawled up into bed with me and laid your head on my breast and went to sleep, like a little boy, as I said.

We never talked about it again, and honestly, at the time, I either didn't believe you, or didn't want to believe you. It seemed so ridiculous that you'd kill a man and then tell someone you barely knew about it just because you were drunk and the two of you were sleeping together. I didn't know back then that sometimes, when people have done bad things, they will tell you these bad things right up front—not to be honest with you, but to see if you will still love them, if you will still tolerate them, after they know you've done bad things.

I think, now, that you did kill that man. I know you better now and have my own reasons to be afraid of you. I remember exactly when I started to believe it: months later, I overheard you on the phone, arranging to have the milk-eater, who still owed you money and had gone back to Vancouver, beaten if he didn't pay up.

That was why, later on, I was scared, very scared, actually, that you'd kill me, too. To shut me up.

I mean, you very nearly did, anyway. It was pretty close, although maybe not in the way a man like you is used to thinking about. I was about half-dead after what you did, half or a little more, for a long, long time.

You can't leave a storyteller only *half*-dead, though. Not without becoming a part of the stories they tell. That was a very foolish, arrogant thing for you to do.

—

A funny thing about being with you, Lucky, was how much you talked about sex versus how much of it you actually wanted to have.

Two-thirds of the time you were so whisky-dicked I might as well have gone out and pleasured myself on the trailer hitch instead of trying to get anywhere with you. Sometimes I'd let you fuck me in the camper bed, which for me was a new and exciting sensation, having a cock made out of flesh instead of silicon inside me, but I liked to be on top, and I think that bothered you. You were always talking about how your cock was average length but extra fat (honey, I'm gay, not stupid; I knew it was just *average* average, the Subway sandwich of cocks, not the worst meal you could have, but there are definitely better). After we fucked, I would lie awake and make myself come, because you always came too fast for me to get mine, an experience which was new to me as a queer person. How do straight women deal with it?

You said part of the reason you wanted to be with me at that time was that you wanted to learn how to eat pussy—you suspected you were bad at it.

You were wrong. You were terrible. I tried to teach you, but you ate cunt the way a monkey eats an orange slice—lips pulled back, teeth bared, tongue bopping up and down like you didn't realize *to eat out* is a euphemism. Much later on, I realized the problem was that you didn't actually know where my clit was, and when I had this epiphany I threw my head back, laughed, and felt terribly sorry for you.

More than your poor technique—and your irrational annoyance when I tried to correct you—you seemed at best bored and a worst a little nauseated by the act. You didn't like my hairy snatch and you were absolutely disgusted, would not even look at me, if I was on my period. One time I made a crack about "earning your red wings" and you positively turned *green*. Another time, you asked me if I was feeling all right, and I said yes, I was just crampy and starting my period, and you recoiled like I'd said I had the goddamn clap and admonished me for talking to you about it.

Although you were squeamish about my pleasure, you certainly weren't about your own. Accustomed to having a lot of oral sex, I handed out blow jobs like after-dinner mints, a gift—and it *was* a gift, Lucky, no one is *owed* a blow job—that you rapidly came to expect from me. It will never cease to amaze me how the men and boys least capable of pleasing a woman's body seem to feel the most entitled to receive pleasure from it.

What I remember most about fucking you, though, what I think about all the time, because it's so *you*, so very indicative of the kind of piece-of-shit asshole you are, is that night we were both a little drunk and very horny, and you were fucking me and I said you could come inside me, but partway through I changed my mind and I didn't want you to. I was scared. I said *please don't*. So, you pulled out and shot off on my belly, and we went to sleep.

In the morning I woke up to you sticking it in me again—this was unusual, as you usually only had the stamina for one round a day, and I was dry and it hurt—but I went with it and rolled on top of you and started bouncing up and down, taking it.

And after a few short pumps, you came. You came right inside me. Without asking.

I wasn't on birth control, you knew that, and you didn't give a fuck and just shot your fucking load without a word about it. I've always assumed this was because you felt somehow owed—I'd said you could and then I changed my mind, but you were going to have it anyway.

I didn't know what to say, so I said nothing. That doesn't happen in lesbian relationships. I had no fucking idea how to deal with it, and I think you knew it, too, you selfish prick.

I did say, however, that you surprised me. I remember saying this very softly, because I wasn't sure how you would take it.

"I mean you can say you're a feminist or whatever," you said, blinking slowly in your post-orgasm glow, "but it's been my experience that women are happiest when you come in them. They're crazy without it. That's why women go nuts on birth control. They need it. It's natural."

Funny, how eating my unshaven pussy was gross, but you nutting without my permission inside me with your sweaty, hairy, unwashed dick was the most natural thing you could think of.

Is that how you wound up with a daughter—just sticking it in, humping like a dog, then coming in your ex without asking? Is that why she doesn't speak to you now? How is your daughter, by the way? She must be seventeen, eighteen?

May she be so blessed as to never have a lover as big a fucking pig as you are.

———

It wasn't all bad though, being with you. I was fond of you. You were capable, funny. I'd never had many male friends, and I'd never been a female-presenting adult with a male-presenting partner before. I was shocked at how different it was, being in a heterosexual relationship. When we went to eat somewhere, the staff addressed you, not me. When we went out to drink, men stopped hitting on me—like motherfucking *magic*—the moment they saw your hand on my thigh.

When we checked into a hotel, you were given everything to handle, and you handled everything. I felt safe at the time, in a way I'd never felt safe before.

Best of all, I didn't have to explain myself, or watch out for bigots, or consider when and if it was safe to kiss my partner or hold their hand. So much was assumed, unspoken, sanctified by the implicit approval of other people. Everything in my romantic and sexual life was just so goddamn *easy*, even if you *were* kind of an asshole and I had to get my own good self off.

Toward the beginning of August, you had to go home. I can't remember if you needed to or wanted to, but you went, and you took Fred and Annie—now a well-established couple themselves—with you back to one of the smaller islands off Vancouver Island, where you're from. To do this, the three of you needed to get from Meziadin Junction to Prince Rupert, where you'd catch a ferry. I offered to drive you all, since none of the three of you had a car and I did.

My truck had a crew cab, and you sat up front with me and my dog, and Fred and Annie sat behind us. As we drove we listened to music. Annie is a musician—plays guitar, sings like she's the reincarnation of a long-dead blues queen—and so it was her playlist we were listening to. The song "Jimmy" by Moriarty came on. It's from an album called *Gee Whiz but This Is a Lonesome Town*.

Annie started to sing along. You were in the middle of saying something, but you trailed off in the middle of your sentence. Your face went slack and your eyes went narrow and angry.

Fred said something to Annie, too quiet for me to hear. She stopped singing.

You reached up and turned the stereo off. Silence filled the truck. You turned away from us, looking out the window.

After an uncomfortable moment Fred said *it's the song he and Renee used to sing all the time*, chiming in to explain for you. Renee was the girlfriend you'd had last summer, a French girl you met in bush with Fred, who was also from that country. The French love morels; French pickers sometimes come and treat the western Canadian back-country like they're living a chapter from a Jack London novel. From the bits and pieces you'd told me about her, I gathered the two of you had been planning on getting married. She went back to France at the end of the summer, and you were getting all set to go and meet her. When she got back to France, though, she stopped talking to you. She just disappeared. Told Fred not to tell you where she was, what she was doing.

And then she was gone. Out of reach. It broke your heart, you said, because you never quite knew why.

But I think you do know why. I think you know, and if you don't—I mean if you really, honestly don't—I think maybe I could tell you.

Sometimes, now, when I'm feeling afraid or powerless, sometimes, too, when I'm haunted by the memory of what you did, of the violence of it, of the fear that held me for so long after you were gone, I play that song. I play it over and over, like an incantation, like some old magic, this song that has the power to hurt you and therefore make me strong.

I'm playing it right now, Lucky. Can you hear it?

—

Annie didn't have a driver's licence, and Fred only had a French one (besides which, he drove like an asshole). You had lost your own licence some years ago and still hadn't gotten it back, so it was me who drove us the 400 kilometres or so to Prince Rupert, which is a town on the coast that smells like the sea and in which it is impossible, for reasons I cannot quite articulate, to feel like you should ever leave your drink unattended. We needed the extra money, so we'd picked all day first and arrived in town late, with our fingers still stained purple from the fruit. I was exhausted from the extra work of driving, and after eating dinner, we split up into couples to our rooms in a cheap motel above the restaurant.

We had big plans to stay up the whole night, fucking, but I was so tired—tired from weeks in the bush, from the constant strain of trying to make ends meet in the backcountry, from the physical labour and the bugs, from the long drive, from the hurt of my still-broken heart and the ache of the depression I was just barely keeping at bay with liquor and work—that I fell asleep on the bed while you were in the shower. I'd had a shower before you—the first shower either of us had in weeks—and the hot water and the soft bed and the clean sheets made me so sleepy that I just kind of drifted off in the short time you were in the bathroom.

I remember half waking when you came back out. I remember you crawling into bed next to me and kissing the back of my neck. I remember you pulling a blanket up around the pair of us.

You could be tender, Lucky. I'll give you that. You could be a mighty tender man when you felt like it.

III

You went away and I went away, and for a while we were apart.

You went back to the Island, where you lived by the sea. I've never been to that island, though for a while I lived on another one not far away. I keep getting invited, but I choose not to go. I'm afraid I'll run into you.

I went with the others back to the berry camp. It was nearing the middle of August, and the season shifted, and we moved farther south, to Hazelton. I stayed there a while—it was only me and Patricia and her beau now, and mostly I spent my days by myself, because Patricia was in love, and no matter how much a friend cares about you, three's a crowd when you're freshly in love and basically on a honeymoon. Clay, having discovered I was 100 percent not ever going to fuck him, had left us in a huff of disenchanted male entitlement. He died the following spring.

The rains came, and it was cold. Work slowed. The berries grew harder to find; we had to go deeper into the bush for them. It got darker faster. The nights began to threaten frost. I was already sad, but I grew sadder. I was very alone.

I went home for a while, back up the highway to Whitehorse, tried to get a job and a place to live, but that was even worse. I tried to slip back into my old life, the one I'd had with Gabrielle, but there was no life to go back to. I was living in a room in this horribly filthy house with this awful, geriatric cat who screamed all night and pissed in my shoes and shit on the floor, a cat so sick and skinny that it looked like an old ratty puppet—a possessed old ratty puppet.

I was so terribly, terribly alone.

In the spring, when everything had first gone wrong, I had tried to run. Now it was fall, and I found that I had not left the things I was running from out in the backcountry. They were there all along, loping behind me, silent and dogged as a coyote, waiting for me to limp to a stop. And now I had.

I started drinking. I'd been drinking before, but now I was *drinking*, and drinking hard. I became the sort of hot, horrible mess who calls their ex in the middle of the night, sauced, and demands an explanation for things no one can possibly give an explanation for, who shouts and gets in fights at a certain hour in certain bars, who wakes up on the bedroom floor without their shoes and a whisky bottle smashed against the closet door and a bruise on their face they can't remember how they got.

I hated that person then and I hate them now. I knew what I was doing was wrong. I knew drowning myself in drink wasn't going to fix me, wasn't going to take away the agony of watching Gabrielle disappear after the accident, nor the ache of her betrayal, nor the stink of poverty and failure, the crisis of turning thirty and being a bum in a dirty apartment with nothing—no partner, no job, no money—to show for all the days of my worthless life.

When I drank, I hurt just a little bit less and felt like maybe I might not be a total failure and that perhaps it wasn't all over for me, not yet. That's not an excuse for drinking. I was a horrible person, then. There are no excuses for the way I behaved, although there are certainly reasons, which are not the same thing.

I started walking alone along the river, late, late at night, eyeing the dark, cold water. I started looking at the lengths of rope in the hardware store. I started collecting pills. I was unwell. I had probably been unwell for a long time, longer even than I had been with Gabrielle. It's just that losing her that way had jangled something loose in me, and I didn't seem to be able to put it back together.

And then you started calling me and I started calling you. You missed me. You wanted to see me. You hadn't been able to stop thinking about me. Things weren't working out there for you on the Island the way you'd thought they would, and you'd like to get back out into the bush. You said you knew a place out in the backcountry where we could go for pine mushrooms. The price was high—we'd make a lot of money.

And then, when we were done, if I wanted, maybe I could come back to the Island with you.

Back to the Island, where the water was full of fish and the sea came in and out, and you could walk along and dig for crabs and clams.

Back to the Island, where it was never cold, where you had a place we could stay until the spring.

Back to the Island, where we could plant a garden and plan for the next bush season together.

You dangled the idea before me—bait—and I knew it was bait and took it anyway. I closed my eyes and opened my mouth and swallowed, because I was miserable and sad and alone and so so scared, because I simply didn't know what else to do. I just wanted something to hold on to for a while.

I was using you. I won't deny that. We were using each other.

It was an ugly thing for us to do, but it was an especially ugly thing on my part because I can see now—I can see quite clearly now, looking back—that in your own way, you loved me.

I knew that, and I wanted to love you, even though I knew I couldn't. It must have been really hard for you, and really confusing, to love me as if I were a woman, when really, I was just a little changeling, a shape-shifter queer in your bed who had, just to keep you, taken on the shape of something they were not and could not be—a woman who would want to be with you.

No matter what you did later—and what you did was awful, certainly, but still, no matter what you did then—I'm sorry for that. That I used you and hurt you like that. That's on me. That's my fault, Lucky. I shouldn't have done that, and I'm sorry.

———

So, you flew into Whitehorse and we got in my truck, and I struck camp on the shady not-life I had tried out there, and then there we were: back on the highway again, together.

We drove south through the rapidly cooling country, through the gold burned poplars and the fireweed that lined the roadsides, turned down the Cassiar and fell under the shadow of the coastal mountains. You were in high spirits, chattering away about how beautiful the country was, about how much money we were going to make, about buyers we'd sell to and some scheme about drying our own mushrooms on the side and selling them to restaurants later, in the winter months when they were more in demand. Premium prices, you said. Seller's market. Looking back on it, I can see how it was all bravado and bullshit, and I can see, too, how much you reminded me of my father, which should have been not only a red flag but a goddamn red-flag marching band, but at the time I was either too drunk or too sad to pay much attention to it.

We got as far as Dease Lake before you told me didn't have any money. You asked me could I please buy you some smokes.

I should have known right then that the whole fucking enterprise was doomed. I should have turned that truck right around and driven us back to Whitehorse, or headed south without you, left you standing there on the side of the road in that pretty, cold country 1,000 kilometres from home.

Instead, I went inside and bought you a pack of Players. You usually smoked Canadians, because they were cheaper, but something in them always made me sneeze.

IV

There is something cursed in that beautiful, strange, unfathomable country along the Cassiar Highway, country caught somewhere between the boreal and the coastal, the subarctic and the rainforest— something sacred or profane or both. In those wet, cold forests, you can come through a thicket of devil's club and find a bear lumbering by, silent and mournful and disinterested as a drunk old man, or turn back on your own tracks and see them overlaid with the footsteps of a cougar only a few metres back. Salmon come up to the rivers from the sea and, at the right time of year and the right place, look like herds of silver horses viewed from a great distance. In the late summer there are places where the berries come in so thick you can just lie down on the ground and shake them into your mouth like delicious rain.

Whatever old magic is out there—and I'm a superstitious queer, as you know, prone to listening to my gut, to turning back at the prickle of danger on the back of my neck, to saving my skin at the last minute like a wiry old cat—let me tell you, too, that there is something *awful* in those woods. Some spirit restless and malevolent, which, if you are in a bad way, if you are weak or stupid or foolish, as we were, will creep into your camp at night and fuck up your life. If it does, most likely, I think, you deserve it. We deserved it, certainly, and I felt in that place that there were bad ghosts everywhere. Sometimes, when I travel that stretch of road, I still feel it, and when I do I burn the fire extra hot and sing as I come into my camp in case there might be a bear, and I am extra respectful and extra clean. I cut no green wood and I dig my cat holes extra deep, and am extra kind and polite to strangers, because I feel, always, that I'm being *watched*.

Was it me, Lucky? Was it my shaky hands and my cracked heart and my frayed nerves that brought the disaster on us, that invited the bad spirit into our bed? Or was it you, who once professed to have killed a man, you with your black secrets that were not really secrets and your masculine terror of—not necessarily failure, but the *discovery* of failure? Either way, it was you that the bad ghost crept into, little by little and then all at once.

It was small things at first. You were irritable and exhausted. You slept and slept. We were both so tired all the time—working out in the slopes, bushwhacking into that damp cedar country, and working the miles and miles of backcountry with our heads down. Hunting pine mushrooms was physically demanding, cold, wet work—but you seemed exhausted spiritually as much as physically. Maybe I did, too, I don't know; I was too busy worrying about how we were going to put gas in the truck to think much about myself. You started sleeping later and later, stopped wanting to have sex. You complained of food cravings—you wanted yogourt, red meat, jujubes, none of which, of course, we had way the fuck out there, 150 kilometres from a grocery store any which way you looked.

And then one night I came back and you were just … lost. Lost to me, lost to yourself, just *lost*. That's the only word I have for it. I went down to the buyer camp, "the Zoo," as the pickers called it, to sell our mushrooms from that day. I was gone for about an hour and a half. Shot the shit with the buyers, drank a beer—an Old Milwaukee, the can dripping red and white and cold from sitting on ice—as was customary, and by the time I got back it was dark, and something in you had just wandered off and gone.

You'd drunk every fucking thing in the camper that night—all the beer, half a box of red wine, a mickey of Fireball you'd kept for Irish coffees. When that was gone, you went into the cupboard and took out the bottle of wild blueberry–infused vodka I'd made in the berry season and was keeping as a gift for a friend and drank that.

You were so restless and mournful I couldn't even be mad at you. I certainly didn't dare try and stop you.

You only ever talked about yourself when you drank; most days, you were so quiet, so reserved about your feelings, but when you got drunk it was like someone had opened the tap and everything gushed out. Tonight, someone had not only turned the tap, but broken the spigot; you sat there next to the fire, drunk as fucking balls, sitting in a camp chair in that ragged red-plaid bush coat of yours, its holes patched with duct tape, and just talked and talked and *talked*.

You talked about your daughter and how you weren't allowed to see her anymore. You talked about how much you loved her and how you were so afraid to fail her.

You talked about all the women who had hurt you, all the women you'd thought would be forever-women but weren't, and how you didn't understand women and couldn't understand how you kept failing and failing at keeping them.

You talked about how you desperately wanted a son, and how sometimes you thought maybe I might be the one to give you one—me, or someone strong like me. That was the phrase you used. *Me, or a strong woman like me.* You talked about how you might never have a son, and how if, in a couple years, you turned thirty-five and still hadn't had one, you'd get a vasectomy.

You talked about your mother, and how much you loved her and missed her and worried about her back on the reserve. You talked about how your father loved your mother terribly, how she was Indigenous and he was white, and how to prove he would do anything to be with her, he'd slept on the front porch of her house, slept rough out in the cold and the Island's winter rain, until he'd won her father's respect and was allowed to come in. You talked about how worried you were that you'd never have a love like that—a love that could be tallied and proven.

You drank and drank and you talked and talked. I sat quietly and nursed a beer you'd forgotten in the back of the camper and nodded and tried to listen. I could see, or thought I could see, that this was what you needed—somebody to listen.

You got partway through the blueberry vodka and then you started talking about your people back on the Island. You talked about how most of them were dead, how years and years ago so many of them were killed by the smallpox the white people gave them, or were taken away to residential schools and never returned, or were driven to suicide by poverty and despair. You talked about how your bloodline would probably die out in your lifetime. You talked about how you missed the Island, and how you were sad and angry that you couldn't speak your own language. You talked about how unfair it all felt, how angry it made you.

I didn't know what to say, of course. How the fuck would I know what to say? What could I have possibly said that would have been the right thing? And would it even have mattered if, by some untapped magic, I'd pulled the right words out of thin air? Would you have heard them through the·liquor? You were so drunk, and you were so sad. I'd seen you drink before, but never this much. You'd started crying, but it was a quiet crying that made tears run down your rough face, made your black eyes gleam.

I reached over and squeezed your thigh. I said *I'm so sorry, Lucky*. I said *maybe you should come to bed*.

And then your eyes got hard, and your mouth drew tight, and then you got angry. Just like that: quick danger, like the sudden *chunk* of a bolt-action rifle being cocked. Maybe it was the wrong thing to say, and if it was, I'm genuinely sorry for that, because I could see you were hurting. I could see you were hurting *so* bad, but maybe it was just that you looked at me and saw me—my pale skin, my blond hair, my blue eyes, a Settler through and through, a Northern European mutt. Maybe that was what made you mad, and honestly, if that's what it was, I don't blame you. I'll take that. I'll take that as my due.

Either way, you started in on me—told me I was an idiot, I was a bitch, a cunt, a whore. I tried to pull away from you, but you snatched my wrist and yanked me toward you to keep me in place. You said *you're just a stupid little white girl—you're just a stupid fucking white girl and you don't know fucking anything.*

And suddenly, I was very afraid of you. You were squeezing so tight—you had those big, broad hands, and your one hand could have wrapped twice around my wrist—and it hurt. I realized, suddenly, what a risk I had taken in coming out here alone with you, out to the backcountry without cellphone service to an off-grid site no one but you knew the location of. You were twisting my wrist and pulling harder now, and the tips of my fingers were tingling, and as calmly as I could, I said *Lucky, you're hurting me* and as quickly as you'd gone away, you came back to yourself—*snap snap*—and let go.

You sat there, quiet, a stunned, blank look on your face, and then you stood up and staggered off into the bushes. I could hear you throwing up, so I got up and went into the camper and poured you a big mug of water from the jug. When you came back, I gave it to you and you drank it, and then we got into the camper and got undressed and went to bed. We lay in bed for a while, and you kept talking about the same things you were talking about before, moving on this cycle of tenderness and rage, alternating between telling me these deep, difficult things about yourself and being angry with me for hearing them. After a while you touched my leg and asked me if I would suck your dick, and I did, not because I felt like it, but because I thought it would mollify you, and it did. I sucked you off and you came in my mouth and then you drifted off to sleep and I was left alone with my thoughts and my aching wrist.

At the time, I was really bitter about what you said, although I never said so. I resented being called *stupid white girl* and I resented your anger. I felt I was being held in some way accountable for something I didn't feel I had anything to do with directly. Which means, of course, that you were right—I was a stupid little white girl, and I didn't know anything about anything you were talking about, and I'm sorry.

—

I know what you're thinking: you're thinking this is taking an awfully long time. You're thinking *fucking get on with it, Lor, pull the trigger if you're gunna.* You always were very impatient. It's not about pulling the trigger, Lucky. It's not about hurting you. I would have thought that would be clear by now.

What this is about is the way two people can be hurt by the same system while fighting against the same system, about the ways those hurts can turn each person against the other, about how someone can be an enemy and a lover and a stranger and a friend all at the same time.

It's about the story. The story—the whole story, from beginning to end—is very important. As a culture, we deal so much in half-stories these days. I want to tell the whole one.

I'm a storyteller, and every good story—every true story, anyway—is equal parts an act of forgiveness and an act of revenge.

So don't get your panties in a twist. It's coming. You know what you're about to do. We both know, and as that's the case, I have to ask, do you think I deserved it?

I'm asking honestly. I don't have an answer; I genuinely don't know how you feel about it. Do you feel good, Lucky, about what you're about to do in this story?

You might not know this, but a couple years later—I mean a couple years after you and I stop talking—Patricia will see you. She'll be working as a waitress at a restaurant on Vancouver Island, and she'll come over to serve a table and you'll be one of the men at that table. You'll look at each other, and although neither of you will say anything to each other, you will be unable to meet her eyes and be visibly uncomfortable, embarrassed. Patricia will give the table to someone else so she doesn't have to serve you, and you will say almost nothing the whole time you are there, then you will pay for your food and leave very quickly.

Which makes me think that no, you don't feel good about it.

What's funny is that I'm genuinely sorry about that, too.

—

Jesus fucking Christ, so many bad things happened so quickly after that, didn't they? It was like once the bad luck started, it couldn't be stopped. It was like tsunami of misfortune, and no matter how fast we ran, we couldn't get to higher ground in time.

First, it started to get cold at night, so cold the little propane heater in the camper couldn't keep up. No matter how many blankets we added or how close together we slept, you, me and the dog, we woke with chattering teeth, so we strung up tarps off the camper to act as a heat bounce and slept with the door open and a huge fire going. It kept us warm, but sometimes the wind would blow the wrong way, and smoke would fill the camper, and we'd wake coughing. Honest to god, it was a damn miracle we didn't suffocate in our sleep. Later, it started to rain, harder and more often, and it became difficult to find dry wood to burn. There wasn't any place to buy any, and even if there had been, we didn't have any money to buy it. We took to stealing it from burn piles and bush plane runways and places where they had cut the brush at the side of the road, but it was often wet and green, and the problem with the smoke got worse and worse.

Then there was the truck—the battery was starting to go, and the transmission was on its last legs. If you didn't accelerate fast enough out of first it would stick into second, and then we'd have to pull over and crawl beneath the undercarriage, unhook the automatic transmission from the electrical system, count to ten, rehook it, then jump in and fucking *floor it* right into third. Then we discovered the tail lights had stopped working only when that pig cop pulled us over outside of Hazelton. He was a racist fuck, questioning and questioning you, and you felt so small and embarrassed and angry, and I felt awful because it was my fault, I'd been tired and driving too fast, that's why we got pulled over. He wouldn't let us go on until we fixed the tail lights, but there was nowhere to buy anything to fix them with. When he finally went away, I wanted to try to creep home in the truck, but you said we couldn't because he would be waiting for us just up the road, and I knew you were right. It was dark and getting so cold; we'd dropped the camper at the site to save gas going back and forth, and so it was just us and the dog in the cramped cab without blankets, just our damp bush coats, with no place to sleep and no place to go. I called

BCAA and they towed us back to Hazelton, and we spent money we didn't have on a room for the night at the Robber's Roost Motel and drove back in the morning. We never did get the lights fixed because we couldn't for love nor money figure out what was wrong with them.

And then, one night in mid-October, it snowed, and the ground froze.

All the mushrooms died and nothing new would come up. The season was over, and we were *fucked*.

Without the mushrooms, we didn't have a way to make any money. We had—what? A grand between us, which was about eight tanks of gas, if we bought no food. Eight tanks of gas for a truck whose lights didn't work and whose battery was dying, and bags of dried mushrooms and no propane left and nowhere to goddamn go.

If we were going to get back to the Island, even, we'd need gas money, food money, fare for the ferry—very expensive, with the truck and camper. We talked about that, remember? We were going to sneak you in the back of the truck, lying low under some blankets, but we were scared of what might happen if you were caught, and we scrapped the idea. Even if we did get there, then what? We had no work, no money coming in.

I can still see your face that morning, Lucky, when we woke up and peeked out from under the tarp and saw that the fire had gone out and the snow lay thick and wet like the down from a pillow someone had cut open: wide-eyed, broken-hearted. A child's despair.

I mean, yeah—we were well and truly screwed.

You wanted to keep going, though; you had us pack up and head off, slipping and sliding on my bald-ass tires in the wet snow, off the down the highway again. The season was still going farther south. We could make a go of it in Lillooet or Pemberton. There were matsutake there, too, you said, high in the hills of that pine and sage country. We'd start over again, you said.

Honestly, I should have told you that was nuts, because I knew when you said it that it was a stupid idea. We didn't know that country, had never worked it, knew no one, had no connections; the odds we would make it out with enough to eat, let alone a profit, were piss poor. My only other choice, though, was to turn the truck around and limp back into Whitehorse, where there was nothing waiting for me—not a place to sleep or a job or anything—and moreover, where would that leave you? Stuck with me in a Yukon winter without even a smoke to your name, or else standing on the side of the road trying to hitch your way home.

So, we pooled our pennies, put what we didn't have on my credit card, and went off again. Down the highway, outrunning the snow. We went by way of the Lillooet pass, the truck's faulty transmission grinding and clunking and stuttering, its worn brakes overheating so badly on the way down you could smell the pads burning.

And then we were there and we found a buyer, and the buyer said *sorry, season's over early. No mushrooms.* A wrinkled old man on a porch somewhere outside of Pemberton, drinking a can of beer. You didn't believe him at first. You said we should look and I said *where* and gestured at the miles and miles of country we didn't know, the hills neither of us had ever been to, and you realized we were beaten and sat in the passenger side of the truck and looked out the window, silent and brooding.

Neither of us knew what to do.

On the map I saw there was a campground nearby called Owl Creek—a rec site, so it was free. I took us there and we set up camp, and you set to drinking in the back of the camper, and I went down to the creek and went fishing to clear my head. I caught nothing. There was an old apple tree there that had gone wild, so I climbed up into the gnarled branches and filled my pockets. Little yellow apples, tart and sour. We ate them for breakfast and between meals, something to put in our mouths and suck and chew, even if they were so acidic, they hurt our stomachs.

We stayed one day, then two. You came up with new schemes and then shot them down yourself, finding all the reasons we might do this or that and then all the reasons we shouldn't do this or that all on your own. I listened quietly but found it exhausting. You weren't being realistic—all your plans involved getting out of here, but we only had enough money for one, maybe two tanks of gas, about 800 kilometres of travel with the busted transmission and the camper on. No matter what we did, we'd need more money to keep going, so on the morning of the third day, I called a friend who lived in Whistler, explained our situation, and asked if she could help. She had a boyfriend at the time who worked in construction, and they desperately needed labourers—come to Whistler, she said. She'd hook us up.

I agreed eagerly—in part because we needed the money and in part because I had been with you and only you for going on two months now, and I needed some friends and some space and a good cup of coffee once in a while. I'd taken the call down by the creek, and when I got off the phone, I walked back up the bank and popped into the back of the camper, where you were sitting, smoking a cigarette.

I told you I'd found us a job and that I thought we should go to Whistler to work it.

You blinked around the curling blue smoke and said you wouldn't do it. You wouldn't work as a labourer. All they'd see, you said, was a *dirty Native*—those were your words—and you wouldn't lower yourself to it. You'd worked construction crews before, and you wouldn't subject yourself to that again.

I was quiet. I didn't know what to do. I just knew that we were in serious fucking trouble, that we needed money and we needed it *now*, or we were going to run out of gas and then out of food and then—

Then what? What would happen? The not knowing was the most terrifying part of all.

You thought for a minute, and then you said we should split up. You'd go back out into the hills by yourself and pick pines and make money up there, and I should go work in Whistler with my friend. You'd send me money when you made it, but you'd need me to lend you some money until then, so you could get set up.

I think the mistake I made, Lucky, was that I laughed. I threw my head back and laughed, a barking, angry, dry little laugh, because I knew perfectly well what you were doing. This was hard, and you didn't want to be responsible for it anymore. You were going to take the money, and I might see it again, and I might not; you already owed me a couple grand for fuel and hotels and food and smokes and liquor. Now you wanted most of what we had made together—which was really *my* money, since you owed me on top of it already—so you could fuck off back into the bush and leave me to deal with the mess alone.

You had no cellphone. You had no truck, no driver's licence. You didn't even have a bank card. You could just disappear.

I saw right though you, you goddamn bastard. That's what made you really angry. I saw you were scared, and I saw you didn't know what to do, and I saw you were a coward, and *you couldn't mother-fucking stand it.*

And so I said *no, that's not what we are doing.*

And you were fucking *furious.* You absolutely goddamn lost your shit.

In saying no to you, in questioning you, I had dispelled the version of yourself that you wanted me to believe you were—that *you* wanted to believe you were. By questioning you, I threw your whole hustler/bush guy/provider mystique under the bus, and that meant that not only had *I* questioned your ability to get out of this, *you* had to question your ability to get out of this.

And that scared the fucking shit out of you, which you never did forgive me for.

We got into a terrible fight—we'd never quarrelled until then, and it came as a wicked surprise. You were really used to people, women especially, just taking you at your word, just letting you lead, and for a long time I'd been happy to do that, too. Now, though, we were in a serious fix, and you just wanted to go galivanting off as if we didn't have some responsibility to each other at this point, and I was not going to back down on this. I was not going to give you the money, nor was I going to drive you around to all the places you wanted me to take you so that you could scout, nor was I going to let you just bail out on me, owing me and leaving me on my own in a town I'd never been to before. You demanded just the opposite, refused the construction job, refused any kind of job with a wage. You were going back up into the hills, you said, you were not going into the city, and you'd come back when you had the money.

Like fuck you would. Did you think I hadn't been out in the bush as long as you? I was just as tricky, just as sharp, just as lean and hungry and fierce as you, and I don't think you realized it until then.

I despise fighting. Nothing two people who care about each other can do is so wildly wasteful as fighting.

You slammed your hands, you stomped your feet, you refused to budge. It went on and on. Finally, in a fit of exasperation, I threw my hands up and said *fine, fuck, whatever, Lucky. I give up. I give up on you, just do whatever you want, I give the fuck up*. I meant it, too. If you wanted to go, fine. If you couldn't see you were abandoning me—or, more likely, if you didn't care—then fine. Lesson learned about you.

You went very quiet. Your face got dark and sad. You said fine. You guessed that was it, then.

I said what was it, then, and you said that when a woman says she gives up on you, that's all there is, it's over, there's nothing you can do. And I said there's nothing you can do about *what*, but you turned and stalked out of the camper down to the creek. I never did find out.

Alone, I fed the dog, who, frightened by the commotion, was hiding under the table. I sat in the camper (my camper, on my truck—none of this was yours, you yourself had nothing, which I see now was part of the problem) and drank a beer. I smoked one of your cigarettes, even though it hurt my throat and made me sneeze. Cheap, dirty smokes that tasted like shoes and tar and made my head light and fuzzy.

When you came back, your eyes were black, and you were resigned. You would not go into the hills, you said. It wasn't fair to leave me, you said, as if this was your own conclusion and not what I'd been shouting at you for an hour. We'd go into town and even though you hated the thought of it, you'd take the construction job until we could save enough money to go on.

And then you kissed me, and we got quiet, and we stayed one more night and pretended everything was okay and that things weren't tight and tense and horrible. In the morning we got up, and I took Herman for one last swim in the creek while you broke camp, and then off we went into Whistler.

You tried to be cheerful, but you were a lousy actor. You were sad and angry, and although I understood, I also *didn't* understand, which made me feel stupid and shitty. I feel bad now, and I felt bad then. I know how much you didn't want to work there, I know why. I just honest to god couldn't see another way out, and also, honest to god, I don't think there was one.

I didn't understand, then, that this was an unforgivable indignity to you. I'm really sorry for that. I wish there'd been another way.

It wasn't your fault, you know. I can see now how you thought it was your fault, the tremendous failure of that season, but I hope you know I never blamed you. I've been in the bush long enough to know—and, in fact, it's what I love most about it—that nothing out there is ever personal. Good things happen or bad things happen, mostly just because good and bad things happen, and not because you did or did not deserve them.

I never blamed you, Lucky. Really.

I think you blamed me, though. It's okay if you did.

I really should have just let you go. I should have just swallowed the money, should have just straightened up and gone off on my own, but I was afraid. I was afraid of starting all over again without anyone at all, even someone I was coming to realize I couldn't trust.

I would have let you go, though, if I'd known how you'd punish me for making you stay. I'd have packed you a lunch and waved you off as you lurched down the road, blessedly out of my life.

V

Looking back on it now, five years later, I can see what happened next rolling down toward us from a long ways off, see it coming like a prairie storm, black and huge, slow-moving but inevitable.

We took the construction job. You were so bitter about it, and I'm really sorry, Lucky, I *know* and it sucked but what else was there to do short of getting jobs at a gas station or McDonald's or something, if we even could have with our unwashed hair and tattered clothes? You were more skilled than me, bigger and stronger than me, and the men at the site liked you, even though you didn't like them. We were building this huge, stupid house on the top of a hill surrounded by other huge, stupid houses on the tops of hills. The house was not really a house so much as a mansion—it had a fucking waterfall in it, remember that? A waterfall so that the owner would have something to look at while they went up and down the floors in a goddamn elevator.

There were no places to live in Whistler, and even if there had been we wouldn't have been able to afford the astronomical rents. Instead, we lived at rec sites on the weekends, throwing a tarp over the firepit so we could get it going in the never-ending rain. During the work-week, we lived in the Whistler visitor's centre parking lot, Lot 4. You weren't supposed to live there, but lots of people did—there were ski bums there, waiting for the season to start, but also other homeless people and travellers, even some families, small kids playing at night under the street lamps their parents had parked under. The parking officer turned a blind eye, so long as you were out before eight a.m. so the tourists wouldn't see you. If you weren't, you got a warning, and then a ticket. Later, the construction foreman let us stay overnight in the camper on the construction site, which was nice because it meant there was a plug-in and we could have electric lights instead of the kerosene lamp, and we didn't have to commute in the mornings, but once we were there we had to stay there, because they locked the gate.

Fuck, I hated Whistler. That shitbox, that glittering, overpriced bauble. At night, walking through the empty Olympic Village, the shops all shuttered and dark, the faux cobblestones slick with rain, the place was creepy. It had the air of an abandoned movie set, of a dollhouse from which all the dolls have been removed. Rich people in big, shiny cars, in huge houses they barely ever lived in, fucks from Vancouver walking around in suits and sneering at the waitstaff, who lived four or five to an apartment and made minimum wage. Stores locals couldn't afford to shop in and restaurants locals couldn't afford to eat in, and everywhere you went, tacky, pretentious, ridiculous tourist shit.

May the mountain slide down upon it and bury that godforsaken temple of the rich, may each summer-empty mansion catch fire and burn to its foundation, may each haughty shop be overrun by rats with glittering, jealous eyes.

I mean, maybe I'm just biased because that's where we finally got beaten, where the cold and the hunger and the hopelessness of the situation finally broke us. There's just something about eating tuna and ramen noodles, something about shivering at night because it has rained for twenty-eight days straight and the propane won't dry the camper out and there are mushrooms—literal mushrooms, white things blooming horrid, Lovecraftian spores—growing out of the walls, something about your clothes always being wet and your boots rubbing your feet raw, something about sneaking around to shit in a goddamn ditch at night because all the bathrooms are closed, something about living like animals while you *build a motherfucking mansion* for some rich cunt that just makes you a little hostile, you know?

It certainly made you hostile. You were never easy, you were always angry, and since there was no one else to take it out on, you took it out on me. You drank all the liquor, you smoked all the weed, you ate all the food. You got a little potbelly and lay around on the camper bed when we weren't at work, watching downloaded episodes of *Brooklyn Nine-Nine* and *Family Guy* on my old laptop. You watched me cook and clean, you watched me walk the dog, you watched me fret and worry and look for other jobs.

Our relationship had been on the rocks since Owl Creek, but now, in the suffocating death grip of poverty, it rapidly devolved into something rotten, something that festered and *oozed*.

In the cramped eight-by-ten camper, the air simmered with unresolved tension. Whenever I tried to talk to you about it, to divine what was wrong, you'd shrug and roll away from me; if I pressed you, you exploded. At first, this was only when we were drinking, but later it was all the time. You'd tell me I was a worthless bitch, a scheming whore, that I was trying to manipulate you.

We fought and fought and fought—about food, about money, about work, about each other. There was no place for us to get away from each other in the camper, so I started going for long walks, spending time with my friend who had got us the construction job, trying to make friends, but whenever I went out I came back to find you angry and brooding, certain I was talking about you behind your back, that I was telling everyone what a piece of shit you were.

That was never true, Lucky. In fact, when people raised questions about the way we were living, or about the increasingly hostile, even verbally abusive way you spoke to me in public, I defended you, made excuses for you. I assured everyone everything was fine. I said things like *he's a complicated man, but he cares about me* or *it's difficult to understand, but he's doing the best he can.*

"Complicated" is the right word for our relationship at this time, anyway. We had stopped having sex, stopped kissing or holding hands, and you had all but stopped speaking to me, apparently still angry about my having "given up" on you at Owl Creek. Yet, you refused to leave my bed, although there was a fold-out you could have slept on, even when I asked you to, and you continued to sleep wrapped around me at night even when I didn't really want you to. You didn't want to be with me anymore, you said, but when I started talking about a girl I thought was cute or checking women out, you got cold and angry.

All talk of my going back to the Island with you had long since ceased. It was now mutually understood that, once we had enough money, you would pay me what you owed me and we would go our separate ways. We were working and working and working, eight- or ten-hour days for eighteen dollars an hour in the never-ending drizzle, but we never seemed to get up the funds to actually be able to part from each other. Some of this is because, as anyone who has ever been homeless knows, being poor is *expensive*. It costs to not be able to pay the interest on your credit card, and it costs to buy only a few dollars' worth of groceries at a time instead of getting the bigger, more economical sizes, and it costs to buy takeout because you don't have electricity to cook with or hot water to wash with and because you're so fucking tired from working in the cold and the rain that the thought of something as simple as boiling water for noodles is overwhelming.

Moreover, you spent money as fast as we made it. I wanted to save, but you always wanted to spend. You wanted to go to hotels in Vancouver on the weekend so we could have showers and dry out, you wanted to order pizza, you wanted to go out for drinks with the boys and buy weed from the good dealer and ...

And and and, so many ands, until by the end of each week we barely had ten dollars to our name, and you were rationing smokes and glaring at me as if it were somehow my fault. You had started just taking my debit card, though, since you didn't have a bank account of your own, and at night while you were asleep I'd open the banking app on my phone and go through the daily list of expenses you'd racked up with my lip between my front teeth.

I didn't dare tell you no, by this point. I couldn't take one more fight, one more hurled insult. I was having panic attacks; I cried at the smallest things. The stress of poverty, coupled with the stress of constantly being on my toes around you, had weakened me, not only mentally, but physically; I had a constant cough, woke up with my chest rattling in the damp nights, was weak and exhausted and ran a low-grade fever all the time. I went to the doctor one day, and he told me I had pneumonia, gave me a round of antibiotics, but when I got back to the camper I told you he'd said it was just a cold and took the medicine in secret. I was afraid of what you'd do if you found out I was that sick—afraid of what, exactly, I don't know. I was just afraid all the time, in those days.

Mentally, I was even worse off—I was anxious and depressed, even low-key suicidal a lot of the time, and given the circumstances, why the fuck *wouldn't* I be? You could sense this and used it to belittle and disarm me. You said things like *it's no wonder Gabrielle left you, you're so fucked up* or *if you're going to kill yourself, I wish you'd do me a favour and just do it.* If I tried to talk to you about the way you talked to me and treated me, you'd get angry and shout and bang your fists on the walls and tell me I was being fucking crazy. Other times, you'd look at me blankly and tell me none of that had happened, or if it had, it hadn't happened the way I remembered it—I was being dramatic, and moreover, I was sick and not thinking clearly. Around this time, you got more and more angry whenever I went out without you, especially if I went to go see my friend. You made me promise never to talk to her about you.

Do you know what gaslighting is, Lucky? Because you're *really* good at it.

What confused me the most—what still confuses me now—is the way you absolutely refused to let me break up with you. You didn't want to sleep with me and you didn't want to be with me, but you didn't want me to date other people and you didn't want to sleep away from me. It's hard to figure now exactly what it was you did want. There was also the night a girl asked me out for coffee and I accepted, and when I came home you were drunk and furious, screaming and shouting at me that I was a whore. You chased me out into the parking lot where the dog and I leapt into the cab of the truck and I locked the door from the inside—I had the keys—and you smashed your fists against the glass so hard the truck rocked back and forth, covered the windows in flecks of spittle as you screamed at me to come out. I honestly can't believe no one in Lot 4 came out of their vehicle that night to see if you were murdering me, but I also can very much believe it, because in order to help someone, you have to have enough to help yourself, and *enough* was in short supply for everyone.

When you realized I wasn't about to let you in, you went back into the camper and slept in my bed. I slept on the bench seat spooning the dog, huddled beneath my coat. In the morning you made me apologize to you for the scene I'd caused and swear I wouldn't see anyone else until you left for the Island.

These were all warning signs, of course, for what you would eventually do.

What did you *want*, though? What was the end game? I never knew. I still don't know.

VI

Well. We're here now. We've come to it. You know what comes next, although you say you don't remember quite all of it. That's what you said, right? That you couldn't remember and that I was making this all up? You've refused to hear it, before. You've hung up on me and blocked my number when I tried to talk to you about it. You've said *this is just what women do* and you hung up.

That made a lot more sense later, when the police told me you had another complaint on file, a complaint just like mine. But I'm getting ahead of myself.

You wouldn't hear me then, but you're going to hear me now, Lucky.

It was November 2016. Leonard Cohen had just died, and Donald Trump had just been elected president of the United States. You and I were out drinking at the Cinnamon Bear with a few of the guys from the construction site; I seem to remember they had some kind of a deal for shots of Fireball, but maybe you were just drinking Fireball.

It was a work night. I went home early. I was tired. We were drunk. You wanted to stay. You were going to shoot some pool. You asked for my credit card. I gave it to you, and I went home, alone, back to the camper. It was raining. It was always motherfucking raining. The cobbled streets were slick and black.

I let the dog out and then I crawled into bed, into the upper bunk that hung over the truck cab. I went to sleep.

When I woke, it was several hours later. I remember looking at my phone and seeing it was nearly three in the morning. You were at the door, banging it back and forth, trying to get in. You had a key, but the door had long ago ceased to hang true in the frame, and it needed to be pushed in and wiggled around a little to get it open, which you were having a very hard time doing.

I called your name—your real name, not "Lucky"—just as you got the door open and came in. You didn't answer me, only closed the door behind you, and then you stood there, your face hanging slack as a wet shirt, your eyes black and glittering with liquor. You were lit, wrecked, bombed; you were so shithoused you swayed back and forth where you stood. With your oversized, tattered bush coat on and your hair long and wild, you looked like a scarecrow bobbing back and forth in the wind. It was dark in the camper, but the lights were on in the lot—they never went off—and your face was backlit in the too-white light. You were looking at me, but you seemed to be thinking hard about something. Your mouth hardened into a tight, thin line as you started forward, kicking off your wet boots.

And then you were in the bed with me, and your hands were moving all over me. They were not soft, they were clumsy and rough and hard. I was stiff in the bed next to you. I didn't know what to do. You hadn't touched me in a long time—you'd had your dick sucked, sure, but you hadn't fucked since the fight at Owl Creek, and I didn't know what this meant or what to do. I turned to try to look at your face, and the look on it—distant, cold, and angry—scared me, so I stayed quiet.

You moved on top of me. You were saying something, but you were so drunk it was hard to understand you—something about how I'd been a bitch, something about how I was a mess. You rolled on top of me, put your hand on my chest, pushing me down. Your eyes were glazed and empty and it gave me the creeps—it was like looking into the face of a badly made doll. You took my hand by the wrist and guided it down to your dick, which you had freed from your boxers. It was semi-hard, clammy, and slick as the flesh of an oyster. I wondered if it was sweat, or if you had gotten so drunk you'd pissed yourself.

You slurred *is this okay?*

It was not fucking okay, but you were so big, so big and hot and heavy on top of me, and your hands were so strong. I was scared. I was scared of what would happen, of what you would do, if I said no.

So I said yes, it was fine, even though it wasn't. I kept stroking you. I was afraid to stop.

You pulled my panties off, positioned yourself between my legs, and, before I could stop you, lined your cock up and shoved it into my asshole.

It *hurt*, Lucky. You weren't lubed and you weren't wearing a condom, and it fucking *hurt*. I squealed and tried to push you off me, but you leaned forward, aiming to smash more of yourself into me. You were only partway in and I dug my nails into you, I pushed back hard. I thought maybe you were so drunk that you'd made a mistake, that it had just kind of slipped in there on its own—we'd never had anal sex before, had never even talked about it—but you pushed forward harder and harder, trying to drive yourself into me in deliberate, annoyed little jerks, like you were trying to get into a pair of pants that had shrunk in the wash. You muttered something about how it had to be my ass, that it was the only way to keep me from getting pregnant. I couldn't get pregnant, you said. I didn't want to have your baby.

That's exactly what you said. I didn't want to have *your* baby, like this was somehow a personal affront.

That was true. I absolutely did not want to have your baby.

You pushed down harder on my chest. It was starting to get hard to breathe. I was starting to panic. I managed to say, in a low voice, that there were condoms in the drawer. I don't remember how I did it, but I convinced you to get out of my ass—god, how it *hurt*, you weren't gentle going in and you weren't gentle going out—and put on a condom. I put the condom on for you, and while you watched me do it you started to cry. You didn't seem to realize you were crying, but you were, slow, cool tears running down your haggard cheeks.

When I asked you what was wrong, you said, in a small voice—a voice I can still hear now, a voice alarmingly like frightened child's, full of uncertainty and pain—that I couldn't wait for you to be gone. That I couldn't wait to get rid of you.

I didn't say anything to that. There wasn't time. You pushed me back down against the bed. You seemed even heavier than before, somehow, and I struggled to breathe as you slid all the way forward. You stopped crying now and looked down into my face with wet, unsteady eyes.

Your voice a man's voice again, low and sad, almost tender. You said, in that voice, *she doesn't love you, you know*. You had one hand on my collarbone, your fingers spread across my throat. I was very aware of the pressure there, of how bad this could turn and how quickly.

I thought of your admission that you'd killed a man and wondered again if it was true.

By "she" you meant Gabrielle, of course.

I hadn't realized you were jealous of her before that moment. I had drastically underestimated your emotional investment in me. I hadn't thought it mattered to you that I still loved her. I'd thought you understood that, whatever we were doing, at the end of the day, I was fucking *gay*.

That's my fault, Lucky. I didn't realize how careless I'd been with you, and for that, yes, for *that* I'm genuinely at fault. I'm genuinely sorry.

You said *if she really loved you, you wouldn't be here*. And then you sank into me. I was dry, and it hurt. It hurt, and what you said hurt, because it was true. It was true in all the ways it could be true.

If she really loved you, you wouldn't be here.

All the fight went out of me. It was like someone had unplugged me. I went far, far away. I lay there and let you pump and grunt and rut like a dog, stupid and hairy and panting and male. It didn't take you long. You came, and you pulled out of me. I took the condom off. I tied it off. You rolled over and passed out. I threw the condom into the plastic bag tied to the handle of a dresser that we used for a trash can. You were snoring by the time I rolled back over—big, drunk, half-choked snores. It would almost have been funny, under different circumstances. Fred Flintstone's snores.

I lay there on my back for a while, staring up at the ceiling, at the stains the mould left as it grew and spored out and died on the wallpaper. My cunt hurt. My asshole hurt. The places on my chest and arms where you had grabbed me and pushed me down hurt.

What would you have done to me if I'd said no? Do you even know?

I couldn't have said no to you any more than I can say no to paying the rent. I couldn't have said no to you any more than I can say no to buying groceries. I couldn't have said no to you any more than I can say no to pulling over for a cop. It's all the same thing: extortion, coercion, dressed up as a decision that is yours to make.

We're all stuck in these bad places with these choices that aren't really choices. I think you'd understand that, if you took the time to think about it. I certainly do. Think about it, I mean.

———

For a while, I lay there, unsure what to do. You were more unconscious than just asleep. A thin line of drool ran down your cheek. After ten or fifteen minutes or so, I slipped out of the bed, pulled the bag of garbage with the condom in it off the hook, and dropped down onto the floor of the camper. I dressed quickly in the dark, took the dog, my phone, and my wallet and slipped out into the parking lot, where it was still night and still raining. I didn't know where I was going, I just knew I couldn't be there with you anymore. I threw the bag of trash into the first bin I came to, which I think was on my side of the street, close to a set of stone stairs.

I don't know why I threw it out. For a long time, I would be vague about the details of what you did. For a long time, I would tell people—friends, the police, myself—that it hadn't gone as far as it had, that it wasn't as bad as it was, even though I knew, deep down, deep down, down where I pressed that awful memory into the black muck of my heart, that it *was* that bad, that bad and worse. It's just that I felt it was my fault, in some way, and felt ugly and used and hurt and ashamed, so terribly terribly ashamed, with my asshole hurting and my cunt aching and your goddamn jizz in a plastic bag in my hands. I think, maybe, I'd hoped by throwing it away, I could forget about the whole thing, conceal if from everyone, even myself. That didn't work, of course, but I suppose it was worth a try.

I went over to the Olympic Village and stood in the shadow of a store light, scrolling through available hotels on my phone. There was some kind of conference in town, and there was hardly anything left, and what was left was going for prices I wouldn't have been able to afford even in my old life—$300, $400, even $500 a night. Even if I could have paid for it, which I couldn't, I doubt they would have let me inside, a small, exhausted, dishevelled person in a filthy coat with a dog on an old piece of rope.

I walked around for more than an hour, just going up and down the empty streets in the rain, my reflection gliding over the darkened glass of storefronts that gazed back at me like blind eyes. As I came into a square at one end of the maze of closed shops and restaurants, I saw two men standing at the edge of a fountain. The fountain wasn't running and had been boarded up for the winter, and the men, both in suits, were leaning against it and having a cigarette.

I approached them slowly. I said *excuse me* in my brightest, clearest, most I'm-not-crazy voice. They stopped their conversation and looked up at me. One of them had a red-striped tie, the other wasn't wearing a tie at all. They were both white and in their late thirties or early forties, with the neat little pouch bellies of office workers.

I asked if they knew where there was a hotel with rooms that weren't so expensive. I explained that I was in trouble. I explained that my boyfriend had come home drunk and furious. I said that he had hurt me, although I did not—could not—tell them what I meant exactly by that. I said I was afraid.

The two men exchanged confused, perhaps even annoyed, glances.

One smiled at me gently and said, in the kind of voice you'd use to speak to a child, that he was sure my boyfriend hadn't meant anything by it, he was sure it was all a misunderstanding, he was sure my boyfriend would be sorry in the morning and it would all work out.

The other man nodded. He said I should go home. He said my boyfriend was probably worried about me.

May their balls blacken and fall off, as shrivelled as raisins. May their prostates swell and split inside them. May their wives cheat on them and give them each a virulent, antibiotic-resistant dose of the clap.

I went back to the camper. There was nowhere else for me to go. It was the closest thing I had to a home. You were asleep in my bed. I undressed. I gave the dog a bowl of water, kissed his little nose.

There was nothing else for me to do. It was cold and raining. I ached.

I crawled back into bed next to you and slept.

———

Do you remember what you said to me in the morning, Lucky, when you woke with that sheepish, frightened expression on your face, when you saw the bruises on my arms, the way I held myself away from you?

You asked me what you'd done. I told you a little, but I didn't want to tell it all. I don't entirely believe that you didn't remember. I think you remembered a hell of a lot more than you let on, but you asked me to tell you. We were lying in the bunk and my back was to you, and you reached out and pulled me against you. Maybe you thought I wanted to be held, but I didn't—not by you, certainly. I just didn't think I'd be able to look at you and talk at the same time.

When I was finished, you held me tight, and you cried into the back of my neck. You held me tight and cried into the back of my neck as if this were not something that you had done to me, but something that had been done to *us*. As if you, too, needed comforting. Maybe you did.

We lay quietly for a time. After a little while, you sat up. Your face was bright and determined. You'd stopped crying.

You took my hand and said *everything is going to be all right now.*

You said you knew you had been unfair to me lately, that you had been cruel and hurtful, but it was all going to be all right now. You hadn't been able to forgive me for what I had said at Owl Creek, for giving up on you, for not letting you go off to pick pines again while I worked in town, but now you *could* forgive me. You'd had to do what you did, you said, because I needed to be punished for the way I had acted, and now that you'd punished me, you felt better. We could be like we were before. You were going to get us out of this mess, and we were going to go to the Island. You knew it had been hard, but everything had been set right again. I wasn't well, I was depressed, and I had been taking it out on you, but hopefully now I could see that it was my fault, too, how hurt and angry and frustrated you were with me, how much you cared about me to put up with how difficult I was.

You talked about this at length, and as you talked, I was quiet. Something inside my chest felt bruised. It all made sense, of course. It must be my fault—it certainly *felt* like my fault.

I started to cry. I wasn't really sure why I was crying. I apologized. I said I was so sorry for the way I had acted. I wasn't sure what I was apologizing for, why everything had gone so wrong with the words "I give up"—to this day, I have no idea what that has to do with anything, if it ever did, why those three words were an act of treason deserving of this—but I did. I apologized to you.

You nodded. You accepted my apology. I was so tired. I was so sore. I thanked you. I said I could see, too, that you'd needed to do what you'd done. You stroked my hair. You said it was all going to be okay.

Then you asked me for a blow job, and I gave it to you.

You're a goddamn bastard, you know that, Lucky?

You're a goddamn bastard and a rapist.

—

You know what happens after that, don't you?

The peace you promised me lasts maybe a week before it breaks. Pretty soon you're back to screaming at me and calling me a bitch and telling me I should kill myself, only now I'm so tired and worn out and shell-shocked I don't even argue with you, I just let you do whatever you want, which somehow only makes it worse. You get angrier and angrier, and in short order we are one of those couples fighting in parking lots that no one will make eye contact with, that everyone ignores as they go back and forth with their takeout coffees, but about whom their wives will say to their husbands in hushed tones on the way home *do you think we should have done something?*

You keep spending money like it's going out of style, so unbe-knownst to you, I start making calls, gathering resources: a little from a friend here, a little from my father there (at this time, I am still speaking to him). I pawn some jewellery I have hidden in the truck, sell clothes, books, anything I have that still retains some minor value, and when I have enough, I lie and tell you *we* have finally saved enough. We never mention my going back to the Island with you again, but you don't have a way to get there, so it's just assumed that I will drive you, which I do.

I think you're as relieved as me for this all to be over, but to my surprise, when we get into Vancouver, you demand first one day in a hotel with me, then two—it's money that we don't have, but that I am too afraid to not to spend. We shower, we get takeout, we watch television. Our room has two beds, and we eat in one bed and sleep in another. I am sad and hurt and anxious, and I don't know why. You seem relaxed and happy for the first time in weeks, but on the morning of the third day, when I take you to the ferry terminal, you are suddenly wistful, almost reluctant to part. When you go to get on the ferry, I get out of the truck in the drop-off zone, you tell me that I mean so much to you, that you're going to miss me, but that you're sure we'll see each other next season. Then you kiss me goodbye, shoulder your bag, and start up the ramp to board the ferry.

And then I get in my truck with the bad transmission, get in my truck with barely enough money to eat and put gas in that truck for a couple weeks, get in my truck with a pile of debt you've racked up on my credit card—smokes, beers, hotels—that I was too terrified to ask you to pay back because it might make you angry or because it might force you to stay. I get in my truck and I *haul fucking ass* across the country to Montreal.

I said I was going to go stay with a friend, but what I was really doing was running the fuck away from you.

—

In the weeks and months that follow, I slip into a deep, deep depression. I'm anxious and irritable. I get in a serious car accident that destroys my truck and leaves my frayed nerves further shaken. In Montreal, I live with a friend, M, who is an alcoholic, and together we descend into a winterlong drinking binge. Whole days—whole *weeks*—dissolve in a haze of cheap dep wine and even cheaper vodka.

During this time, you text and call, and call and text, and text and call. You're upbeat, jovial. You check in all the time to "see how I'm doing." I answer you because it's my habit to respond to you, but in the back of my head I can't figure it out. You spent months acting like I was garbage, like you hated the very sight of me, but here you are talking about how much you miss me and how great next season is going to be, asking me if I have contacts in the Yukon wildfire service so we can map out fires early for morel picking. You ask how things are going in Montreal, you ask about my friends, you ask about my day. It's like you're a totally different person, a person much more like the one I met at the beginning of the summer, although perhaps even a nicer, more thoughtful one than that.

You talk about everything we're going to do *next year*. In your head it's certain, fixed, that I will be going out with you and a whole new crew next year. You don't want to bring Patricia or her beau or her sister, nor anyone else I worked and picked with last year—they'd only slow us down, you say. You just want me to come.

You need a woman with you, you say, because having a woman brings so much warmth to a camp. You need me to come.

And then, slowly, a fear of you—deep, profound—seeps in through the armour of drugs and booze I've been wearing. I start to dread the buzz of a text message from you, I start taking longer and longer to answer, which you start to notice and which starts to irritate you, so you text more and more often. I start dodging your calls, pretending I don't see your emails. I don't want to talk to you, or about you. I don't want to think about you.

My stomach hurts all the time. I have terrible insomnia, and when I do sleep, I have nightmares. I start smoking a metric ton of weed, and when that fails to soothe me, red wine and sleeping pills at night. I tell myself I can't find a job in Montreal because what little French I speak sounds like someone trying kill a frog in a blender, but the reality is that I *can't* work. I don't bathe. My clothes are rumpled, shabby. The littlest thing makes me cry. I burn myself with matches. I can't stand to talk to men. Loud noises make me jump, and then after I jump I'm furious, every nerve ending like a lit firecracker. I think about dying all the time.

It will be months more before I am finally told that these are all symptoms of post-traumatic stress disorder; in the meantime I'm a hot mess of anxiety, hypervigilance, and searing, seething, uncontrolled *rage*, which has no other outlet but me and my own body.

And then one day, you call, and I answer. You're going on about a plan for the next season, and suddenly I say—as if the words are being said by someone else, as if I have no control over whether or not they get said or not—that we need to talk about what happened in Whistler. There's a weighted pause at the other end of the line before you ask me what I mean, and I say *what you did to me in the truck. I need to talk about it.*

Before I can talk about it, of course, you are in a cold but potent rage. I'm a bitch. I'm crazy. I'm a liar. I made the whole thing up.

None of that ever happened. I'm just a crazy cunt, doing what crazy cunts do.

I'm very calm. It's like I'm watching someone else move my mouth for me. I say I just want to talk about it.

And then you tell me I'm a bitch again and never to call you. You hang up. I call you back. I call you. I call you again. It rings and rings. I call you again, but this time it goes straight to voice mail, and I know you've blocked my number. I go on Facebook, but you've also blocked me there.

And then you're gone, disappeared. We will never speak again, and I will never get an answer—hell, I will never even get a lie *disguised* as an answer—as to why you did what you did.

VII

But you know all that, don't you? Here's what you probably don't know.

A day passed, then two. At first I felt better—I mean, at least I was really free of you now, at least you were out of my life. Slowly, though, the fear crept in. I thought about you arranging to have your friend the milk-eater beaten up in Vancouver. I thought about the money I saw people offer you, several times, to beat up other people—money you said you didn't take, but I couldn't be sure that you didn't. I thought about all your rages, about your uncertain temper, about the man you said you killed, and then I got very, very afraid. I'd given you the address of the apartment I was staying at, and you knew many of my friends—what if you sent someone after me, or after them, to shut me up? Even if you didn't do that, what if I ran into you again one day in the bush, ran into you someplace where there was no cellphone service and no one around?

Would you have paid someone to hurt me? Would you have hurt me then? Now? Did you think about killing me? Would you have killed me, if it would have shut me up?

I didn't know what else to do, Lucky, so, like an idiot, like the stupid little white girl you had often, quite rightly, accused me of being, I called the police. What I wanted was to file a report, so if you did try anything, there would be something on the books. I wanted a restraining order—which in Canada is called a cease and desist—so you couldn't come near me or contact me.

Do you know what happened after that? You'll think this is very funny.

Fucking *nothing* was what happened. I mean, nothing I asked for, anyway.

I never got a cease and desist, never got an official file on the books, nor was I ever able—although I'm not sure it's what I even wanted—to press charges against you.

What I did get was absolutely fucking *dehumanized*, *objectified*, and *humiliated* by the fetid pieces of rancid pork flesh who squeeze themselves into their uniforms and call themselves "police."

I called the RCMP first, but they told me they couldn't take my statement because, even though the incident occurred in Whistler, I had to report it to the Montreal police, since that was where I was right now. So I called the Montreal police, who informed me that now that I had formally reported, I *had* to go through with an investigation and press charges if possible, whether I wanted to or not. They sent two heavily booted, armed white men with badges to my door, despite my having said this was precisely what I did *not* want. They didn't so much take a statement from me as interrogate me, aggressively and repeatedly, for more than an hour. One officer, the older of the two, clearly did not believe me. He asked me things like *if it was so bad, why did you stay? Why are you reporting now? If you sleep with women, why were you sleeping with a man? Were you drunk?*

He asked me these stupid, sexist, degrading questions so many times that his partner turned to him and told him, in French, to shut up.

When they'd left, I cried and cried, because I felt exposed and violated all over again. They went back to their offices, where they misfiled their paperwork with incorrect contact information.

Because of this, it would be five weeks before the Whistler RCMP—now in charge of the case I hadn't wanted to make a case out of in the first place—got in touch with me.

When they did, they asked me to repeat my story all over again to another man—I did not once speak to a woman in the entire time I dealt with police from any division—in as much detail as possible. I asked why I had to do it again, as I had just gone through this with the Montreal police. The answer was "protocol." By this time, I was beginning to become as concerned with my own safety as I was with that of others—if you'd done this to me, would you do worse to another person?—so I pressed forward, in no small part because the young male officer in charge of my case kept assuring me that this was the right thing to do, not just for myself, but for others. I submitted to a phone interview, then, at their request, a written account of events because I couldn't be interviewed in person, being on the other side of the country. I also submitted text messages, emails, and even pages from my journal when they asked for further evidence.

It was so degrading to have my personal life torn open and nosed around through by a bunch of male strangers, especially male strangers who kept insisting they were "on my side" even as they poked and prodded for holes in my story.

I submitted everything. And then you know what happened, Lucky?

Nothing. Nothing happened. They couldn't find you. You'd disappeared. No one knew where you were, and if they did, they were, quite rightly, not talking.

Months passed. I moved back to the Yukon. I got a new job as a journalist. I went to therapy. I started to get better. My life was looking up.

And then, one afternoon in late July, I was sitting at a table at the Town & Mountain—the hotel is still open, but the bar is gone now, by the way—and *there you were*. Standing there in the bar, 2,400 kilometres from where I last saw you. You were dressed in bush clothes—tattered shirt, holes in your jeans—and your beard was thick. You were holding a pitcher of beer, bringing it over to a table of similarly dressed men. There had been many forest fires in the Yukon the year before; you had likely just come back from working a burn.

For a minute, everything just kind of stopped, a couple seconds out of sync with the rest of the world, like a blip in a reel of film. There was a taste like cold pennies in my mouth and a sound like the static between radio stations in my ears. I must have gone white, because the person I was sitting with—an intern new to the territory, I was showing her around—asked me if I was all right.

I put my beer down on the table. I said *we have to go right now*.

I got up and left. I don't even think I paid for my beer.

The sheer arrogance of it, Lucky. The *audacity*. To rape me and then walk around my small town, drinking and carrying on and acting like you had every right in the world to be there.

It's hard to remember what happened next. I think I called someone—a friend, maybe? Next thing I know, I'm at the police station, explaining, yet again, that I need them to help me, to protect me. They sent someone down to look for you, but you were already gone.

The Whistler dispatch called me. I spoke to the officer handling my case. He explained, again, that there was little they could do for me if he was here. I said I was afraid to go out in the backcountry, afraid to go camping—a huge part of life in the North—afraid to walk home at night. What if I ran into him? Or, more likely, what if he saw my byline in the paper and deduced where I worked? I was living alone in a cabin outside of town—what if he followed me home?

The officer listened. There was a pause. Then he asked me, quietly, if I had "access to a firearm." I said no, I did not. This remains, to this day, the most logical and reasonable question any police officer ever asked me.

A few days later—weeks? Time didn't mean much then—I got another call from the Whistler RCMP. They said they were dropping the matter; the Crown had decided it didn't have a chance at a conviction.

The reason is extremely funny. You'll love this, Lucky.

There was an inconsistency in my testimony, they said. Apparently, in a text message sent to you and submitted as evidence, I had said you *tried* to fuck me in the ass, but I claimed in my written testimony that you *had* fucked me in the ass.

Apparently, your cock about a third of the way in, unlubed, did not meet the legal definition of "fucked in the ass."

I suppose the Crown would be the expert on that, wouldn't they?

Honest to god, that's what broke me. All this suffering, all this exposure, all this fear and then—nothing. Dismissed. You were still around someplace, or maybe you weren't. I started drinking again. I started drinking *all the time*. I kept a box of wine in my car, and when my nerves got too bad, I'd sneak out into the parking lot and shotgun huge glasses from old paper coffee cups in the back seat. The nightmares, which never quite went away, worsened. I dreamt you were in my cabin at night, I dreamt you were coming to kill me with an axe, I dreamt you were waiting to leap out at me in the back seat of my car. I grew paranoid, exhausted. I stopped sleeping, stopped eating. I lost weight. My hands shook all the time. I was suicidal.

As there was nothing anyone could do, the local RCMP suggested I "take a vacation" and leave the territory for a while until I could be sure you were gone. I took leave from work for three weeks. It didn't do me any good. By September—my thirty-first birthday—I suffered a complete nervous breakdown. I quit my job in January. I simply couldn't work anymore.

Thanks a lot, Lucky.

———

It took me years to get over what you did to me. I mean as "over" as anyone ever can be about these things. Over it enough to see it clearly, anyway.

You were just part of the story, of course. Poverty, that great crippler of all fortunes, and class were a big part of it; if I'd had money saved up, if I'd had a safety net, if I'd had a career that paid more, things might have gone differently. My queerness was another. If I'd had more experience with men, I might have understood the danger I was putting myself in (or I might not have), or I might have had a better relationship with my family and been able to ask them for help.

The police, with all their misogyny, male posturing, and bungling, were another.

We believe you, but also we don't believe you.

I'd be driving and I'd suddenly think *is this all there is? Do I really not matter?*

And the answer is that, no, I do not matter. Under a capitalist patriarchy, my body was not my body. My body was a cunt, and my cunt was property. The rules of the game were written to protect the men who broke them; the game was rigged. It's *always* been rigged.

All cops are bastards.

But you know that, Lucky. You're Indigenous. I'm the fucking white moron who didn't know until then. That's on me.

I'm sorry I called the police, Lucky. I wish I hadn't. I didn't know what would happen when I did, because I was young and stupid and scared. It was, I understand now, a shitty thing for me to do, because if they *had* found you, I have no confidence at all that you, as an Indigenous man, would have received a fair shake. I think you would have been punished in ways that a white man would not be, and what would that have been but more injustice and another kind of harm and another kind of hate?

I didn't want for you to be punished. I wanted you to be *accountable*.

What fucking good would punishing you have done me, have done anyone—your family or your daughter or your community? How would putting you in jail have made things better? What you did can't be undone.

I just wanted to feel like I was going to be safe from you—like women would be safe from you—which is something that, even now, I don't. Sometimes I'm out in the backcountry, and I come up over a ridge, and I think *what if he's on the other side?*

So, I'm always armed. I've always got a knife, and I know how to use it. I don't want to carry one and wish I didn't feel like I have to, but you made it so that I will never, ever be able to entirely relax again, so ... here we are. You out there somewhere, doing whatever, and me here in Whitehorse, drinking a beer with a knife in my boot I don't want to need, but can't leave the house without. If I were an American, I'd have a gun.

You're a selfish, irresponsible, homophobic, woman-hating man-child and rapist with delusions of grandeur, Lucky.

You're also an impossibly lonely, impossibly frightened, impossibly hurt human being, one who has suffered and struggled and is, in his own way, just trying his very best to get by in a system designed to make that as hard as possible for everyone who isn't a straight, white, middle-class or higher male.

I can hold space for you to be both. God knows I myself am something of an asshole. God knows I myself am something of shapeshifter. I am prepared to think of what you have done as a kind of friendly fire.

I forgive you, you know. Maybe you don't think you need to be forgiven, but I do forgive you. I feel sorry for you, and I forgive you, and I hate you.

One of the worst things about what happened with you, with the police, was that when I first started thinking and writing about this, when I first started trying to sort it all out on paper and in my head and my heart, what everyone kept saying was *you can't use his name.* If I were to say your name on the record here, in print, or out loud, without a full trial and conviction, without the blessing of the system which holds a knife to our throats, *I* would be punished. I would be held accountable in ways that you were not, for saying what I know is true.

Names, though, are a funny thing. I had a different name when all this happened. I have a newer, perhaps truer name now. Even if I never tell a single soul alive who you are, you know who you are and what you've done, and so do I.

I think, in telling this story as honestly and truthfully as I know how, I've revealed more about you and who you are—and about me, too, and the world we live in, and the way the system hurts us and crushes us and pits us against each other—than your full, legal name ever could.

I've called you by your name.

I've called *it all* by its name, Lucky.

This Has Always Been a War

"And the great owners, who must lose their land in an upheaval, the great owners with access to history, with eyes to read history and to know the great fact: when property accumulates in too few hands it is taken away. And that companion fact: when a majority of the people are hungry and cold they will take by force what they need. And the little screaming fact that sounds through all history: repression works only to strengthen and knit the repressed."

—JOHN STEINBECK, *The Grapes of Wrath*

THE CARAFE SAT, sweating, on the tasting room counter. It was full to the top with ice water, into which someone had sliced fresh English cucumber, paper-thin wedges of green suspended luminously amid the crushed ice. Next to the carafe was a stack of small, finely crafted rose-tinted glasses, turned upside down, one atop the other.

A man—tall, in a linen shirt and polished, point-toed leather shoes—was talking with the sommelier standing behind the counter, who nodded as she poured a glass of wine the colour of watered honey. The man had one arm draped lazily about the waist of a slim, dark-haired woman in a light summer dress printed with blue flowers. With his free hand he reached out, took up an empty glass from the stack, flipped up the lever on the spigot with his ring and pinky fingers and let the water pour into the glass, then turned the spigot off with the same two fingers, all the while never removing his arm from his companion, who was listening to the sommelier and nodding. The man raised the glass—the water was very cold, you could tell because the outside of the glass had already developed a thin layer of condensation—and put it to his mouth.

He took a big, greedy sip. My throat tightened with animal desire.

I could see all this from where I was standing outside, in the dust of the parking lot. I was barefoot, wearing tattered black Carhartts rolled up to just below my knees, a tank top, and a green ball cap with a dirty-finger-stained brim that said CARIBOO—a brand of cheap beer—in large, raised white letters. I was holding a water bottle, which I had just finished filling from the garden hose that hung around the back of the tasting room. It was nearly 40 degrees Celsius with the humidity, and when I first turned on the hose, it came out like bathwater. I'd run it for a few minutes until it turned tepid, though not cold. I'd drunk off half a bottle, refilled it again, then leaned forward and let the water run over my head, wetting my short-cropped hair.

We—the workers who tended the acres of vines, green and broadleafed in the neat, tight rows stretching along the gentle slope of the hill going down toward Okanagan Lake—were not allowed in the tasting room to fill our water bottles from the tap. We were not to use the indoor washrooms, which had running water, but the green porta johns: stinking, crawling with flies, hand sanitizer half-boiling in a plastic fitting on the wall, the plastic walls trapping the sun like a greenhouse, more vile than even the worst, most rundown outhouse I had ever used. When you went inside the stench of shit and piss, magnified by the tremendous heat, was like putting a hot, thoroughly used plastic bag over your face. While on my period, emptying my DivaCup in there—leaning forward, half squatting to pull the thing out of myself, trying not to touch anything because there was no water to wash myself with, trying to wipe any remaining blood away with the thin toilet paper—was an act of equal parts endurance, discipline, and desperation.

Standing there, looking through the front windows of the tasting room as I was, even at a distance, I was breaking another rule of the vineyard: I was supposed to come and go around the back of the building, not cross the front, as I had. It was considered distasteful for patrons to see the vine workers up close. Just the other day, I had been reprimanded because a customer had seen me on the tasting room porch—I'd had question about the care for a row of vines I was about to begin trimming and was searching for the winemaker—and complained about my "disgusting" feet, which were bare in the 35 degree noonday heat.

As I watched, his throat bobbing up and down, the man drained the glass of the cold, clean water and set it back on the counter without looking at it. He was still focused on the sommelier, who was pushing a few ounces of the white wine toward him across the cool black slate of the countertop in a wineglass she held at the base of the stem with two fingers. Everyone was smiling.

I ran my tongue over my sunburnt lips, the coppery, chemical taste of the hose water lingering in my mouth.

My job at the vineyard was "thinning." I made fifteen dollars an hour working five to nine hours a day, depending on the heat and what other jobs I had lined up. After taxes, an hour of my work would buy me a dozen eggs, a loaf of bread, and *maybe* some cheese or butter, but definitely not both. Two would buy me a hot meal and a cold beer or two. Four would buy me a bag of dog food. Eight would buy me a tank of gas.

Once the thinning was finished—two or three weeks at most—I would need to find other work, but for now this was what I was doing.

I worked in Naramata, British Columbia, a small but very rich village high up on a winding hill along Okanagan Lake, where the houses of the wealthy popped up all in a line on either side of the road, like fairy ring mushrooms. Naramata's closest city centre—a place to buy groceries, access the library, have your car serviced—is Penticton, about fifteen kilometres away. Each morning, I came into the vineyard around dawn. There was no bus system, and so when my truck—a cantankerous old Toyota I had bought for a song off a guy in Kamloops and later turned out to have been stolen—was running, I drove into work. When it wasn't (which was often) I walked the eight-kilometre round trip in the half dark of the morning and the blazing heat of the afternoon down the side of the shoulderless, winding road, my dog, Herman, trotting along next to me, panting with his long pink tongue hanging like a loose ribbon.

When I got into the vineyard, I'd go directly to the row I had left off on the day before. I carried a pair of small, curved snips in a leather holster. With these, I would start at the top of the vine trellis—slightly above my head—and cut off large, green clusters of unripe grapes, cool and hard as pearls. I'd work my way down, snipping at the base of the cluster, carefully brushing aside the leaves, sure-handed, gentle, mindful not to cut the vines themselves in the tangle, until only a prescribed amount of fruit remained.

At first, I had been too gentle—I can be overly sentimental about silly things, and it hurt my heart to cut the fruit before it had a chance to ripen, as if I were somehow cheating the plant, and I would sneakily leave a few extra clusters hidden behind the leaves. The winemaker—a tall, kindly New Zealander with a black-and-white collie Herman would sometimes play with while I worked—inspected my rows, shaking her head and removing the fruit I had tried to spare. The fruit closest to the top would never ripen fully, even in the relatively (by Canadian standards) warm climate of the Okanagan; the growing season was too short, the intensity and duration of the heat too brief for the vines to reach their full production. To promote ripening and sugar content in the final harvest, the vast majority of the fruit had to be culled, with the fruit closest to the base the best and most likely to reach the desired maturation. How much I left and how much I kept depended on a lot of things: the type of grape, the age of the vine, the placement of the fruit.

You had to cull the fruit at the top, or else the plant—and the wine—suffered, she explained. Afterward, I did as instructed and cut ruthlessly.

Up and down. Cut, cut, toss. An errant young tendril, curled like a pig's tail, carefully tucked back into the trellis. The broad green leaves, papery and growing fragrant as the day warmed. The rows and rows and rows of vines laid straight like lines of music on the gradual slope of a hill that tilted down toward the blue-green expanse of Okanagan Lake.

As I worked, a trail of discarded fruit formed, but even as it was crushed under my feet, broken open, sticky and rotting in the sun, it attracted no flies. Traditionally (and still in some vineyards) the unripe grapes would be collected and pressed into *verjus*, a non-alcoholic, lightly acidic sort of vinegar used in salad dressing or condiments, but when I'd remarked on the waste, the winemaker shook her head. The vineyard was not set up to process it, she said, but, moreover, even if it was, you might not want it for precisely the same reason the flies didn't: the pesticides rendered the green grapes undesirable.

I asked her if she thought it would be safe for me to take some of the fruit home to try to make something with it myself.

She said maybe, but she wouldn't, so I never so much as put one to my lips to see how it tasted.

———

There was no place to live in Naramata—the vacancy rate was nearly zero, and unless you knew someone, finding a room to rent—especially with a dog—was almost impossible. Even in Penticton, where things cost a little less, the vacancy rate was less than 2 percent, and working-class people who lived there year round crushed as many people as possible into their houses, so there was very little space to be had. There were no campgrounds, and even if there had been, most farm-workers would not have been able to afford them, as a campsite ran thirty to fifty dollars a night all throughout the Okanagan—about two to three and a half hours of my work as a thinner. By contrast, if you have an apartment that costs $1,200 a month, you pay forty dollars a day to live there, so thirty-five a night for a flat piece of earth to pitch a tent on is a pretty steep price to dole out for an itinerant labourer working for low wages and unstable employment apt to dry up at any moment.

That year, when I first started working in the vineyard, I had been living out of my truck, way up on a logging road on a hill above the village. There was a bylaw in Naramata that made it illegal to sleep in your vehicle anywhere within the municipal limits. This, like the lack of campgrounds for workers, was very much on purpose, because while they wanted and needed the work labourers like me provided, they didn't want tourists to see a bunch of degenerate, filthy fruit pickers and vine cutters sleeping rough on the beaches or scooched together in the back of their vans, so they made it as hard as possible for us to both work *and* live in the village. Whether or not this was an *actual* bylaw in Naramata or simply an unspoken agreement between the cops and the village was never really clear to me, but everyone knew that if you tried to spend the night in town, a booted and armed pig in his air-conditioned cruiser would pull up and bang on your window and make you move along. The logging roads were safe—from cops, anyway—as they were technically outside of the city limits. It was terrifying, though, until you got used to it, to be awoken in the early morning by one of the big logging trucks rumbling in and out, kicking up dust and stones that pelted your windows like hail.

It was sure pretty up there, though, above the village at night, with the sky red and the crickets singing in the sage. It was also uncomfortable, hot, and sometimes frightening as a perceived female to be alone out there, where anything could happen to you and maybe no one would find you for days. I slept with a knife tucked under my pillow. It took a long time to get into work in the morning, too, constantly having to break my camp, packing and unpacking my stuff, and making and unmaking a bed in the back.

When another farmer I had worked for earlier in the season offered to let me stay on his farm, I jumped at the opportunity; it was both safer and more convenient.

—

Earlier in the season I had picked cherries for this farm. The workers had camped together in tents in the orchard, sleeping under the shade of the fruit trees. The season was over now, and all the other pickers—working-class Mexicans and Québécois, mostly, interspersed with the odd rich kid on a gap year—had gone. I lived alone outside the bunkhouse.

During the cherry season, the bunkhouse was where the workers could wash up and cook their meals. It had a small electric stove, a dusty, worn couch, and a rickety, sloping porch that pickers sat on to drink and eat their meals in the hot summer evenings. The roof was uneven and leaked terribly when it rained. I can't remember if the toilet had been disconnected or didn't work, or if there just was no toilet, but either way, there was no bathroom. In the cherry season, the farmer had a solar shower you could use—a big tank that ran a stream of sun-heated water down over you, which you accessed by shimmying down the side of the dusty hill—and porta johns, but now that all the workers were gone, the farmer had removed them, so I pissed and shit in a President's Choice Dark Roast coffee tin that I kept in the back of my truck and emptied into ditches.

In the beginning, I tried to live in the bunkhouse, but after a few nights I gave up and went back to my tent, a green two-person Marmot with a tuck-taped fly. It was too hot inside the bunkhouse. The still air hung in the two-room building like a dusty miasma, and it was absolutely infested with mice—on my second night, I awoke to the sensation of a clawed foot lightly skittering across my cheek in the dark, soft and itchy and horrible. It was also haunted. Several workers, myself included, had seen the outline of a tall, thin man in a long coat in the evenings, a pale shape that clung to the corner of your eyes and seemed to shift whenever you tried to get a good look at it. One room in particular exuded such an unsettling, uneasy aura that it gave me goose pimples to walk into—an act my dog absolutely refused to do. I still cooked my meals in the kitchen during the day, although if I had to be up before dawn, I often just used the camp stove to make coffee—I didn't like to be in there when it was dark.

I paid seven dollars a day to stay there—about fifty dollars a week, or $200 a month—an amount that always seemed to me an oddly uneven number. I assume it was calculated to offset the cost of my electricity and to allow the farmer to make a small profit, although I don't think he really needed my fiver and toonie each day, as he himself had two houses.

The first was the original farmhouse, a gorgeous old home with a wraparound porch and a view of Okanagan Lake—breathtaking in the evening, when the sun spilled across the water in pools of rose and lavender—in which he had installed his mother, a spry old woman I often saw in the mornings watering the flowers of her lush garden as I left for work. The second was a new house that he was still in the process of finishing, much larger and fancier than the original farmhouse—less a house than a mansion, actually, mushrooming out at the base of the hill like the cap of a matsutake. Although I never saw it myself, more than one picker said the farmer had ordered a room built especially for his dog, with heated floors.

Of all the farmers I worked for over the years, this one was far and away the best. He paid his workers on time and paid everyone exactly the same wage, whether they had papers or not. There was a cool, quiet patio up at the old farmhouse where you could go and sit, with limited Wi-Fi for pickers to send emails and look for other jobs, and he and his wife and his mother kept it pretty and clean, with flowering plants and white fairy lights strung about the veranda.

I think about it sometimes, that house and that porch overlooking the orchard, when I am very sad and need to remember that, for some people, such happiness—stability, beauty, comfort—is possible.

All this to say that, although he was a capitalist and a landowner, the farmer was not an asshole. The farmer was, in fact, very nice. It's just that he was nice in the only way that rich people who don't understand the advantages of their richness—and who assume, in some way, that wealth is their right—can be. They can be kind, but their kindness has holes in it.

I am not saying that the farmer was a bad person. I don't think that's true at all.

I just want to know why one man should have two houses and an orchard full of fruit when other people in his village don't even have a bed and a place to keep their beer cold.

———

That afternoon I finished working in the vineyard around two. It was terribly hot, and I often left in the afternoons when the sun became too intense—for both me and the plants, whose star-shaped leaves grew delicate in the brutal heat. I'd pick up working again at one job or another in the evenings, when it was cooler.

That day the sun was especially fierce, and it was hard to breathe because of the smoke drifting over from the forest fires burning on the other side of the lake, so I was especially tired and moving especially slowly. I got out a cold can of beer from the fridge in the bunkhouse, then took it to the sloping, broken-down porch in the shade to sit down with a book. Herman lay down in the shade of a Rainier, the sun coming in through the arrow-shaped leaves dappling the top of his broad, smooth head. Rainier cherries—smaller, sweeter, pink and yellow instead of heart's blood red—are my favourite, but they don't ship as well or produce as much as Bings and Vans, so not a lot of orchards grow them.

I cracked my beer and leaned back against the wall of the bunk-house, spreading my book across my knees. I was reading a dog-eared copy of *The Grapes of Wrath*, an old edition from the sixties. On the front cover was a gaunt man in overalls on a dusty dirt road with a fruit basket on his hip.

The dramatic blurb on the front read, "A way of life long gone." I thought that was extremely funny.

———

Here is how you pick cherries as a professional:

You are given a ladder, a bucket, and a harness. Some places make you put down a deposit and rent the harness from them if you don't have your own, but this farmer was kinder than most and just took your name down; you had to return it before you got paid. The harness fits over your shoulders like a vest and has a pair of clips on it, into which the bucket fits. You get up at 4:30 a.m., while it is still dark and cool, make a cup of black coffee on your camp stove by the light of your headlamp, and jam a granola bar into your mouth. Then you walk with your coffee and your full mouth into the row of trees you were assigned.

As the sun comes up, you lean your ladder against the tree—hopefully in such a way that it is safe and steady (I myself have fallen only once)—and shimmy up it into the branches. Once there, you begin picking, working amid the red clusters of cherries, which can be as big and heavy as a basketball. You find "the spur," a little nub that connects a bunch of cherries, usually two or three, to the branch of the tree, take it between your thumb and forefinger, and gently twist with your whole hand, all the way to the wrist. The spur will come free, and the cherries, still on the stem, will come with it.

When you have the fruit in hand, it goes in the bucket—*gently*. Cherries bruise or split, which leads to spoiling, very easily, so you need to place them in the bucket, not just chuck them in. You can always find a new—or shitty—picker in a row of trees, because you can hear the *ding ding ding* of the cherries as they smash into the bottom of their bucket. You also need to be careful not to strip the leaves or the little buds farther up the ends of the branch, as those are next year's cherries.

When the bucket is full, you shimmy down the ladder again, unclip the bucket, place it at the base of the tree (in the shade, for the love of god, in the shade!), clip on a new bucket, and go back up again. When you get to be good at it, your fingers just know where to go, and you work half-blind and two-handed by feel, moving from cluster to cluster and branch to branch. If you're small and light and confident, like me, and if the trees are old enough, you can actually step off the ladder and into the crotch of the tree to work directly amid the bunched fruit. It's customary for good workers to start at the crown, the most difficult place to get to, and work down until you can pick from the long-hanging branches, standing on the ground. Farmers expect trees to be stripped to the best of your ability; you can't move on to the next tree until you clean your current tree, or else everyone would just be "cherry picking" the best and easiest fruit. It helps if you work in a team of two, one of you small and the other tall, so you can get both the high and inside fruit.

Work usually ends between 10:30 a.m. and noon, depending on how hot it is; when the sun is high and the temperature rises, the fruit warms, the stems just refuse to stay on, and the flesh becomes soft and more easily bruised. The boss rings a bell, everyone comes in, and you tally up how many buckets you picked—a full bucket is generally considered to be full to the rim, with a slight dome, like the head on a properly poured beer. The number is recorded and added to your previous tally. You are paid $2.75 a bucket.

How much you can pick depends both on your experience and how productive the trees are. In this orchard, I generally picked eighteen to twenty-five pails—fifty to seventy dollars' worth—per day, although I was much slower in my first season and made far less.

When you pick cherries, one of the most important things, besides not bruising the fruit, is to keep the stems on, because removing them leaves microtears in the flesh of the fruit, which again, makes it spoil much faster. Also, in an age of sour-cherry candies and canned cherry pie filling, customers like to see the stem on the fruit as a sign of its real-farmness; without stems, the cherries are dramatically devalued.

You're welcome, usually, to eat the cherries that accidentally get destemmed (it's inevitable that some will), but lots of pickers refuse to eat the fruit—the residue of pesticide, acrid and brown, sticking to our fingers, and the faint bitter almond scent of it amid the recently sprayed leaves, makes it unappealing. Many of the seasoned pickers I knew did not eat the cherries. In my first season, I did eat them, until someone pointed out to me that no bees, nor flies, nor wasps were eating any of the fallen fruit on the ground. After that I would only eat them if they were thoroughly washed.

In that country, fruit is grown to be sold, not eaten.

———

In the beginning, when I first started working in the vineyard, I was coming in during the evenings, too, and working when it was cooler—but then there was an incident.

One evening at around seven, I was working in the rows. The sun was lowering over the lake, turning it orange and scarlet, and the vines cast long shadows. I was listening to a podcast as I worked, and I could hear a tractor moving several rows away—not an unusual sound—although the vines were too tall for me to see what it was doing. The wind was blowing toward us, down the slope, toward the lake, and I remember thinking there was an odd smell, odd but familiar, because I had often smelled it in the early mornings on my way to work without knowing what it was. I was nearing the end of a row, which brought me out near the vinting room. As I trimmed the last few plants, I heard the tractor getting closer, also nearing the end of its row, several rows up. My dog, tired from a long day in the sun, was napping close by.

The door to the vinting room flew open so hard it struck the wall behind it with a slam, startling me. I looked up to see the winemaker, also evidently working late, come rushing out, looking very alarmed, at the same time the tractor emerged from around the corner. Sitting astride the tractor, smoking a cigarette, was a skinny, shirtless young man I knew to be a jack of all trades to the vineyard owner, a fixer of machines and a planner of picking schedules as well as a worker—a "straw boss." Seeing the winemaker, he stopped, idling the tractor. There was a large plastic container of something on the back.

What he had been doing was *spraying*.

The winemaker demanded to know what the straw boss was doing. He was applying pesticide, he said—the owner was concerned about a certain kind of fungus.

The vineyard owner had apparently forgotten to tell the wine-maker that they had scheduled a round of pesticide application, so she had asked several of us—myself and a pair of Mexican men who did not speak English—to be in the fields that evening. We'd all been exposed.

The winemaker asked the young man where his protective gear was; he was supposed to be wearing long sleeves and pants to keep the stuff off his skin, along with gloves and a mask, but he was shirtless, in shorts, wearing only a ball cap. The straw boss said this was how he always applied the pesticide and that he had never worn anything special to do so before.

The winemaker ordered him to kill the tractor, which he did, and sent him off into the vinting room to get a mask. When he'd gone she turned to me, and I could see she was angry. She asked how long I'd been in the vineyard. I said about forty-five minutes.

Frustrated and worried, the winemaker explained this wasn't the first time they'd had problems with pesticide use and safety. When she'd first started working here, they had been using a much more potent chemical to control fungus and insects, which required a minimum seventy-two-hour window after application during which no workers should be allowed in the rows for their own safety. She wasn't told it had been applied, and somehow some of it had gotten into her eyes; likely she had touched the vines while inspecting them, then thoughtlessly, unaware of the possible danger, rubbed her face. She turned her head a little and pointed under her eye. When we'd first met, I had noticed something oddly asymmetrical about her face, but it would have been rude to stare or ask outright, and she often wore sunglasses. Now I saw the skin just under her right eye was sunken in, as if someone had taken their thumb and pressed down into wet clay. The tissue in and around the mucus membrane had deteriorated as the result of the pesticide exposure—the doctor wasn't sure why, but suspected it was an immunological response to the toxin. It had effectively eaten part of her face.

After that she'd made them switch to a milder pesticide, the one they used now, but it still had a twelve-hour re-entry window, she said, and it wasn't safe for us to be here—especially with pets. She gestured at Herman, who was lying in the shade of a freshly sprayed row. She was quite fond of Herman.

The winemaker suggested I go home and shower, change my clothes, maybe give the dog a bath. I didn't have a place to take a bath. There were no public showers in Naramata. Neither were there any public showers in Penticton, nor any pay facilities, unless you were staying at one of the fancy tourist campgrounds. There was a community sport centre, a slick building with a pool and, of course, showers, but when I had tried to access the facility in the past I'd been told that unless I was a member or bought an expensive day pass, I couldn't use them.

I went back to the farm, got a change of clothes, a towel, and shampoo, and took myself and Herman to the beach.

I had us wade out to a little bay around the corner—as much privacy as we could afford—stripped to my underwear, and sudsed us both up as best I could, rinsing us off in the sun-warmed water. Herman loves to swim, but he hates having a bath; he stood stiff-legged and miserable as I tried to get all the shampoo out of his fur, pouring water over him from a tin cup. When we were as clean as we could be, I changed into a different pair of clothes—they weren't clean, I didn't have any clean clothes left—and washed my work clothes with biodegradable dish soap in the lake, too.

When I was finished the dog and I spread out together under a willow and took a nap. I was most worried about Herman, who was closer to the ground and weighed less than me, but we both appeared to be fine. We were very tired—I remember we slept very hard—but with the work and the heat, we were often very tired.

The spray used in the vineyard and in many orchards in the region was a fungicide produced by Bayer and sold under the brand name Luna, composed of a mix of fluopyram[42] and pyrimethanil. Used to control (kill) funguses and nematodes, fluopryram works by inhibiting an enzyme found in the inner mitochondrial wall of cells, as well as in the outer cell walls of bacteria, while the fungicide pyrimethanil[43] works by disrupting the biosynthesis of methionine, an amino acid (one which is, incidentally, also essential to humans). Luna is toxic to birds, aquatic organisms, and "non-target terrestrial plants."[44]

Safety instructions for the product note that one working with or around Luna should "avoid contact with the skin, eyes, or clothing. Wash thoroughly with soap and water after handling and before eating, drinking, chewing gum, using tobacco, or using the toilet. If product comes in contact with clothing, remove all contaminated clothing, wash skin with soap and water, and dress in clean clothing. Launder applicator clothing separate from other laundry ... During mixing, loading, application, clean-up, and repair activities, workers must wear long-sleeved shirt and long pants, shoes plus socks, and chemical-resistant gloves."

Although the re-entry period for workers following application is listed as twelve hours, that's only for activities which do not involve actually *touching* the plants. For all other activities—including thinning—the safe re-entry period is twenty-four hours.

We were all back in there working the next morning.

—

After the incident with the sprayer, I stopped going into the vineyard in the evenings and found work for myself as a handyperson and gardener. I liked this work—I've always loved plants, loved working with my hands and being outdoors—and I could set my own hours and charge more money for my time. I'd done this before, when I lived on

Salt Spring Island, and once I had one or two clients, I quickly had three, four, five clients (which was usually all I could manage) because people liked my work and recommended me to their friends. I specialized in "repairing" lawns and gardens—making neglected lawns green and lush again, weeding and revitalizing forgotten flower beds—but I also did things like general maintenance and tree planting, repairing fences, laying patio stones, and chopping wood. Naramata and Salt Spring Island are much more similar than either community might like to admit, the primary difference being that on Salt Spring, people are embarrassed to be thought rich, even if they are, and in Naramata people are embarrassed to be thought *not* rich, even when they aren't. I found clients as quickly in Naramata as I had on in Salt Spring.

One of my clients was the wife of a ridiculously wealthy older man who owned several wineries in the area. I found her odd, because although she was very rich and, by the white, cis-heteronormative standards of beauty to which she presumably ascribed, very pretty, with her manicured nails and her good clothes and shoes and her hair professionally cut and highlighted, she always seemed both unhappy and nervous. She fidgeted, she rushed, she always seemed to be harried and running from one place to another. She rarely smiled, and when she did, it never reached her eyes. She had a beautiful home and a beautiful family in a beautiful part of the world, but I never heard her laugh or say a kind thing about anyone. Mostly, I worked for her at her home, but I also worked periodically at a few of the wineries her husband owned—bottling and labelling, mostly—so I saw her around a lot. It was sad to me that someone who had so much could still seem so unhappy.

Together, the couple had an elegant ranch-style home on the top of a hill, from which you could see the sprawling green of the wineries below, the red or black roofs of the wineries themselves, and beyond that, the flat, cool green-blue of Okanagan Lake. I was only ever inside the actual home once; I think I was particularly dirty from cutting some prickly thing at the front of the house, and she invited me to use the washroom to clean up. I was stunned by its opulence. Hardwood floors and cupboards. A bay window overlooking the valley. The sort of sleek, modernist furniture that is so expensive and fancy that it does not need to try to look expensive and fancy. A marble countertop— real marble, which I had never seen before—upon which sat a crystal bowl of fruit. Thick rugs. Professionally framed photographs. Fine wineglasses hanging in the kitchen, expensive-looking knives and kitchen gadgets. Everything so clean and cool, air-conditioned. When I got into the bathroom, I let the water in the sink run for a minute and then bowed my head and drank the cold water greedily.

Once I had washed up, I dried my hands on toilet paper and flushed it, because even though I longed to touch the impossibly soft- and thick-looking towels, they were white, and I knew it would take more than a quick scrub to get the deep-set filth from my hands. I crept in and out of the house stiff-legged and nervous, like a cat that knows it's gotten in someplace it's not supposed to be.

Although the house was immaculate—they had a cleaner, of course—their yard was neglected and sad, much in need of a tender hand. The flower beds were overrun with weeds, the grass was sun-burned in places and overgrown in others, the small vegetable garden needed watering and fertilizing, and brambles and sage had overtaken the slope at the front of the house. I cut the grass and pulled the weeds, I edged around the patio stones, I trimmed the hedges and carted wheelbarrow after wheelbarrow of brambles to a mulch pile at the back of the house, and I carefully exterminated a *massive* hornet's nest because the inhabitants kept stinging their dog, an impossibly bubbly lab who I'd throw a ball for and allow to shower me with kisses when no one was looking, because, like a garden in need, I absolutely cannot resist a dog.

I liked the work I did there, but I could never quite bring myself to like the people I worked for. I could smell the stink of wealth on them, that animal odour of superiority, of separation that makes the rich behave as if they are a separate species from the common people. They held themselves away from me when they spoke, they didn't meet my eye, and they were often disrespectful of my time, asking me to come in to work and then not showing up, or cancelling at the last minute. Occasionally, they would ask me questions about myself and could not entirely contain the flicker of surprise on their faces when they found I was not only an avid reader, but a published journalist with a degree in literature. Frankly, I don't think they believed me, which was fine by me.

One afternoon—very hot, the sun lowering but still fierce, insects buzzing, the smell of sage heavy in the air—I was working in the garden while the lady of the house was home hosting a small get-together. She and a handful of women—sir was off somewhere, and their teenaged daughter was away—were sitting in the backyard at a table placed in the shade. There was a bucket of ice on the table, in which a bottle of rosé from one of their wineries, doubtless, was chilling; a glass of it sat in front of each of the women, along with a tray of cheeses and charcuterie. I hadn't eaten all day and was very hungry. I could smell the salt coming off the olives, the yeasty fragrance of the fresh baguette, the sweetness of the lightly bruised flesh of the grapes.

I had an edger in my hands—a half-moon blade on a long handle, used to cut the sod from around the rims of gardens and patios—and was turning up a length of crabgrass nearby. I leaned it against a tree, wiped the sweat from my face, and as I paused, the woman of the house called my name. She gestured for me to come closer and so I approached the table, although I sensed I shouldn't come right up to it; it was like being summoned by a teacher at school, their desk between them and you. My employer introduced me, said I did fabulous work, and was *from the Yukon*, a detail I suppose she, like many Southerners, found somehow exotic.

The women were all white, in their mid- to late forties, pretty, and thin in that difficult-to-maintain WASPy way. They greeted me with stiff politeness. I was under the impression, based the snippets of conversation I had caught, that they all worked in the wineries—in management, of course. My employer went on to explain I was working in the vineyards, as well as for her, and that I spent a lot of time mushroom picking in the backcountry. She listed these facts casually, as if explaining the pedigree of a certain breed of dog. I don't think she was trying to be rude. I think she just found me unusual and thought her friends would find it entertaining.

The women asked me a few questions about myself, and I answered them lightly. No one offered me anything to eat, nor a glass of wine, nor a glass of water.

In the bush, if you invited someone over to your fire, and you were all eating or having a beer, but didn't offer them something, this would be considered extremely rude, even an insult. Which, in a way, it was.

Just as I was getting uncomfortable and annoyed with being looked at like a strange zoo animal, one of the women asked me where I was living. She had heard, she said, that it was very difficult for workers to find someplace to live here.

"It is very difficult, yes," I said, before I could stop myself. "I live in a tent on one of the farms, and before that I lived on the logging roads. There needs to be a communal camp for all the workers, so we'd have running water and showers and a place to sleep and cook."

"Oh, well, you know," my employer said quickly, waving one hand in front of her face lightly, as if brushing the idea away. "There's been some talk among the vineyard owners and the farmers of building a camp for the pickers, but it's impossible. Where would we put it that it wouldn't be in the way? It's also far too expensive—and the government won't give us any money for it." She rose, pulling the wine bottle, now empty, from the ice. Her nails were scarlet, freshly painted. "We can't be expected to pay for it ourselves," she added, and then turned, stepping lightly around her chair. She went to the patio window and slid it open, slipped inside, and slid it shut behind her again, presumably to keep the air conditioning in.

I watched her cross her kitchen in her white slingback heels.

I watched her place the empty wine bottle on the cool of the real-marble counter.

I watched her open her clean stainless-steel fridge full of fruit and meat and cheese, brightly coloured glass bottles of fresh juices, shelves brimming with condiments, and select another bottle of chilled wine from a stack of many bottles of chilled wine.

The remaining women, still seated, looked uncomfortable, although I'm not sure they knew *why* they were uncomfortable. I have an excellent poker face. I don't think any of the rage—the seething, snapping, rattling *rage* coiling and uncoiling like a snake in my chest—showed on my face. A wasp had landed on their charcuterie board, was fondling a grape with its thin black legs.

"Excuse me," I said, brushing my dirty hands with their ragged, bitten nails against my tattered Carhartts. I put my hat, which I had taken off, back on, tucking my unwashed hair beneath it, out of my face. I smiled at them, and I knew my smile was not nice. I didn't want it to be nice.

"I must get back to work."

——

That night, when the grass had been cut and the patio stones edged and the tools put away, I drove into town for groceries. It was nearly dark, and the purpling light fell over the great wineries and the big houses in the hills, across the now-empty tasting rooms and the orchards with their locked gates, as I drove down the winding road into the valley. On the lake, the boats of rich people and tourists cut across the blackening water like white birds. The truck had no air conditioning, so I drove with all the windows down. Herman sat on the seat next to me with his large black nose twitching, the scent of the night—sweet earth and ripening corn, sun-warmed asphalt, exhaust, pesticides—washing over us.

The lights of Penticton cut a yellow line through the falling night, and as we drove into the city the landscape changed; the buildings grew shabby and tired and the cars became as rusted and road-chewed as my own. There were people sitting in front of the food bank, some on pieces of cardboard, some on the bare sidewalk with their backs against the wall, while others pushed grocery carts or carried plastic shopping bags with random objects—the sleeve of a coat, the leg of a teddy bear, a licence plate—spilling out through the holes. Some were quiet, sitting with their eyes closed, as if they were meditating, while others seemed animated, nervous, pacing and shouting at each other, at the food bank attendants, at nothing.

Farther up the street the road split into a Y; at this juncture stood the same sign that was always there with a sad, partly deflated blue balloon, a sandwich board sign that read NEEDLE EXCHANGE 5 CENTS.

I passed the library, too, where I had been several times to use the internet or the printer, although never for very long, because I couldn't bring the dog inside. I knew they had a security guard who stood between the twin doors of the men's and women's washrooms; if you were in there too long, they came inside and told you to leave, as I had discovered one day while washing my dust-smeared face. There were naloxone kits in every room of the building, as the fentanyl crisis had spread out from Vancouver and spilled into the surrounding towns.

I drove past the main downtown strip, where the streets were lined with clothing shops and wine bars and restaurants aimed at the rich tourists who came through to see wine country. Outside of these places, large, new, gleaming cars sat, SUVs and convertibles and sedans with tinted windows. It was getting late, but on the patios, people were still sitting under umbrellas, drinking cocktails and eating tapas or pizza, or drinking cold beers in tall, frosted mugs and being served by weary-looking waiters in sweat-dampened shirts. Many of the restaurants and stores had signs in their windows that said *WASHROOMS ARE FOR CUSTOMER USE ONLY* which, as anyone who has ever been homeless knows, really means *STAY THE FUCK OUT, HOBO.*

As I turned down the street that would take me to the grocery store, I passed a ragged woman standing in front of an empty-looking building. She was wearing an oversized T-shirt full of holes and slumped forward, back humped, holding herself up against a chain-link fence. She was crying loudly, her mouth open in a keening wail, the sores on her face raw, red, and oozing, the backs of her hands covered in scabs. The sound of her crying rose and fell in an arc that took a long time to fade away after I'd passed her. Herman shuffled, restless, in the passenger seat, ears up, unnerved by the sound of her distress.

At the grocery store, I bought eggs and ramen noodles. I bought a handful of vegetables, a loaf of bread, soy sauce, a tin of coffee. I bought nothing fancy, nothing expensive—no meat, no milk, nothing that would spoil quickly. A bag of dog cookies for Herman. Granola bars. I went into the liquor store, bought a flat of cheap beer. I went to the gas station, filled the tank, bought a small bottle of orange juice, carb cleaner, a protein bar. I went to the pharmacy, bought hand sanitizer, dish soap. I had a yeast infection from the heat, from the lack of showers, from the stress, and I bought a single dose of over-the-counter fluconazole to treat it. I bought a pack of tennis balls, also for Herman, because he loved to play fetch at the lake.

When I was finished, I pulled into the parking lot of the grocery store again. I parked, killed the engine. Sitting in the cab of the truck, I took out a scrap piece of paper and my receipts and started adding them up, doing the math with a pen swiped from a Motel 6. When the figures were totalled, I saw that I'd spent not only everything I'd made that day, but everything I'd make tomorrow, too, not counting my seven-dollar-a-day rent at the farm and the gas to and from Penticton.

The insurance for my truck was due at the end of the week. Herman would need more dog food soon. I had an ache in my teeth that I suspected was a cavity. I was almost out of my asthma medication, a steroid inhaler I had been using at half the recommended dosage to ration it out, because it was $120 to refill. I needed new laces for my shoes, which were too small and cutting up my feet—this was why I often worked barefoot—and my last pair of jeans was wearing thin at the crotch and the knees. The truck needed new shocks and an oil change. There was something wrong with the ignition, and I was worried it would fail each time I went to start it—and indeed, several days later, it would.

Any day now, the work in the vineyard would dry up, and I'd have to move on. More cherries, maybe, the later organic crop in Oliver, or pine cone picking—they grow them into seedlings for tree planters—in Salmon Arm. That meant more gas money and time spent travelling around to look for someone who needed workers. And then that work would dry up, and I'd have to look for more work, and then I'd find something, and then what? Winter? I was trying to put away enough money to go back home, to get up to Whitehorse, but if I couldn't do it fast enough, the snow would come, and I had no money for hotels and it would be too cold to sleep in the truck and then—

And then what?

I sat in the parking lot with the truck turned off and the windows rolled up and my hands clenched tight around the steering wheel, trying to do the math, trying not to cry, then doing the math again. Maybe I shouldn't have bought the beer, but the thought of trying to get through a day living the way I was—through the heat, through the dirt and the boredom, through the loneliness and the endlessness of it—without something to look forward to, to take the edge off, even just one cold drink at the end of the day, was crushing. The beer was twenty-four dollars. Maybe I shouldn't have bought the dog cookies and the tennis balls—they were nine dollars—but Herman was such a good dog, and I loved him, and he protected me and kept me company, and his life was so much shorter than mine, and I wanted him to have good things, too. Besides, what good was an extra five, or ten, or thirty dollars—what would that get me? Part of another tank of gas to keep working, another bag of groceries that were food, but not meals?

You could cut down on everything, you could save with a razor's edge until you have removed every single dollar not spent on the barest necessity, you could shave it down until there isn't a single thing, not one single bright spot of pleasure left in your whole life and then—

And then what?

As I leaned over the wheel, a thin woman in a too-large T-shirt with dark circles under her eyes came out of the grocery store. She was pushing a cart which contained bags of groceries and a screaming half-naked child, their tiny fists held over their head in rage as they squalled. The woman pushed the cart along, coming to a stop next to a rusted-out grey Honda Civic, boxy and full of holes. She began to unload the groceries without changing her blankly resigned expression or trying to comfort the child, who continued to cry. When she started the car up and drove away, I could hear the whine of a fan belt that needed replacing, the rattle of a loose muffler.

I put the keys into the ignition of my own truck, turned the engine over, and took a deep breath. I wiped the tears from my face, blew my nose. I scratched Herman's ears, and he licked my salty fingers. Then I put the truck into gear and drove out of town.

———

That year—2018, the last year I worked in Naramata—was the year much of the Okanagan burned. No one seemed to remember exactly when the fires started, only that once they did, it seemed like they would never stop. In the evenings you could sometimes see the dark shapes of helicopters passing overhead on their way to drop water bombs or flame retardant. The wind blew smoke from across the lake into the hills. In the mornings there was often a thin patina of ash on my car, or in the fine hairs of Herman's muzzle.

That night as I traced the winding road upward back into Naramata, I drove through a soft haze of smoke, faintly bluish and curling in twisting plumes that bounced my high beams back at me, like driving through a snowstorm. The lights of the houses—big, expensive homes with tiled pools and high fences and their many windows fluttering in my passing headlights like the eyes of a person on the verge of sleep—shimmered in the dark.

I thought, as I drove, of the people who lived in those houses, rich people who wore good clothes and good shoes, who ate good food and smoked good cigarettes and drank good liquor, people who looked nervously about them and locked the doors of their good cars and averted their eyes when they drove through certain parts of Penticton.

I thought about what it would be like to go into one of those houses and run a bath, and sink into the water and wash my hair, and eat something from the fridge, and lie down in a big bed with soft, clean sheets, and go to sleep.

I thought about the people in town sleeping out on the sidewalks, and I thought about the woman in the parking lot with the crying child and the raised fists. I thought about the fires and about my aching hands and back and about what I would do when the work here dried up. I thought about the Mexican men in the vineyard who had been sprayed when I had been sprayed and wondered how they'd told them—*if* they'd told them—that they needed to wash and change their clothes when no one else spoke Spanish.

I thought about how it was that a handful of people could have everything, while so many people did not have enough, or anything at all.

I thought about all the workers in the fields and all the people I met on the road, all the fruit pickers and vine cutters and labourers who grew food they didn't get to eat and made wine they didn't get to drink.

I thought about how it's this way not only here, but everywhere. I thought about all the delicious plates of food I had served to tables, only to go back into the kitchen and eat soda crackers or stale fries. I thought about all the wild food I harvested and sold, destined for restaurants I was too poor to eat in. I thought about the house in Whistler I helped build for a rich woman to live in while she skied three months a year, while I myself lived in a dirty camper without running water, heat, or electricity.

I thought about the rich women in the garden drinking chilled rosé with their manicured nails gently resting on the stems of their wineglasses, nibbling food with feigned disinterest. Looking at me with their distant, curious eyes. I thought about my employer in her summer dress and her sunhat, rolling her eyes and saying *we can't be expected to pay for that* and then going back into her cool, fine house built by the hands of labourers like me.

And then, I was angry, a wave of rage like an electric shock, so potent the hairs on the back of my neck stood on end. I was coming up the top of a hill and there was a pullout on the shoulder, a lookout over the whole of Okanagan Lake and the lights of the city below, and I cut across the road into it, braking so sharply my tires squealed on the asphalt.

I sat there with the truck idling, frayed and furious and so, so, so tired. The night below was a bruised blue. In the far distance, there were lights that could have been either towns or fires.

And then I thought—dangerously, half delirious with exhaustion, with smoke, with the stress of living this way—*what if we just stopped?*

What if working-class people just stopped working?

What if we refused to build the buildings and grow the crops and bring the coffee and fix the machines and drive the cars and cook the food?

What if we refused to pay our rent or our loans with the impossible interest rates, or to give up our cars and houses and possessions when the bank came to take them?

What if we refused to let the upper classes have so much more than us, and told them that they couldn't anymore?

What if we, the people, the working-class people, the poor people, just walked into the houses of the rich, the nice houses with the polished floors and the steel appliances, and said *this is ours now—it always was*?

They would tell us we couldn't have any food because we didn't have the money to pay for what we'd grown.

They would evict us from our homes, and debt collectors would come and take what was left of our things.

The police would come and attack us, arrest us, and if we resisted, they would gas us or beat us or shoot us. They would say we were thieves and terrorists and violent criminals. They would imprison us against our will. If they ever let us out—and they might not—they would put a mark on us so that no matter what we did for the rest of our lives, people would know that we had once disobeyed the system and been caught.

We know this because it has happened before. Because it happens all the time. Because it's happening right now.

We are not paid fairly for the things we make, yet things can be denied us or taken from us if we cannot pay for them. If we refuse to obey the rules of the people who have those things, we will be punished. If we refuse to be punished, we will be imprisoned or killed.

We are told, when these things happen, that this is justice. We are told we have behaved immorally and illegally. We are told that we have made *bad choices* for which we are responsible. The conditions in which we live, with low wages, a crippling housing crisis, a shortage of time, of freedom, of light, are posed as the result of a moral failing on our behalf, not of a system designed to exploit our labour, time, environment, and bodies for as little compensation as possible.

Serve us or starve.

Work or be evicted.

Obey us or live in misery.

What part of that sounds like a choice?

Some people say capitalism is the only possible system because it's the best system possible. It isn't fair, but it's the best we've got. It's the law, and we all have to live by the law whether we like it or not.

Other people would say it doesn't matter if capitalism is fair, because nature is not fair. There have always been wolves and rabbits, hawks and mice, shepherds and sheep.

Your children can go without food, you can be forced out of your home, you can freeze in the winter or cook in the summer, your teeth can rot right out of your head, a loved one can get sick and die without medication, all because the numbers in the bank don't tally up to enough to make your life worth living.

If things are the way they are because this is the only system we have, then we need a new fucking system.

If things are the way they are because this is the law, then we can change the law.

If things are the way they are because we are animals, because this is the natural order of things, then we should be able to do as animals do and fight for what we need, what is ours, as the makers and doers of this world.

And what if we did?

What if we stood together?

What if we were finally prepared to fight back?

If the rich will not give us what is ours—if they will not pay us fairly, if they will not let us eat what we grow, live in the houses we build, and use the energy, goods, and services our hands and feet create in ways that allow us to live good honest lives—what if we *made* them?

What if we stormed their houses and kicked in their doors and threw the rich people into the streets? What if we turned those seized houses into apartments where many families could live, instead of just one wealthy one?

What if we took their farms and their vineyards and their orchards, stopped growing things to *sell*, and started growing things to *eat* so there was enough for everyone?

What if we stormed the banks and burned them down, and in their place we laid down sod and planted trees where people could sit and play?

What if we called the police what they really are, paramilitary capitalist forces, and seized their stations? What if we turned those stations into medical clinics or libraries or just tore them down altogether, salted the earth, and walked away?

What if when the police shot at us, we shot back—not one of us, but ten of us, twenty of us, a hundred? What if when they marched on us and pushed us back, we pushed forward—a thousand of us, a hundred thousand, a million?

It might not be—almost certainly would not be—peaceful. As we've seen, it's not possible to protest "peacefully" against a state that views dissidence as a nuisance and dispatches police to enforce "law and order." "Law and order" in a capitalist state means the maintenance of an unjust status quo which values the protection of middle- and upper-class property over the safety of working-class bodies; it's the defence of capitalist enterprise at any cost.

Recent police violence in both Canada and the United States, such as that enacted against unhoused people living in Toronto's Trinity-Bellwoods Park, who were forcibly removed by armed officers, expose so-called democratic governments for what they have become—class-based oligarchies designed to defend the interests of the wealthy—and the police for what they are in that system—the dogs of the state, to be unleashed on working-class bodies who dare to balk against their upper-class ersatz masters.

This organized violence is perpetrated most often against people of colour, as racism, along with misogyny and queer- and transphobia, is baked into capitalism, a philosophical system of economic oppression which requires both readily available markers of class and a mind-set in which the exploitation of certain sets of bodies by other sets of bodies is normalized and perceived as justifiable. In recent years, however, the choke chain capitalism places around the throat of the working class has been pulled tighter and tighter as police and the state attempt to "correct" dissent, becoming bolder—even brazen—in their willingness to violently and publicly supress the bodies of people of colour and their white, working-class allies. This includes beatings, intimidation, forced curfews, and the use of chemical weapons such as tear gas[45] and pepper spray, as well as widespread repression of media, even arresting or brutalizing journalists actively reporting at the front of these conflicts.[46]

Given these facts, it may be that we have passed the point where a peaceful resolution would be possible.

That's uncomfortable to think about.

Police and state violence aside, the problem runs deeper, to the rotten, selfish heart of a capitalist culture which lauds wealth as a virtue and the wealthy as morally unimpeachable, regardless of how such wealth is acquired. Having lived and worked to serve the rich for so many years of my life, I don't think the rich can be reformed any more than a glass of milk, once spoiled, can be unspoiled. A landlord who evicts a tenant who cannot pay, while he himself has a home and many apartments, is a landlord and not a human being, just as a business owner who refuses to pay her staff a living wage and allows them to live in poverty in order to maximize profits is a business owner and not a human being.

To free ourselves from capitalism might mean violence, but that violence would be—is—self-defence.

I'm not calling for war. This is already a war.

This has always been a war.

———

I sat up there on the shoulder of the road for a long time. Herman grew bored and lay down on the bench seat. I put my hand on his head and gently rubbed his ears. It felt nice to be up there with my windows rolled down, perched above the farms and the towns, the houses and the fields, the sky and the lake. From time to time a car would pass, the sound of their wheels like the humming of bees rushing toward me and then rushing away.

I drove back to the farm. The gates were closed, but not locked, which meant it was not yet ten. I unpacked my groceries and then sat on the stoop of the bunkhouse with my headlamp on, drinking a warm can of beer and looking out into the dark orchard. Along the edges of the treeline, something moved, and I turned my head in time to see the slinking shape of a coyote making its rounds. Herman lay on the porch beside me, ears up, watching the place where the animal had been, but he didn't rise.

I finished my beer. I went behind the bunkhouse, unbelted my pants, and took a piss in the dust. The lights in the big house were on. The lights in the farmhouse were off.

I crawled into my tent, hung the headlamp from a hook over my head. There was a moon, but the smoke blotted out the stars, and the wind was dry. I couldn't remember the last time it had rained. My limbs were heavy. I undressed. Herman lay down on my discarded shirt. With my boots off, I could see that the blisters on my feet had burst, leaving open red sores. I was out of Band-Aids.

I lay down and went to sleep.

———

That night, the smell of the smoke from the fires—the fires that would not stop burning, the fires that covered everything, the fires that went on forever and ever in every direction—crept into my dreams.

I dreamt a bird flew through the fires eating the country on the other side of the lake. I dreamt that the bird—black, huge, more a shadow of a bird than a bird—crossed the lake in huge, dark wing-beats. I dreamt that, as the bird flew over Naramata, a single feather from its long, flowing tail fell. The feather was on fire, and when it hit the ground, it caught in the sage and scrub, and the fire leapt up and swept through the whole valley like the back of a hand sweeping all the glasses from a table so they go clattering down.

All the houses—all the fine, expensive, big houses—were empty. I was standing in the garden of my employer, but they, too, were gone along with everyone one else.

The fire burned through the orchards and through the yards, and as it burned, there was a terrible sound. At first I thought it was the roaring of the fire, but it got louder and louder and closer and closer, and it was not fire at all, but the furious barking of dogs. As the fire moved, it pushed the dogs with it, and the dogs—huge dogs of all colours, lean, amber-eyed dogs with tails like whips—came through the fire, panting and drooling and barking. It didn't touch them or burn them. I knew, in the logic of dreams, that the dogs had come with the fire from someplace far away.

The dogs went into all the houses. They tore up the tile and the drywall. They chewed through the shingles and the patio stones, they gnawed on the copper wiring in the walls. A huge silver dog ran around with a whole fan blade in its mouth. A red dog carried away a sofa cushion. A piebald dog ran about dragging a widescreen TV by its cord.

The dogs ate up the fancy houses until only their frames were left—skeletal, pale, looming.

And then the fire caught them, and they burned, too. Burned them right down to ash.

—

I did eventually get out of Naramata, and I did eventually get out of poverty. This was done mostly through sheer good fortune, suffering, and the small graces allotted the hungry with a penchant for making their own luck.

Nowadays, I work for another rich person who does not realize they are rich. At the start of the pandemic, they said to me *I don't know what I'm going to do, I have two mortgages*, while I was fretting about what would happen to me if I couldn't make the rent on my basement apartment.

Like many wealthy people, they don't think of themselves as rich, because they've never been poor.

I've been so lucky. I'm often lucky, in my own way, even when it looks like I'm not.

Today, as I write this, the fires are burning again. Ontario is on fire, and British Columbia is on fire. California is on fire and Washington is on fire and Oregon is on fire.

There are fires, now, even now, burning south of Penticton, eating up the grass, eating up the trees. The smoke drifts through cities and chokes people. It hangs like a haze in the air, toxic and miserable. It chokes out the sun.

And I think about those houses high on the sage hills, those houses with their cool marble countertops, with their fridges full of food and wine chilling on ice, with their owners as just as cool and bloodless as their houses. I think about them drinking that wine and gazing down on the valley, impassive, unmoved, as the people who live in that valley suffer in the heat, cough on the smoke, and die. Staring down on the valley as if the fire were not tearing across the earth, swift and angry, moving through the undergrowth, across the fields, along the roads, roaring with the sound of a thousand hungry dogs all baying together in the night.

As if the fire were not moving steadily toward them.

The Lame One

"Everybody knew Bagheera, and nobody cared to cross his path; for he was as cunning as Tabaqui, as bold as the wild buffalo, and as reckless as the wounded elephant. But he had a voice as soft as wild honey dripping from a tree, and a skin softer than down."
—RUDYARD KIPLING, *The Jungle Book*

I'M FLOATING NEAR THE DEAD CENTRE of Squanga Lake on a bright, sunny afternoon in a little green canoe. The water is calm, and on one side of the boat I can make out the shape of green, gleaming bodies moving beneath me. A shoal of pygmy whitefish. Not what I'm looking for, but nice to see.

Summer has come late to the North—the lake ice didn't break up until late May, as cold and wet and rainy as a Vancouver winter—but today is a bluebird day, and I've snuck out of town to fish for pike. I've been working a hard drop-off on the western side for about an hour without a single bite, so I change tactics and decide to switch over to the marshier, sunlit easterly side. This means paddling across.

The lake is much wider than I thought it was, and the wind is against me, but the strain is a pleasure. The muscles in my arms work steadily to move the little boat across surface of the water, which is blue-black where it is deep and blue-green where it is shallow. I troll as I paddle, my rod tucked under one leg, the line taut as the canoe pulls it along.

About two-thirds of the way across, my lure snags on the bottom. I stop paddling, let the tension off, and wriggle it around so it comes loose. I reel it in, but as I do so I see a wicked snarl has formed in the line. I'm not even mad about it; it just happens sometimes. I pull the rest of the line in by hand, inspect the tangle and, finding it an unsalvageable mess, pull my knife from the sheath on my belt and cut it a few centimetres below the problem. I cut free the wire leader next, from which the lure, a flashy five-of-diamonds-patterned ruby-eyed wiggler, still dangles. I then carefully wind the several feet of line around my hand, tie it off, and tuck it into my tackle bag. Animals, especially lake birds, get tangled in discarded line and die slowly and painfully as it wraps around their wings, legs, and beaks; if you're the kind of asshole who leaves your line out there just floating around, you don't deserve to be out on the water.

Pulling the outfit across my lap, I open the catch on the reel, rerig the rod, and retie the leader. Pike have multiple rows of very sharp curved teeth, like sharks, and you need a metal leader when you hunt them, as they can turn on the line when hooked and bite clean through it, leaving an injured fish out there trailing the lure you've lost, a suboptimal situation for both of you. Since I haven't been getting any bites on the wiggler, I decide to swap it out for something else, take out my tackle case, and go through my large game fish lures for something a big old boy might find appealing. The thought strikes me: I've had some of these lures for nearly ten years. I got into fishing when I first moved to the Yukon in May 2012, when I was twenty-five; it's now June 2021. In September, just a few months away, I'll be thirty-five.

For a moment, I'm paralyzed with existential dread—how is that even possible?

Thirty-five somehow seems so much more terrifying to me than thirty ever did.

Also, I'm genuinely surprised to still be alive.

Less than three years ago, I was homeless, living in severe poverty in the back of my truck, drinking myself within an inch of my life. My recovery was a slow, grinding crawl full of missteps and backslides. Half of that recovery time has been spent in the middle of a global pandemic that, even as I write this, we aren't sure will ever be over and that—unsurprisingly, has severely impacted my mental health, along with everyone else's. Up until a year and half ago, I was constantly financially insecure, holding down a serving job and working nights while I struggled to support myself as freelancer without secure housing, a financial safety net, or even a credit card, constantly aware that I was just one killed story, one blown tire, one missed rent payment away from being homeless again.

All that aside, I'm a two-time sexual assault survivor with severe anxiety, struggling daily with the effects of post-traumatic stress disorder. I grew up in an abusive, unstable, misogynist, religious, and queerphobic household—all factors that dramatically increase the risk of suicide or other violent death for a person like me.[47] I've also worked in difficult, unsafe conditions in quasi-regulated industries— bushwork, construction, farm labour, restaurant service—which more than once placed me in highly dangerous, even potentially life-threatening situations.

I'm a visibly queer and non-binary person who grew up in a time and place when that was even more dangerous than it is now, who has lived and worked in communities and settings where my queerness was often a threat to my safety.

I should, statistically speaking, be dead. Probably more than once.

And yet, somehow, here I am, fishing out on Squanga Lake, rooting around for a lure on a sunny day, nearly thirty-five.

I straighten up in the canoe seat. Overhead, a bald eagle turns in a wide, lazy circle, riding the thermals, wings spread so that I can see a gap in the fan of feathers where they have lost a primary. I watch them. They make a funny mechanical cry, an *ah-ta-ah* chittering. They are talking to their mate, who I don't see, but must be around. I love it when they make that sound. Eagles mate for life. Eagles fall in love.

So much of what has made my survival possible is circumstantial. I'm white, for one thing; undeniably, being a white person with the social privileges that brings contributed to my survival. Although I am no longer straight- or cis passing, I was for much of my adult life, and this, too, probably helped to save me. Even though I have little family and none with whom I am particularly close, I have an incredible set of friends who have supported me emotionally, physically, and occasionally financially, when I was the hungriest and needed it most.

Another part of why I'm still here is pure, stupid luck. I'm one of those uncannily lucky/unlucky people who always manage to get themselves both into and out of the most unlikely of situations with only minimal loss of skin.

Only a small part of my survival can be attributed to my own choices and skills; something I learned while I lived out in the bush is that sometimes good things happen to you, and sometimes bad things happen to you, but mostly, things just happen to you. You can be the fittest, most cautious, most competent bushperson around and still get mauled by a bear or drown in a river for no goddamn reason at all other than it's just something that happens. You can prepare and do your best to avoid bad situations, but the amount of power you have to control your fate is limited. The bush—and the wider world—is amoral and impartial to both your success and your suffering. Some people find that hard to stomach, but I find it tremendously comforting. Often, things just *are*.

But there is a tiny part of making it against the wildly stacked odds to the contrary, an itty-bitty speck, that is my own doing. Predominantly, I think it has to do with a decision I made when I was at my lowest point, when I was hurt and sick and impossibly, fiercely, indescribably angry. I made this choice when I was turning that anger against myself, over and over, in all the ways a person can.

Improbably—and so much of my life could be described by that word, "improbable"—I owe this decision to *The Jungle Book*.

———

I don't understand the movie adaptations of *The Jungle Book*.

They're always so focused on Mowgli, as if he were the hero. He *is* the main recurring character around which the plot revolves, yes, but he's not the *hero*.

Perhaps it's our tendency to (incorrectly) centre human experience as the most valid and most valuable, as somehow more "real" than animal experiences. Perhaps, too, it's our Western colonial roots, since you don't have to squint too hard to see Mowgli as a thinly veiled allegory for the supposedly "natural" superiority of the British over their Indian "subjects." Rudyard Kipling, who penned the novel in 1894, grew up in colonial India, during which time the book is set, and was an unapologetic supporter of British colonialism (in other words, a racist douche weasel) who later admitted he'd lifted wholesale many of the stories in *The Jungle Book* from Indian folktales.

But I'm not that interested in Kipling, nor in how he intended the book to be read. That's the thing with books: once you put them out there, they're not entirely the writer's anymore. What I'm interested in is what the book means to me.

The thing is, Mowgli doesn't actually *do* a lot in *The Jungle Book*. Shere Khan—the tiger, for those of you somehow not familiar with the story—chases off Mowgli's woodcutter parents when he makes a spring for them and mistakenly lands in their campfire, giving toddler Mowgli an opportunity to wander off—he doesn't really "escape" as that implies intention—into a wolf den. Incensed by the injustice of killing a helpless infant, Raksha the she-wolf refuses to turn him over to Shere Khan when he demands it, opting instead, in an act of valour and kindness, to raise him alongside her own children.

It's the wolf pack who raises him and protects him, not only from Shere Khan's hunger, but from all the other creatures who might harm him: poisonous snakes, Kaa the python, the monkey king and his people. When it comes to the final showdown between the tiger and Mowgli, he wouldn't have been able to save himself without the knowledge, strength, and support of his friends; without them, he'd be nothing. Even this nonsense about the other animals being unable to look him in the eye—supposedly evidence of his natural superiority and the reason Shere Khan hates him—is just that, fucking nonsense, a fabrication of a colonial mind whose real understanding of the wild world was stunted by prejudices he didn't even know he had. As someone who has spent considerable time in the backcountry, I invite anyone who truly believes human beings have natural "dominion" over any other living creature to try that look-them-in-the-eye shit with a grizzly. Go right ahead. Fuck around and find out. I'll send flowers to your family.

The cover of my copy of *The Jungle Book* depicts Shere Khan the tiger, locked in combat with Bagheera the panther, Mowgli's protector, confidant, and best friend. Claws out, Bagheera is taking a furious swipe at Shere Khan, who appears almost startled, put off balance by the other big cat. That the scene never actually occurs in the actual text—Shere Khan and Bagheera exchange very few words and exactly zero blows—is irrelevant. The cover artist divined the heart of the story better than any filmmaker ever has.

The primary struggle in *The Jungle Book* isn't between Mowgli and Shere Khan. It's between Shere Khan and Bagheera.

Which is to say, the book is actually about the struggle between a hurt, lonely individual blinded by rage, and a hurt, wrathful individual nonetheless guided by compassion.

———

Here's where I first read *The Jungle Book*: sitting in my friend's apartment sometime before midnight in the no man's land of time that falls between Christmas and New Year's Eve. M, my friend of nearly ten years, had done her best to make me feel at home, but the apartment was small, and the couch had become my whole world. I slept on the couch, and I ate on the couch, I worked on the few freelance pieces I could sell from the couch and watched TV on the couch. Sometimes I brought home strange women from Tinder or from the bar and fucked them on that couch. Afterward, when they'd left and I was alone, I lay on my back on the couch and stared up at the ceiling and wondered why nothing felt like anything anymore, why food tasted like Styrofoam and beer tasted like tap water and even sex left me aching and empty and sad.

I was alone in the apartment. It was a Friday and M, a bartender at a burlesque club, was at work. She probably wouldn't come home tonight. The apartment felt empty and too quiet without her, but I was grateful to be alone. M had been hovering over me the last few days, speaking to me in that half-angry, half-upbeat tone she thought made her sound light and jovial, but really made her sound frustrated and frantic. She wanted me to do things—to go out drinking and dancing with her and her friends, to have a few beers and play poker over at D's house, to grab a bottle of wine and watch *Star Trek* with her—but I didn't want to do any of those things, except the drinking part, and my steadfast refusal to cheer the fuck up and start acting "like Lor" again, was wearing on her.

That was reasonable; it was certainly wearing on me. I hated the person I had become: debilitatingly anxious, prone to unstoppable crying jags and fits of rage, to breaking bottles, to standing on the platform of Metro stations, watching the approaching train and looking down at the tracks. That was why I did what I had done, and why M's "just buck up!" attitude had gotten so much worse lately.

A few nights earlier, on Christmas Eve, I had been house-sitting for a friend of M's, a carpenter and set designer who'd gone home to Saskatchewan to see her family. While at the house, I'd tried—with limited success, obviously—to kill myself. M, quite reasonably, had not known how to deal with that, so we just didn't. In fact, to this day, more than half a decade later, we've never talked about it.

Partly, I think, this is because M doesn't know how to broach such a serious topic. Partly, it's also because when she found me, instead of taking me to the emergency room, she rolled me into bed and left me there to either make it or not on my own. I don't blame her for that. Some things are just too much for some people to handle. Some things simply don't have an explanation that will satisfy anyone.

Tonight, I was alone for the first time in days.

I didn't know what to do with myself. Lately, the stimulation from music or television, no matter how mindless, was too loud, too grating for my jangled nerves to handle. Next to the couch, M had arranged a selection of books, spines out, next some *Star Trek* knick-knacks—M was a huge *Star Trek* fan. Most of them were books I gave her several years ago, when I'd moved out of my Dalhousie Street apartment, back in the days when we lived down the street from each other. It didn't look like she had ever read any of them, as they appeared to be in the exact same condition they had been when she fished them out of the box I had intended to send to the Salvation Army.

There, next to a bobblehead Mr Spock, was *The Jungle Book*. I pulled it off the shelf. The paper was old and yellowed. I couldn't remember where I'd gotten it from—some used bookstore, probably one of those dollar-a-book bins. I had never read it, either. I'd been having a hard time reading lately; my concentration was shot. But maybe, I thought, a kids' book might be easy enough for me to follow.

There was a bottle of cheap wine on the table, because there was always a bottle of cheap wine on the table. I poured myself a glass. M kept very nice wineglasses, even though the apartment itself was rundown and dirty. I leaned back, took a sip, and began to read.

—

The earlier movies based on *The Jungle Book* miss something important about Shere Khan: his birth name, the one his mother gives him, is *Lungri*, which means "The Lame One." Shere Khan has been lame in one foot since birth. He can't hunt wild game well, so he eats cattle instead, which gets him in trouble with humans and earns him the scorn of his fellow jungle creatures, who mock him for it. This detail is included in the 2018 Netflix production, *Mowgli: Legend of the Jungle*, which shows the tiger with a curled and deformed front paw, and in the 2016 live-action remake of the 1967 animated film, Disney also tries to throw a spin on this by giving Shere Khan scars on his face, supposedly received from a human. However, this take misses the point somewhat; there really isn't any reason for Shere Khan's vicious hatred of Mowgli besides the fact that the tiger is hurt and angry and insecure. It's not *Mowgli* the tiger hates, it is the perceived disrespect shown to him by the other animals when they refuse to turn the boy over to him.

We all know people like Shere Khan—people who will remember even the smallest slight until the end of time, people who complain they have been "disrespected" as a reason to keep that grudge alive, people who are always angry about the things that have been done to them or the way things are going for them. Often, they have a really good reason to be angry—bad things have happened to them, life has been unfair, they don't have all the resources or love they need to be at peace—and they take it out on other people, harming not only others, but also themselves.

It's much rarer, though, to know someone like Bagheera.

There's a scene at the very beginning of *The Jungle Book*, not even twenty pages in, where Bagheera reveals something essential about himself. He bids Mowgli reach beneath his jaws and feel a little scar there—the image of the small boy tenderly reaching out to touch such a delicate place on such a tremendously powerful animal has always moved me—and explains his secret: Bagheera was born in captivity, in the menagerie of a king, and the scar is the mark left behind from the collar he wore during his imprisonment.

"I too was born among men," Bagheera tells the boy. "I had never seen the jungle. They fed me behind bars from an iron pan till one night I felt I was Bagheera, the Panther ... and broke the silly lock with one blow of my paw, and came away; and because I had learned the ways of men, I became more terrible in the jungle than Shere Khan."[48]

Bagheera, unlike Shere Khan, has every reason to despise Mowgli; humans hurt him, caused him pain and suffering, and took away his freedom. Instead of letting this experience make him bitter and cruel, however, Bagheera allows it to make him wise and strong, even as he carries the mark of it all his life. He's respected but, more importantly, he is just; he despises the tiger not because he is a cattle-eater, but because he is cruel and cowardly and arrogant.

Bagheera is just as physically powerful and as strong as Shere Khan, but instead of being feared and hated, he is beloved and respected. He's never angry or vicious, as Shere Khan is, but *wrathful*; he exacts revenge only for acts of injustice, not for personal slights or wrongdoings. Which is why he saves Mowgli and continues to protect him all the days of his life—because it's right.

Shere Khan chooses hatred and rage, which not only makes him bitter and miserable, but leads to his destruction: "a dog's death," crushed by the very cattle he steals, universally despised by everyone and unmissed. At the end of the story, he's literally skinned and laid out on the council rock, a symbol of Mowgli's triumph over his would-be killer and the bitterness and anger he represents.

Bagheera chooses love and compassion, which keeps him alive and happy, as well as prosperous and beloved.

———

I read *The Jungle Book* in one sitting.

I thought about it for days, weeks, after I'd finished it.

I turned it over and over in my head like a puzzle. I turned it over and over because something in me wouldn't let it go.

And then one morning, I woke up and realized that, like Bagheera, I could choose.

When I had tried to kill myself, it was because I was hurting, yes—hurting very badly—but it was also because I was so *angry*. So much had happened; some of it had been in my control, and some of it had been out of my control, but none of it felt right or fair or good. I was angry, and that anger was making me sicker, because it had no place to go. I was just levying it at myself, ripping my own self apart, drunk all the time, unable to dig myself out of the hole I had crawled into, helpless against my own fury.

My anger and hurt were reasonable, even rational—I had been raped, abused, betrayed, humiliated, and impoverished—but it wasn't doing me any good. Not me, or anyone else. My anger was, in fact, killing me.

I would always be angry, probably, and I would always be hurt. But I could choose what to *do* with that anger and hurt.

I could choose rage and bitterness, like Shere Khan, and be a menace to myself and everyone else, accomplishing nothing but my own ignoble death—most likely, at the rate I was going, by my own hand.

Or, I could choose compassion—compassion and *wrath*. I could be angry, but that anger could be just, and productive. I could do good things with it. I could turn it not on myself, nor even the specific people who had hurt me, but on the *reasons* had been hurt.

Patriarchy. Queerphobia. Classism. Capitalism.

My wrath could be useful, not just to me, but to other people.

I could make my wrath a knife to use however I wanted.

A knife is a tool or a weapon, depending on how you hold it.

—

Maybe you think it's stupid to take so much meaning from an old children's book about an orphaned boy and a vengeful tiger and a thoughtful panther. If that's the case, that's fine; books have always been very important to me, but I know not everyone feels that way. I will remind you, though, that there are other people who base their lives on *Lord of the Rings* or *Star Wars*—the Church of Jediism, after all, is a legally recognized religion in the United States, despite the fact it's based on a film franchise now owned by Disney. In that context, I don't think it's so very strange that I could have an epiphany based on a children's book.

Also, if you do still think it's strange, you can get fucked, because I really don't care what you think, you joyless shell of a human.

It would be nice to say I came to this conclusion—that I could choose compassion and wrath over rage and bitterness—and then everything immediately got better overnight, but that's not how things work. There were many more months of healing ahead of me, of getting up and falling down, of uncertainty and pain and failure.

The difference was, though, that now I knew the choice was there: I could break the lock on my own cage at any time.

And when I was ready, I did.

———

So now, here I am. On the lake. About to turn thirty-five. The eagle still turning overhead. The sun still shining. The canoe rocking back and forth slightly as I let it drift.

I take a new lure from my tackle bag: a gold-plated Croc with a long vertical orange stripe, an old lucky favourite. I clip it to the leader and look up from my work to survey the lake. I've floated a significant way down, closer to the shoreline. It doesn't look like there's much of a drop-off, nor any choice reedy habitat for pike, and so I'm about to pick up my paddle to move myself along when I notice a gull. The bird circles a spot on the water awkwardly—gulls are not exactly graceful birds—and then, suddenly, dives, skimming over the surface of the water before darting straight up. It has a small silver fish about the length of my little finger in its beak, some kind of fry, either whitefish or grayling, I can't tell from where I'm floating. The gull quickly throws its head back and swallows it in one bite, then swings back around again in a wide loop, dives again, and comes back with another morsel. The fry must be schooling there, just below the surface.

I think about this for a moment. Pike like fry. I watch the gull make a third pass, swallow another would-be fish. I pick up the rod, gauge the distance between me and the school and, deciding it's reachable, cast out with a curt snap. With a plunk, the lure lands just to the left of where I believe the school is and immediately starts to sink. I wait until I feel it touch bottom, then give the lure a little jerk upward, some tantalizing motion before I begin the retrieve.

The strike hits so hard it nearly yanks me forward, and I jerk the rod up and to the right at an angle over my shoulder, a reflexive motion I've done so many times I don't even have to think about it. The line tightens. The rod bends. The hook is set hard. There's a fish on there. A *big* fucking fish.

I loosen the drag a little so the line won't break, then open the catch for a second or two, spooling out some line to give the fish play. This is my favourite part—either one of us could win or lose now. When I fish for pike, I only ever use barbless single-tine hooks—think a perfect J with a sharp end—regardless of what the regulations for a particular lake are. This means that, although there's a higher risk of losing the fish than there would be if I used a barbed or treble hook, there's a far lower risk of wounding the fish, which is very important to me as I want to *eat* the fish, not *hurt* it.

The fish dives, nose down, jerking the rod. I give it more line, feel it dart, roll. It's most definitely a pike on there; it lunges, rips, then "lunks out," diving farther down and lying still, like a log. It's tired. I begin the retrieve. It fights, but I've got it now, steadily moving it closer to the surface, inch by inch. When I can see the dark shape of it, long, blade-like, writhing, I tuck one end of the rod under my knee and reach for the net. I dip it into the water with my right hand, controlling the fish with my left. I sweep the net forward, and there it is, it's in, I'm lifting it, we are straining together as I deposit net and fish into the bottom of the canoe.

The pike flails. I let go of the handle of the net and pull out my knife, which is long and slim. With my left hand, I take the fish just behind the head like you would a snake, careful of the snapping jaws—they can give you a nasty bite—and pin it in place. At my touch, the fish stills. We take a breath together. I say *thank you* and then I take the knife in my right hand, slide it behind the gill plate, turning the fish 45 degrees for leverage as I do, and jerk the blade down into the cranial cavity. The pike gurgles, jerks, then is still. Dead.

Some people, believing that fish don't feel pain—or that they don't feel pain in the same way do, as if that matters—will bash a fish over the head, bludgeoning it to death, or else keep it alive on a chain until they are ready for it. But fish do feel pain, and they do feel fear, or something like it. I think it's important to do everything—even killing—with thoughtfulness and compassion.

The fish is beautiful, long and silver with darker black-green stripes. Pike in different lakes often have distinct markings or colour patterns, like regional differences in dress. He is the length of my arm, from fingertip to shoulder, and about as wide as the palm of my hand. A mature male, old but not too old, pulled from the bitterly cold water, perfect for eating.

I wipe the blood off my knife onto my jeans, then rinse it in the lake water and dry it on my other hem before putting it back in its sheath. I breathe a minute, feeling my heartbeat as I run my fingers down the cool, heavily scaled length of the fish.

Sometimes, when I am given something so beautiful as this fish, as this moment, it seems as if it's all too good for me, as if I have somehow cheated my way into this place, and I'm overcome with the hugeness of it, the perfectness, the improbability of it all. That I should be dead so many times—by accident, by my own hand, or by another—but I am not, that I have lived through homelessness and violence, illness and loneliness, and such terrible, terrible anger and pain to be here on this sunny day, just another animal doing what all animals do, eating and breathing and hunting and being seems ... *impossible.*

But I am here. I chose, and I'm here because chose compassion.

I take the fish back across the lake. I open him up and gut and clean him. I tenderly rinse him and wrap him in a cool wet cloth, then lay him on ice to keep him fresh. I wash my hands in the lake. I drink a cold beer from the cooler, sitting at a picnic table. I watch the gulls eat the guts that I tossed back into the lake. I eat a granola bar. I feed a piece to a whisky jack, who has been asking for a bite very politely.

When I am rested, I load the canoe and drive home. I take the fish out of the ice and lay him on a cutting board. I scale him, little silver armour plates spattering up and down my arms. I rinse him under cold water, wipe the cutting board down, then lay him back on it. He's ready.

Very carefully, with a knife I keep very thin, very sharp, oiled and clean just for this purpose, I cut him into pieces. I work slowly and methodically, getting as much meat as possible. The spine and head and tail will be boiled down into dog food. When I'm finished, I have several perfect fillets, all piled on a plate. I clean the knife and put it away.

Some of the fillets I give away, to feed people I love. I keep two for myself, which I cook, battered and fried generously in butter. The flesh is firm, and the skin is crisp, curled from the high heat of the pan. It's good.

It is all so good.

Acknowledgments

An incalculable amount of work goes into writing a book—perhaps especially a first book—not only from the writer, but from so many people who believe in that writer, and this book is no exception.

Endless and heartfelt thanks to my agent, Stephanie Sinclair, who took a chance and believed in me and this scrappy, angry little book, even when I wasn't so sure I believed in myself. A huge hug and a round of thank-you beers to the folks over at Arsenal Pulp Press, who have been so kind, thoughtful, and willing to explain to me—the most neurotic and anxious of all possible Type A's—what was going to happen every step of the way during the publication process. Big thanks especially to my editor, Catharine Chen, who very patiently and continuously reassured me that this book was much better than I thought it was and put up with my journalism-born tendency to scrutinize every single comma, em dash, and period like it's the last goddamn sentence I'll ever write.

This book would not have been possible without the generous support of the Advanced Artist Award for Yukon artists, which provided some of the funding that kept me afloat while I was writing early drafts of these essays.

Thank you to the unflappable Jackie Hong, greatest crime reporter in the North, for all the pots of soup, slices of pizza, and shots of bourbon. You always had a shoulder to cry on, an encouraging word, and a stiff drink at the ready for me, even when I was completely and utterly insufferable.

Thank you to the crew at Woodcutter's Blanket, to Gabbi and Taia and Willow and Chantel, who often let me crawl in at fifteen minutes till close and work for an hour, and who knew that the sound of my head hitting the bar top meant I was stuck and needed another beer.

Thank you to D. I am sure you have forgotten me, but I have not forgotten you and all that you did and tried to do for me.

Thank you to Kwanlin Dün First Nation and the Ta'an Kwäch'än Council, on whose traditional territory I work and live.

Thank you to the land—the rivers and lakes, the backcountry, fields, and mountains—which not only fed and sheltered me when I had no one and nothing, but educated and shaped me in ways too complex and subtle to explain.

Thank you to the kind folks at *The Guardian*, in which an early draft of "The Hour You Are Most Alone" first appeared.

Last, but certainly not least, thanks to my dog, Herman. You have been my comrade-in-arms, my foot warmer, my shadow, and my little brother for all the thirteen years of your life. You were also an irreplaceable silent witness to many of the events in this book. I couldn't have done it without you, buddy. Good dog. Good, good dog.

Endnotes

At Your Service

1. "Minimum Wages for Tipped Employees." U.S. Department of Labor. Last updated Jan. 2022. Online. https://www.dol.gov/agencies/whd/state/minimum-wage/tipped

2. "The Chart: The Percentage of Men and Women in Each Profession." Matt Rocheleau. *Boston Globe*. March 2017. Online. https://www.bostonglobe.com/metro/2017/03/06/chart-the-percentage-women-and-men-each-profession/GBX22YsWloXaeIIghwXfE4II/story.html

3. "Waiters & Waitresses." Data USA. Online. https://datausa.io/profile/soc/waiters-waitresses

4. "Food Service Managers." Data USA. Online. https://datausa.io/profile/soc/food-service-managers

5. "Unskilled Labor." Julia Kagan. Investopedia. Online. March 2021. https://www.investopedia.com/terms/u/unskilled-labor.asp

6. "Ontario Minimum Wage Hike in Effect, Liquor Servers and Students Get Pay Bump." Canadian Press. Online. Jan. 2022. https://globalnews.ca/news/8483240/ontario-minimum-wage-2022-15-an-hour/; see also "Living Wage by Region." Ontario Living Wage Network. Last updated Nov. 2021. Online. https://www.ontariolivingwage.ca/living_wage_by_region

7. "The Case against Tipping in America." Vince Dixon. *Eater*. Online. https://www.eater.com/a/case-against-tipping

8. Ibid.

9. "The Average Restaurant Profit Margin and How to Increase Yours." Stephanie Resendes. *Upserve*. Online. Sept. 2020. https://upserve.com/restaurant-insider/profit-margins/

10. "Gratuity (Still) Not Included." Kathryn Campo Bowen. *Eater*. Online. Sept. 2020. https://www.eater.com/21398973/restaurant-no-tipping-movement-living-wage-future

11. "Gabe Stulman Reverses No Tipping Policy, Brings Back Gratuities at Fedora." Ryan Sutton. *Eater*. Online. May 2016. http://ny.eater.com/2016/5/9/11643446/gabe-stulman-no-tipping

12. "Why Tips Won." Nikita Richardson. *Grub Street*. Online. Dec. 2018. https://www.grubstreet.com/2018/12/restaurant-tipping-returns.html

The Happy Family Game

13. Jennifer Koshan, PhD, University of Calgary. Interview with author. Mar. 2021.

14. "Reducing the Number of Indigenous Children in Care." Government of Canada, First Nations Child and Family Services. Online. Last updated Jan. 2022. https://www.sac-isc.gc.ca/eng/1541187352297/1541187392851

Where the Fuck Are We in Your Dystopia?

15. "J.K. Rowling Book Burning Videos Are Spreading Like Wildfire across TikTok." Emma Nolan. *Newsweek*. Online. Sept. 2020. https://www.newsweek.com/jk-rowling-books-burned-tiktok-transgender-issues-1532330

16. "A Timely Novel of Anti-progress by Louise Erdrich." Ruth Franklin. *New York Times*. Online. Nov. 2017. https://www.nytimes.com/2017/11/21/books/review/louis-erdrich-future-home-of-the-living-god.html

17. "How Feminist Dystopian Fiction Is Channeling Women's Anger and Anxiety." Alexandra Alter. *New York Times*. Online. Oct. 2018. https://www.nytimes.com/2018/10/08/books/feminist-dystopian-fiction-margaret-atwood-women-metoo.html

18. "*Red Clocks* by Leni Zumas Review—If Abortion Were Outlawed in the United States..." Katharine Coldiron. *The Guardian*. Online. March 2018. https://www.theguardian.com/books/2018/mar/29/red-clocks-by-leni-zumas-review

19. "A Twisted Fairy Tale about Toxic Masculinity." Laura Miller. *New Yorker*. Online. Dec. 2018. https://www.newyorker.com/magazine/2019/01/07/a-twisted-fairy-tale-about-toxic-masculinity

20. *"Blue Ticket* by Sophie Mackintosh—A Dark Fable about Free Will." Aida Edemariam. *The Guardian.* Online. Sept. 2020. https://www.theguardian. com/books/2020/sep/23/blue-ticket-by-sophie-mackintosh-review-a-dark-fable -about-free-will

21. "Why Bisexual Women Are at a Higher Risk for Violence." Reina Gattuso. *Teen Vogue.* Online. Dec. 2019. https://www.teenvogue.com/story/why-bisexual -women-are-at-a-higher-risk-for-violence

22. "Why Are Some LGBTQ Girls at Higher Risk of Becoming Pregnant?" Keren Landman. Center for Health Journalism at USC Annenberg. Online. April 2018. https://centerforhealthjournalism.org/2018/04/23/why-are-lgbt-girls -higher-risk-becoming-pregnant

23. "How Many Same-Sex Couples in the US Are Raising Children?" Shoshana K. Goldberg and Kerith J. Conron. UCLA Williams Institute. Online. July 2018. https://williamsinstitute.law.ucla.edu/publications/same-sex-parents-us/

24. "Sexual Violence & Transgender/Non-binary Communities." National Sexual Violence Resource Center. Online. Feb. 2019. https://www.nsvrc.org/sites/ default/files/publications/2019-02/Transgender_infographic_508_0.pdf

25. "Interview: Sophie Mackintosh: 'Suddenly I Really Wanted a Baby—I Resented That It Felt Outside of My Control.'" Claire Armitstead. *The Guardian.* Online. Sept. 2020. https://www.theguardian.com/books/2020/sep/ 05/sophie-mackintosh-suddenly-i-really-wanted-a-baby-i-resented-that-it-felt -outside-my-control

26. "ICE, a Whistle Blower and Forced Sterilization." NPR. Online. Sept. 2020. https://www.npr.org/2020/09/18/914465793/ice-a-whistleblower-and-forced -sterilization

27. "Forced Sterilization of Indigenous Women an Ongoing Problem: Senate Report." Canadian Press. Online. June 2021. https://toronto.citynews.ca/ 2021/06/03/forced-sterilization-of-indigenous-women-an-ongoing-problem -senate-report/

28. "The New Wave of Anti-trans Legislation Sure Looks a Lot Like Eugenics." Evan Urquhart. *Slate.* Online. March 2021. https://slate.com/human-interest/ 2021/03/anti-trans-legislation-eugenics-sports-puberty.html

29. "*Gather the Daughters* by Jennie Melamed Review—A Misogynist Dystopia." Sarah Moss. *The Guardian*. Online. Aug. 2017. https://www.theguardian.com/books/2017/aug/12/gather-the-daughters-jennie-melamed-review

30. "We Need to Talk about Transphobia in Canadian Media." Mel Woods. *Xtra Magazine*. Online. Oct. 2021. https://xtramagazine.com/power/transphobia-atwood-cbc-star-211187

31. "Dystopian Dreams: How Feminist Science Fiction Predicted the Future." Naomi Alderman. *The Guardian*. Online. March 2017. https://www.theguardian.com/books/2017/mar/25/dystopian-dreams-how-feminist-science-fiction-predicted-the-future

Other People's Houses

32. Zumper. Online. Accessed May 2021. https://www.zumper.com

33. Ibid.

34. Ibid.

35. Ibid.

36. Ibid.

37. "Facing 'Gruesome' Housing Shortages, Some Gulf Islanders Call for the Empty Homes Tax." Andrew MacLeod. *The Tyee*. Online. Feb. 2021. https://thetyee.ca/News/2021/02/10/Gulf-Islanders-Empty-Homes-Tax/

38. Zumper. Online. Accessed May 2021. https://www.zumper.com

The Hour You Are Most Alone

39. "How Does Anxiety Short Circuit the Decision-Making Process?" Christopher Bergland. *Psychology Today*. Online. March 2016. https://www.psychologytoday.com/us/blog/the-athletes-way/201603/how-does-anxiety-short-circuit-the-decision-making-process

40. "How Low Income Affects Routine Decisions." Association for Psychological Science. Online. Feb. 2018. https://www.psychologicalscience.org/publications/observer/obsonline/how-low-income-affects-routine-decisions.html

After the Hungry Days

41. "Whitehorse Residents Paint Picture of What Dismal Rental Market Looks Like." Kaila Jefferd-Moore. CBC News. Online. July 2019. https://www.cbc.ca/news/canada/north/vacancy-rate-in-whitehorse-1.5218398

This Has Always Been a War

42. "Fluopyram." David Lunn. Food and Agriculture Organization of the United Nations. Online. https://www.fao.org/fileadmin/user_upload/IPM_Pesticide/JMPR/Evaluations/2015/FLUOPYRAM__243_.pdf

43. "Pyrimethanil." PPDB: Pesticide Properties DataBase. University of Hertfordshire. Online. http://sitem.herts.ac.uk/aeru/ppdb/en/Reports/573.htm

44. "Luna Tranquility." Bayer Crop Science. Online. https://fingal.ca/wp-content/uploads/userfiles/labels/Luna%20Tranquility.pdf; https://www.cropscience.bayer.ca/products/fungicides/luna-products/luna-tranquility

45. "In City after City, Police Mishandled Black Lives Matter Protests." Kim Barker, Mike Baker, and Ali Watkins. *New York Times*. Online. March 2021. https://www.nytimes.com/2021/03/20/us/protests-policing-george-floyd.html

46. "Covering Police Violence Protests in the US." Committee to Protect Journalists. Online. Aug. 2020. https://cpj.org/reports/2020/06/covering-police-violence-protests-in-the-us/

The Lame One

47. "Suicide Prevention Month: A Summary of Data on LGBT Suicide." Rachel Dowd. UCLA Williams Institute. Press Release. Online. Aug. 2020. https://williamsinstitute.law.ucla.edu/press/suicide-prevention-media-alert/

48. *The Jungle Book*. Rudyard Kipling. New York: Century, 1920. Print. Page 29.